D1125647

John Paul II and the New Evangelization

How You Can Bring the Good News to Others

Ralph Martin and Peter Williamson, Editors

PUBLISHED BY ST. ANTHONY MESSENGER PRESS
CINCINNATI, OHIO

Unless otherwise noted, Scripture passages have been taken from the *Revised Standard Version*, Catholic edition. Copyright 1946, 1952, 1971 by the Division of Christian Education of the National Council of Churches of Christ in the USA. Used by permission. All rights reserved.

Cover design by Candle Light Studios
Cover photography © L'Osservatore Romano
Book design by Phillips Robinette, O.F.M.

LIBRARY OF CONGRESS CATALOGING-IN-PUBLICATION DATA

John Paul II and the new evangelization : how you can bring the good news to others / Ralph Martin and Peter Williamson, editors.
    p. cm.
  Includes bibliographical references and index.
  ISBN 0-86716-748-3 (pbk. : alk. paper) 1. Catholic Church—Missions—Congresses. 2. Evangelistic work—Congresses. 3. John Paul II, Pope, 1920-2005—Congresses. I. Title: John Paul 2nd and the new evangelization. II. Martin, Ralph, 1942- III. Williamson, Peter.

BV2160.J64 2006
266'.2—dc22

                                        2005035643

ISBN-13: 978-0-86716-748-1
ISBN-10: 0-86716-748-3

Published by Servant Books, an imprint of St. Anthony Messenger Press.
28 W. Liberty St.
Cincinnati, OH 45202
www.AmericanCatholic.org

Printed in the United States of America.

Printed on acid-free paper.

06 07 08 09 10 5 4 3 2 1

Contents

Abbreviations of Frequently Cited Documents / vi

Contributors / ix

Preface by Ralph Martin / xv

Introduction by Bishop Samuel Jacobs / xvii

PART 1: CATCHING THE VISION

Chapter 1 John Paul II and the New Evangelization:
           What Does It Mean? / 2
           Cardinal Avery Dulles, S.J.

Chapter 2 What Is Our Message? / 17
           Ralph Martin

Chapter 3 Why Should Catholics Evangelize? / 29
           Father Tom Forrest, C.SS.R.

Chapter 4   How Must Catholics Evangelize? Evangelization
and the Power of the Holy Spirit / 39
Bishop Samuel Jacobs

Chapter 5   The Fundamental Mission of Every Believer / 49
Bishop William R. Houck

PART 2: PERSPECTIVES ON EVANGELIZATION

Chapter 6   Go and Make Disciples: The United States
Bishops' National Plan for Catholic
Evangelization / 64
Father Kenneth Boyack, C.S.P.

Chapter 7   Evangelization and the Experience of Initiation
in the Early Church / 79
Father Kilian McDonnell, O.S.B.

Chapter 8   The New Evangelization in Africa / 94
Cardinal Peter Turkson

Chapter 9   Which Churches Are Growing and Why? / 112
Vinson Synan, PH.D.

PART 3: HOW YOU CAN EVANGELIZE!

Chapter 10   Six Steps to Effective Evangelization / 124
Susan Blum Gerding, ED.D.

Chapter 11   Employing Charisms in Evangelization / 139
Peter Herbeck

Chapter 12   Catholic Street Evangelism Today / 150
Leonard Sullivan

Chapter 13   Preaching Evangelistic Homilies / 165
Father Bruce Nieli, C.S.P.

PART 4: BRINGING THE GOOD NEWS TO ALL PEOPLE

Chapter 14 Evangelizing the Poor / 176
            Sister Linda Koontz, S.N.J.M.

Chapter 15 Evangelizing Married Couples / 188
            Frank and Gerry Padilla

Chapter 16 Evangelizing Teenagers / 197
            Frank Mercadante

Chapter 17 Evangelizing in Business and Government / 205
            Michael Timmis

Chapter 18 Evangelizing Hispanic Americans / 218
            José (Pepe) Alonso

PART 5: EVANGELIZING AS A PARISH

Chapter 19 The Story of an Evangelizing Parish / 230
            Father Marc Montminy

Chapter 20 Evangelizing as a Parish / 250
            David Thorp

Chapter 21 Transforming the Sacramental Parish Into an
            Evangelizing Community / 264
            Father Ernesto I. Elizondo

PART 6: EVANGELIZATION AND CHRISTIAN UNITY

Chapter 22 Ecumenical Issues in Evangelization / 276
            Father Peter Hocken

Chapter 23 A Great Springtime for Christianity / 288
            Eduardo J. Echeverria, PH.D.

Notes / 296

Index / 314

Abbreviations of Frequently Cited Documents

AA Vatican II, Decree on the Apostolate of Lay People, *Apostolicam Actuositatem,* November 18, 1965.

AG Vatican II, Decree on the Church's Missionary Activity, *Ad Gentes Divinitus,* December 7, 1965.

CA Pope John Paul II, *Centesimus Annus* (On the Hundredth Anniversary of *Rerum Novarum*), May 5, 1991.

CL Pope John Paul II, Apostolic Exhortation *Christifideles Laici* (On the Vocation and the Mission of the Lay Faithful in the Church and in the World), December 30, 1988.

CT Pope John Paul II, *Catechesi Tradendae* (Catechesis in Our Time), October 16, 1979.

DV Vatican Council II, Dogmatic Constitution on Divine Revelation, *Dei Verbum,* November 18, 1965.

EA Pope John Paul II, *Ecclesia in America* (The Way to Conversion, Communion and Solidarity in America), January 22, 1999.

EE Pope John Paul II, Post-Synodal Apostolic Exhortation *Ecclesia in Europa* (The Church in Europe), June 28, 2003.

EN Pope Paul VI, *Evangelii Nuntiandi* (Evangelization in the Modern World), December 8, 1975.

EV Pope John Paul II, *Evangelium Vitae* (On the Value and Inviolability of Human Life), March 25, 1995.

FC Pope John Paul II, *Familiaris Consortio* (On the Christian Family in the Modern World), November 22, 1981.

GMD United States Bishops, *Go and Make Disciples: A National Plan and Strategy for Catholic Evangelization in the United States,* November 18, 1992.

LG Vatican II, Dogmatic Constitution on the Church, *Lumen Gentium,* November 21, 1965.

NMI Pope John Paul II, Apostolic Letter *Novo Millennio Ineunte* (At the Close of the Great Jubilee of the Year 2000), January 6, 2001.

NPPHM United States Bishops, *National Pastoral Plan for the Hispanic Ministry,* November 1987.

RH Pope John Paul II, *Redemptor Hominis* (Redeemer of Man), March 4, 1979.

RM Pope John Paul II, *Redemptoris Missio* (The Mission of the Redeemer: On the Permanent Validity of the Church's Missionary Mandate), December 7, 1990.

SC Vatican II, Constitution on the Sacred Liturgy, *Sacrosanctum Concilium,* December 4, 1963.

TMA Pope John Paul II, Apostolic Letter *Tertio Millennio Adveniente* (On Preparation for the Jubilee of the Year 2000), November 10, 1994.

UR Vatican II, Decree on Ecumenism, *Unitatis Redintegratio,* November 21, 1964.

Contributors

José (Pepe) Alonso is mission director of Kerigma Asociación Misionera Hispana in Miami, Florida, which promotes the evangelization of Hispanics in the United States, especially through evangelization schools and rallies.

Father Kenneth Boyack, C.S.P., is president of the Paulist National Catholic Evangelization Association in Washington, D.C. Father Boyack is the author or editor of thirteen books, including *Creating the Evangelizing Parish* (coauthored with Rev. Frank DeSiano, C.S.P.). As a consultant to the United States Conference of Catholic Bishops' Committee on Evangelization, Father Boyack served as general coordinator for the development of *Go and Make Disciples: A National Plan and Strategy for Catholic Evangelization in the United States.*

Cardinal Avery Dulles, S.J., is the Lawrence J. McGinley Professor of Religion and Society at Fordham University and a former member of the International Theological Commission. Cardinal Dulles has published sixteen books, including *Models of the Church, The Reshaping of Catholicism: Current Challenges in the Theology of the Church* and *The Craft of Theology: From Symbol to System.*

Eduardo J. Echeverria, PH.D., is an associate professor of philosophy at Sacred Heart Major Seminary in Detroit, Michigan.

Father Ernesto I. Elizondo is the pastor of St. Joseph Parish in Manor, Texas.

Father Tom Forrest, C.SS.R., is executive director of Evangelization 2000, a global effort to promote the Decade of Evangelization in response to the call of Pope John Paul II for a "new evangelization."

Susan Blum Gerding, ED.D., is executive director of Isaiah Ministries, which promotes renewal and evangelization and offers a model of clergy and lay preaching teams and local parish involvement. In 1996 she received the Pope Paul VI Award for Leadership in Catholic Evangelization, given by the National Council for Catholic Evangelization. Her publications include *The Ministry of Evangelization; Text, Study Guide and Implementation Process for Go and Make Disciples;* and *Called and Sent: Living the Eucharist.*

Peter Herbeck is the vice president and director of missions for Renewal Ministries in Ann Arbor, Michigan. He has been actively involved in evangelization and Catholic renewal throughout the United States, Canada, Africa and Eastern Europe for the past twenty-five years. He hosts a daily radio show called *Fire on the Earth* and cohosts the television program *The Choices We Face.* He is a frequent conference speaker and author of books and audio tapes about discipleship and life in the Spirit.

Father Peter Hocken is a priest in the diocese of Northampton, England, currently residing in Vienna, Austria. He is the author of several books and articles, particularly on the themes of charismatic renewal, ecumenism, the Pentecostal movement and Messianic Jews. Father Hocken is a member of the executive committee of Toward Jerusalem Council II and a member of the International Theological Commission for the Catholic Charismatic Renewal.

Bishop William R. Houck is the president of the Catholic Church Extension Society in Chicago, Illinois. Bishop Houck served as chairman of the United States Bishops' Committee on Evangelization from 1985 to1993.

Bishop Samuel Jacobs is currently the bishop of Houma-Thibodaux, Louisiana. Bishop Jacobs has served as chairman of the Bishops' Ad Hoc Committee on Charismatic Renewal. He is currently the chairman of the United States Bishops' Committee for Evangelization and chairman of the board of Renewal Ministries.

Sister Linda Koontz, S.N.J.M., is director of the Spirit of the Lord International Mission in El Paso, Texas. Sister Linda ministers to the physical and spiritual needs of the poor of Juarez, Mexico.

Ralph Martin is the president of Renewal Ministries and host of the weekly television program *The Choices We Face*. He is the author of several books on the Catholic church and spirituality and audio albums on the teachings of the saints. He is the director of graduate programs in the new evangelization at Sacred Heart Seminary in Detroit. Ralph is also an assistant professor of theology at Sacred Heart Seminary and a visiting professor of theology at Franciscan University of Steubenville.

Father Kilian McDonnell, O.S.B., is director of the Institute for Ecumenical and Cultural Research and a professor of theology at St. John's University in Collegeville, Minnesota. He coauthored with George Montague, S.M., *Christian Initiation and Baptism in the Holy Spirit*. He is also the author of *The Baptism of Jesus in the Jordan: The Trinitarian and Cosmic Order of Salvation* and *The Other Hand of God: The Holy Spirit as the Universal Touch and Goal*.

Frank Mercadante is executive director of Cultivation Ministries, a not-for-profit corporation founded in 1990 for the purpose of cultivating team-based, comprehensive and disciple-making Catholic youth ministries by training, resourcing and supporting adult and teen leaders. Mr. Mercadante has designed and written extensive youth ministry training materials for adult and student leaders internationally.

Father Marc Montminy is pastor of Ste. Marie Catholic Church in Manchester, New Hampshire, a parish that has experienced a dramatic renewal in the last decade. Father Montminy has promoted spiritual renewal in the diocese of Manchester for a number of years and is the founder of Joseph House, a contemplative retreat center.

Father Bruce Nieli, C.S.P., is former director for evangelization of the National (now United States) Conference of Catholic Bishops. Father Nieli travels throughout America giving parish missions, retreats and conferences as a full-time evangelist and missionary assigned to the Paulist Preaching Apostolate.

Frank and Gerry Padilla are leaders in Couples for Christ (CFC), a movement that focuses on renewing family life with specific ministries to couples, children, young adults, single men and women and others. CFC is also engaged in the work of total human liberation, particularly building vibrant communities among the poorest of the poor, involving shelter, health, education, livelihood and community empowerment. CFC is officially recognized by the Pontifical Council for the Laity and also by the Pontifical Council for the Family.

Leonard Sullivan is the current vice master of the Westminister Catholic Evidence Guild in London, England. He has been a speaker for the Guild since 1950.

Vinson Synan, PH.D., is dean of the School of Divinity at Regent University in Virginia Beach, Virginia. He is a member of the executive committee of the International Charismatic Consultation on World Evangelization. Doctor Synan's books include *The Holiness-*

Pentecostal Movement in the United States, Launching the Decade of Evangelization, The Spirit Said Grow: The Incredible Pentecostal-Charismatic Factor in the Global Expansion of Christianity and *Voices of Pentecost: Testimonies of Lives Touched by the Holy Spirit.*

David Thorp is a past member of the National Service Committee for Catholic Charismatic Renewal in the United States and the former director of the Office for Evangelization of the Archdiocese of Boston. He is director of evangelization for the Spiritual Life Center of Marian Community, a private association of Christ's faithful, in Massachusetts.

Michael Timmis is co-owner, vice chairman and general counsel for Talon, Inc., a privately held company employing six thousand people. He also serves as chairman of Prison Fellowship International and is one of the founding members of the National Fellowship of Catholic Men. He and his wife Nancy have developed self-help projects in Africa and Central and South America, and they are also very active in addressing the educational needs of children in the city of Detroit.

Cardinal Peter Kodwo Appiah Turkson received a doctorate in biblical studies at the Pontifical Biblical Institute in Rome in 1992. He was ordained archbishop of Cape Coast, Ghana, in 1993. In 2003 Pope John Paul II appointed him cardinal. He pastors the faithful in the archdiocese of Cape Coast and serves on the Pontifical Council for Christian Unity, the Commission for the Cultural Heritage of the Church, the Commission for Catholic-Methodist Dialogue and the Congregation for Divine Worship and Discipline of the Sacraments. He is also the chancellor of the Catholic University College of Ghana. From 1997 to 2004, he served as president of the Conference of the Bishops of Ghana.

Peter S. Williamson, Ph.D., completed his studies in biblical theology at the Pontifical Gregorian University in Rome. Peter has been involved for nearly thirty years in evangelization and pastoral ministry in the United States, and more recently in Lithuania and Kazakhstan. He presently serves as a country coordinator for Renewal Ministries and is assistant dean and assistant professor of New Testament at Sacred Heart Seminary in Detroit. He is the coeditor with Ralph Martin of *John Paul II and the New Evangelization*.

Preface

Soon after I began to notice the frequency with which Pope John Paul II wrote and spoke on the theme of evangelization, I came across an article by then Father Avery Dulles, s.j., pointing out the same development. As he says in the chapter he has written for this volume, "The evangelical shift brought about by Vatican II, Paul VI and John Paul II is one of the most dramatic developments in modern Catholicism."

A development this important needed to be explored in a serious way, not with regard merely to its theological significance but also to its practical implementation. While on a trip to New York shortly afterward, my wife, Anne, and I had lunch with Father Dulles. Out of that conversation was born a conference on the subject of the new evangelization and its implementation, which Father Dulles agreed to keynote.

That conference was held in May 1994 near Ann Arbor, Michigan. It surpassed our expectations in every way: in those who agreed to contribute, in those who came (participants represented fifteen different countries) and in the subsequent quality and usefulness of the theological, spiritual and pastoral results.

The publications of the original essays from the conference met with widespread acceptance and went through several printings. Now, in response to demand from the general public as well as university and seminary professors, the Servant imprint of St. Anthony Messenger Press is republishing an updated, revised version of the book. Many of the original contributors have updated their essays, and some new essays are included as well. Some are scholarly, some more popular, but all provide an important contribution in illuminating the nature, significance and practical implications of the call for a "new evangelization."

The pages that follow represent an immense amount of theological insight, spiritual sensitivity and pastoral experience. We believe this volume will serve as an important resource for the years ahead as the new evangelization unfolds.

At the end of some of the chapters we have provided the phone number and address of the particular organization or organizations with which that contributor is associated. We encourage you to contact them for further input as your own response to this important call takes shape.

Ralph Martin
Ann Arbor, Michigan
August 2005

Introduction

Bishop Samuel Jacobs

The call for a "new evangelization" will be one of the great legacies of John Paul II and his pontificate. Not only did he consistently preach about the need for a new appropriation of the initial command of Jesus to the church—to go and make disciples—but he also personally evangelized at every opportunity and in every circumstance. Like his namesake, the apostle Paul, the Holy Father crisscrossed the face of the earth, visiting over one hundred countries in his twenty-seven-year pontificate and boldly proclaiming the lordship of Jesus Christ.

His predecessor, Paul VI, saw evangelization as the very mission of the church. John Paul II lived this reality as a missionary evangelizer.

He proclaimed in his encyclical *Redemptoris Missio*: "The moment has come to commit all of the Church's energies to a new evangelization and to the mission *ad gentes*. No believer in Christ, no institution of the Church can avoid this supreme duty: to proclaim Christ to all peoples" (*RM*, 3). Thus, the basis of all evangelization is the "one gospel given in Jesus Christ."[1]

While the message of evangelization is always the same, the audience is different: the world is different; cultures are different; tools of communication are different. Because of these differences there is need to proclaim the same Jesus to all peoples in a new way with greater zeal, ardor and clarity, using modern means of communication wherever possible.

Because many of those baptized as infants are culturally or nominally Catholic and may never have internalized their faith, they need to meet the person of Jesus Christ through a new proclamation, so that at the root of their relationship with Jesus will be an authentic conversion of heart and mind. Such a conversion is not a one-time event but an ongoing process that leads one into a more radical living of the life of Christ as a gospel disciple.

At the same time, there are many (even in our own country) who have only heard about Jesus as an historical figure or who have never heard anything about him. It is estimated that nearly two-thirds of the world's population may fall into this category. Because God wills all to be saved, these too need to have the personal opportunity of hearing the Good News of salvation in Christ.

It is exciting that the late Pope John Paul II's consistent emphasis on the need for a new evangelization has borne much fruit over the years. Not only has it brought more people today into a deeper faith life, which is the inward thrust of evangelization, but it also has convicted them of their need to share with others their faith in Jesus. This is the mission or outward thrust of evangelization. This mission aspect is at the heart of the church's true identity. In conformity with the Great Commission of Jesus to the church, both young and old have accepted the challenge to share their faith with others and are doing so regularly.

What at one time seemed to be considered a "Protestant" way of ministering has increasingly become part of the very life of many Catholic parishes and movements. In response to John Paul's call for a new evangelization, the United States Conference of Catholic Bishops in 1992 issued their own support document entitled *Go and Make Disciples: A National Plan and Strategy for Catholic Evangelization in the United States*. In it the bishops stated in solidarity with the pope that the essential mission of every baptized Catholic is first to be evangelized and then to become evangelizers of others. In the words of the bishops:

> We want to make it clear that evangelization means something special for us as Catholics. We can see what it means by looking at what happens to evangelized people. Not only are they related to Jesus by accepting his Gospel and receiving his Spirit; even more, their lives are changed by becoming disciples, that is, participants in the Church, celebrating God's love in worship and serving others as Jesus did. (*GMD*, 25)

Over the years many have responded to this call in different ways. Some have recognized the need to receive further training in the fundamentals of evangelization as well as in the practical steps of reaching out to others on a one-to-one basis. As a result, a number of schools of evangelization have begun in the United States and around the world.

I remember approaching my bishop about twenty years ago with the concern that we talk about evangelization but in fact do very little to empower people in the exercise of this ministry. I asked if another person and I could go and get training, so that we in turn could train others. He agreed, and an associate and I went to an evangelization training school for a week, which included practical experience with door-to-door outreach. When we came back we offered the same training over a period of two years to others in the diocese. It was a wonderful experience both to receive and to give.

Others have responded to the call of evangelization by becoming involved in parish evangelization committees, looking for ways to make the parishes more welcoming and inviting. Others are part of parish cell groups that seek to minister to the needs of the members as well as multiply cells through personal evangelization.

It is my hope that those who read this book will catch the vision of Christ for them as members of his church as well as become convicted by the Holy Spirit, the agent of evangelization, of their need to become authentic and effective evangelizers. It is my prayer that these words of Jesus to the apostles in his Easter appearance will resonate in the heart of each reader: "As the Father has sent me, even so I send you" (John 20:21), and that he or she will not be the same. It is my desire that this book will be the beginning of a new journey for many into what John Paul II calls a "new springtime" for the church.

We have been the recipients of a rich heritage of faith. May we in turn share with others what Jesus has done and given to us. Then we all will be enriched.

PART 1
CATCHING THE VISION

CHAPTER 1

John Paul II and the New Evangelization: What Does It Mean?[1]

Cardinal Avery Dulles, S.J.

Can the Roman Catholic church be evangelical? Is Catholicism a religion centered on the gospel?

Half a century ago some Catholics, and practically all Evangelicals, would have said no. Protestant churches, it was thought, could be churches of proclamation and evangelization, but the Catholic church was a church of liturgy and law, centered on tradition, hierarchy and sacraments. In other words, Protestants were viewed as specializing in the word of God and the gospel; Catholics, in the law of God and the sacraments.

This contrast was never anything but a caricature. Luther and Calvin placed high value on the sacraments and the law of God. The Council of Trent, conversely, taught that the whole point of the Catholic system was to transmit the gospel of Jesus Christ in its purity and completeness. The gospel, it was recognized, is the supreme norm for all Christian belief and practice.

For a variety of reasons this evangelical perspective was obscured during the sixteenth century. Christianity in Europe became rather static, according to the principle that the religion of the sovereign was the religion of the people. Western Europe was carved up into Protestant states and Catholic states, where the faith of the citizens was determined more by political and sociological factors than by personal conviction. As far as Europe was concerned, the era of evangelization was closed.

The recently discovered territories in the Americas, Africa and Asia did, of course, become objects of a new missionary thrust, but even there the focus was not so much on spreading the gospel as on extending the churches of the mother countries. The missionary task was almost totally in the hands of clergy and religious, who worked in close collaboration with the princes and governors of the colonial powers.

Several historical developments have gradually resuscitated the idea of evangelization. The progressive secularization of European and American culture, in the course of the last three centuries, prevented the churches from relying as they previously had on political and sociological factors to maintain the faith. In the new pluralistic situation, faith increasingly became a matter of personal decision in response to the testimony of convinced believers.

In order to win or maintain adherents, Christianity had to be proclaimed once more, as it had been in New Testament times, as a joyful message centered on Jesus Christ. Beginning in the eighteenth century, England and the United States witnessed several

Protestant evangelical revivals. In the twentieth century Catholicism has undergone an analogous evangelical renewal, partly occasioned by the de-Christianization of formerly Catholic countries and greatly assisted by the ecumenical and biblical movements.

Vatican II marks an important stage in this recovery. A simple word count indicates the profound shift in focus. Vatican I, which met from 1869 to 1879, used the term *gospel* (*evangelium*) only once[2] and never used the terms *evangelize* and *evangelization*. Less than a century later, Vatican II mentioned the gospel 157 times and used the verb *evangelize* eighteen times and the noun *evangelization* thirty-one times. When it spoke of evangelization, Vatican II generally meant the proclamation of the basic Christian message of salvation through Jesus Christ.

IN THE WAKE OF VATICAN II

Building on the work of the Council, Paul VI dedicated his pontificate to the task of evangelization. His choice of the name Paul signified his intention to take the Apostle of the Gentiles as the model for his papal ministry. In 1967 he renamed the Congregation for the Propagation of the Faith the Congregation for the Evangelization of Peoples. At his burial in 1978, an open book of the Gospels was laid on his coffin, a fitting symbol of his ministry.

Often called "the pilgrim pope," Paul VI was the first pontiff in history to make apostolic journeys to other continents—first to the Holy Land (1964), then to India (1964), next to New York (1965), later to Portugal, Istanbul and Ephesus (1967), to Colombia (1968) and to Geneva and Uganda (1969). Finally, in 1970, he undertook a long journey including Tehran, East Pakistan, the Philippines, West Samoa, Australia, Indonesia, Hong Kong and Sri Lanka.

Wishing to engage the entire church more decisively in the dissemination of the gospel, Paul VI chose as the theme of the Synod of Bishops in 1974 "the evangelization of the modern world." That synod provided him with materials for his great apostolic exhortation on evangelization, *Evangelii Nuntiandi*.[3] Here he described evangelization as the "deepest identity" of the church, which "exists in order to evangelize" (*EN*, 14). While proposing a broad and inclusive concept, the pope made it clear that there can be no evangelization without explicit proclamation of Jesus as Lord (*EN*, 22). It cannot be reduced to any sociopolitical project of development and liberation (*EN*, 31–33).

John Paul II carried this evangelical shift yet a stage farther. Summarizing the main orientation of his pontificate, he declared in Mexico City on May 6, 1990: "The Lord and master of history and of our destinies has wished my pontificate to be that of a pilgrim pope of evangelization, walking down the roads of the world, bringing to all peoples the message of salvation."[4] John Paul had attended in 1979, shortly after his election as pope, the Puebla conference of Latin American bishops on "Evangelization at Present and in the Future of Latin America." While in the papal office, he made 105 foreign trips, including six to the United States.

Beginning in 1983 the pope issued repeated calls for a "new evangelization." Evangelization, he insisted, cannot be new in its content, since its theme is always the one gospel given in Jesus Christ. If it arose from us and our situation, he says, "it would not be 'gospel' but mere human invention, and there would be no salvation in it."[5] Evangelization, however, can and should be new in its ardor, its methods and its expression.[6] It must be heralded with new energy and in a style and language adapted to the people of our day.

In one of his major encyclicals, *Redemptoris Missio* (1990), John Paul declared: "I sense that the moment has come to commit all of the Church's energies to a new evangelization and to the mission *ad gentes*. No believer in Christ, no institution of the Church, can avoid this supreme duty: to proclaim Christ to all peoples" (*RM*, 3).[7] In this encyclical (*RM*, 86) and in many of his addresses, the pope linked the new effort of evangelization with the preparation for the third millennium of Christianity. The decade of the 1990s, he said, was an extended Advent season in preparation for the great Jubilee of the Incarnation (*RM*, 86). In an apostolic letter released just after the end of the year 2000, he eloquently repeated his summons to "a new apostolic outreach...lived as the everyday commitment of Christian communities and groups" (*Novo Millennio Ineunte*, 40).

John Paul II did not seek to prescribe in detail the methods and modalities of the new evangelization, which will inevitably take on distinct hues in different situations. He was content to provide the stimulus for local initiatives. But from a variety of papal statements, it is possible to sketch the basic lineaments of the program.

Like any evangelistic outreach, the "new evangelization" must be centered on the person of Jesus Christ and on the one and eternal gospel. Within this stable framework the new evangelization has at least four characteristics that set it off from the evangelistic efforts of previous centuries:

1. *The participation of every Christian.* No longer reserved to clerics and religious with a special missionary vocation, evangelization is now seen as the responsibility of the whole church. Vatican II had already taught that since the church is missionary by her very nature, evangelization is the duty of every Christian (*LG*, 17; *AG*, 23, 35–36). Elaborating on this point, Paul VI in *Evangelii Nuntiandi* described the distinct contributions expected of the pope, bishops, priests, religious and laity (*EN*, 66–73).

John Paul II made similar distinctions. Bishops, he said, "are the pillars on which rest the work and the responsibility of evangelization, which has as its purpose the building up of the Body of Christ."[8] Priests are by vocation "responsible for awakening the missionary consciousness of the faithful."[9] Members of religious orders and congregations can play a special role because their total gift of self through the vows of poverty, chastity and obedience gives dramatic testimony to the values of the kingdom of God (*RM, 69*).

From the beginning of his pontificate, John Paul II emphasized the participation of all Christians, whether clerical or lay, in the prophetic office of Christ. In his apostolic exhortation on the laity in 1988, [10] he strongly accented the duty of lay Christians to make their daily conduct a shining and convincing testimony to the gospel (*CL, 34, 51*). It is their special responsibility, he said, to demonstrate how Christian faith constitutes the only fully valid response to the problems and hopes that life poses to every person and society (*CL, 34*). In talks to special groups—such as families, women, students, children, the sick and the disabled—the pope illustrated how the special gifts of each class can contribute to the total effort.

2. *Distinct from foreign missions.* In a period when it could be taken for granted that the Western world was solidly Christian, Europe and America were no longer regarded as suitable targets for evangelization. They were considered to have passed beyond that stage to the phase of pastoral care. Since the legal and social pressures in favor of religious conformity have been relaxed, it has become apparent that many Christians, including Catholics, were never effectively evangelized. Baptized in infancy, they have never made a living personal commitment to Christ and the gospel. As adolescents or adults, many drift away from the faith.

Evangelization, in fact, must be directed to the church herself. Paul VI stated this quite bluntly: "The Church is an evangelizer, but she begins by being evangelized herself.... She needs to listen unceasingly to what she must believe, to her reasons for hoping, to the new commandment of love" (*EN, 15*). The members of the church themselves are tempted by the idols of the prevailing culture.

Different strategies are required for dealing with different populations. In large parts of Europe and the Americas, fresh proclamation is urgently needed to fill in what can only be described as a growing religious vacuum. A new paganism, marked by phenomena such as astrology and earth worship, is rampant. Large numbers of young people, especially in the inner cities, are simply ignorant of Christianity, as are multitudes of immigrants and refugees coming from non-Christian parts of the world. These groups stand in need of *primary evangelization*—that is to say, a first proclamation of the Christian message.

Quite different are the needs of people who were once superficially instructed in their religion but have lost a living sense of the faith and are alienated from the church. They require *re-evangelization* rather than primary evangelization (*RM*, 33), in order to fan the embers of their dying faith into flame. They must be socialized, perhaps for the first time, in welcoming communities of vibrant faith.

3. *Directed to cultures.* Whereas evangelization had usually been studied in terms of individual conversion, Paul VI in *Evangelii Nuntiandi* observed that cultures themselves need to be regenerated by contact with the gospel (*EN*, 20). Convinced of the unbreakable links between faith and culture, John Paul II established the Pontifical Council for Culture in 1982. The new evangelization, he delared, must strive to make human cultures harmonious with Christian values and open to the gospel message.[11]

This is not a matter of dominating cultures but rather of serving them. As John Paul stated in his encyclical *Centesimus Annus* in 1991, evangelization "plays a role in the culture of various nations, sustaining culture in its progress towards the truth, and assisting in the work of its purification and enrichment" (*CA*, 50).[12] Where the prevailing culture remains closed and hostile, faith cannot fully express itself, nor can the culture achieve its full potential.

In his visit to Los Angeles in 1987, John Paul II raised some challenging questions about the influence of the gospel on the music, poetry, drama, painting and sculpture of the United States today. He asked whether all these art forms were sufficiently imbued by the

Christian spirit. To bring about this needed development, he added, is primarily the task of the Christian laity. [13]

4. *Envisaging comprehensive Christianization.* The initial proclamation of the basic Christian message is an indispensable first step, but it is only the beginning of a lifelong process. Paul VI set forth a rich and multifaceted program of evangelization in *Evanglii Nuntiandi.*

John Paul II repeatedly defined full evangelization as involving catechetical instruction, moral doctrine and the social teaching of the church. Personal transformation requires instruction in sound doctrine, participation in sacramental worship and the acquisition of a mature ethical and social conscience. A total evangelization, he said, "will penetrate deeply into the social and cultural reality, including the economic and political order.... Such a total evangelization will naturally have its highest point in an intense liturgical life that will make parishes living ecclesial communities."[14] Evangelization in its completeness should lead to what John Paul II, following Paul VI, frequently called "a civilization of love" (*CA,* 10).

OBSTACLES TO IMPLEMENTATION

The evangelical shift brought about by Vatican II, Paul VI and John Paul II is one of the most dramatic developments in modern Catholicism. Partly for that reason, it encounters incomprehension and resistance among some Catholics, who seem deaf to the new summons. Numerous obstacles must be overcome.

In countries such as our own, terms such as *evangelization* and *evangelism* have a Protestant ring. They appear to be the chosen trademarks of revivalist and fundamentalist sects, some of which are virulently anti-Catholic. Catholics distrust the biblicism, the individualism, the emotionalism and the aggressive proselytization of certain Protestant evangelistic preachers.

Vatican II, moreover, has put Catholics on guard against anything smacking of triumphalism. Attempting to be modest and self-critical, many tend to gaze inward, asking themselves what still needs to be reformed in their own church. Diffident about current Catholic doctrine and practices, they often fail to proclaim their faith with confidence. Influenced by the American tradition that religion is a purely private matter, they hesitate to bring pressure on anyone to undergo a deep conversion of mind and heart. Individuals, they assume, should make up their own minds in perfect freedom.

These concerns are not unfounded. Catholics should not be expected to admire or imitate every feature of Protestant evangelistic preaching. They must adopt an authentically Catholic style of evangelization and avoid obnoxious proselytization. But there are many excellent features in Evangelicalism that Catholics would do well to emulate.

In their call for a new evangelization, the recent popes, following the directive of Vatican II, have given the needed impetus. They have, I submit, correctly identified God's call to the church in our day and have hit upon a suitable remedy for the church's present ills.

Excessive preoccupation with inner-church issues has led to conflict and polarization in the Catholic community itself. We Catholics need to recapture the sense of having a message that is urgently needed for the redemption of the world. If some of us are weak and vacillating in our faith, this is partly due to our reluctance to share it. Once we grasp the universal validity and significance of the Good News, we gain a new appreciation for the privilege of being its bearers. John Paul II put it very concisely: "Faith is strengthened when it is given to others" (*RM*, 2).

THE ECUMENICAL DIMENSION

The task of evangelization is complicated by persisting divisions among Christians, but even divided Christians may have much in common. Vatican II called attention to the widespread agreement regarding the central doctrines of the Trinity and the Incarnation, which are preeminent in the "hierarchy" of truths (*UR*, 11).

It should, therefore, be possible for Christians to unite in confessing before the whole world their faith in the triune God and in Christ as Son (*UR*, 12). In their missionary activity Catholics and other Christians, according to the Council, should be able to join their voices in "a common profession of faith in God and in Jesus Christ." The name of Christ, their common Lord, should draw Christians ever closer together (*AG*, 15).

Tensions undeniably exist between Catholics and certain evangelical Protestants who refuse to look upon Catholics as Christians and who deny the validity of baptism unless it is administered to believers who claim an inner assurance of having been personally saved. In spite of grave disagreements such as these, which need not be disguised, Catholics and Evangelicals have an important core of shared convictions.

More than most other Christians, Evangelicals are committed to the divine inspiration of Holy Scripture and to the articles of the Apostles' Creed. They unhesitatingly affirm the divinity of Christ, his virginal conception, his atoning death and his bodily resurrection. They, like Catholics, expect the return of the Lord in glory at the end of time.

In addition to these theological convictions, Evangelicals accept a strict moral code favoring chastity, parenthood and family stability. Together with Catholics, they oppose radical programs of euthanasia, eugenics and population control that would exploit the aged, the handicapped and the unborn. These and other important convergences are spelled out in greater detail in a recent declaration on "Evangelicals and Catholics Together."[15] A significant ecumenical realignment seems to be occurring in this country, enabling Evangelicals and Catholics to collaborate in defending the Christian heritage of our nation.

I have previously maintained, and continue to maintain, that Catholics and Evangelicals can greatly assist one another. Evangelicals can help Catholics to focus on the central Christian message, to achieve a deep personal relationship with Christ as Savior, to form warm and welcoming communities and to proclaim the gospel without embarrassment.

Catholics, conversely, can help Evangelicals to overcome their own imbalances—to avoid a narrow biblicism, to escape from fundamentalistic literalism, to appreciate the value of tradition and to cultivate a richer sacramental life, a livelier sense of worldwide community and a keener realization of sociopolitical responsibility. A new ecumenism of convergence and mutual enrichment between Catholics and Evangelicals holds rich potential for the future of Christianity.

THE CHURCH'S TRUE TREASURE

Many of us acknowledge in theory that we should be evangelizers, but we feel unable to measure up to the demands. We may have tried to bring others to the faith and resoundingly failed. Conscious of scandals within our own church and of the defection of some Catholics, we may feel humbled by the church's present difficulties.

Why do people not see the truth of Catholicism? Are not its two-thousand-year history, its worldwide expansion, its inner unity and its fruitfulness in good works a sufficient demonstration? How can people fail to be impressed by the stability of its structures, the profundity of its theology, the genius of its artists, the splendor of its cathedrals and the beguiling beauty of its liturgies and music?

While these features are humanly impressive, we must confess that if this were all the church had to offer, she would be weighed in the scales and found wanting. People turn to the church, one would hope, with other motives. The true treasure of the church is not what she possesses and produces but the Lord who possesses her and enlivens her with his Holy Spirit.

Saint Paul reminds us that in Jesus Christ are "all the treasures of wisdom and knowledge" (Colossians 2:3); that he is our wisdom, justice, holiness and redemption (see 1 Corinthians 1:30). To evangelize, therefore, is to preach "the unsearchable riches of Christ" (Ephesians 3:8).[16] In the words of Paul VI, "he indeed is the hope of the human race, its one supreme teacher and shepherd, our bread of life, our High Priest and our victim, the one mediator between God and men, the savior of this world and king of the eternal world to come."[17]

The church, therefore, has one inescapable task: to lift up Christ. When she seeks to lift herself up, the church becomes weak, but when she acknowledges her own weakness and proclaims her Lord, she is strong. Moses in the desert lifted up the bronze serpent, and all who looked upon it were healed. Applying this incident to himself, Jesus said that the Son of Man must be lifted up in order for believers to have life in him (John 3:14–15). "And I," he said, "when I am lifted up from the earth, will draw all men to myself" (John 12:32).

The church is privileged to lift high the cross and let the light of Christ shine upon the whole world. Effective evangelization, according to John Paul II, consists precisely in this. "The new evangelization," he said, "begins with the clear and emphatic proclamation of the gospel, which is directed to every person. Therefore it is necessary to awaken again in believers a full relationship with Christ, mankind's only Savior. Only from a personal relationship with Jesus can an effective evangelization develop." [18]

Here, precisely, lies a major difficulty. Caught up in a merely sociological or traditional type of Catholicism, too many Catholics of our day seem never to have met the Lord. They know a certain amount about him from the teaching of the church, but they lack direct, personal familiarity. They have never realized that the deepest identity of the church is to proclaim the gospel.

Many who shift their membership to Evangelicalism do so because Catholicism did not seem to offer them a real encounter with Christ. If they only understood who it is that is really speaking when the gospel is proclaimed from the pulpit, or who comes to them in Holy Communion or who forgives their sins through the ministry of the priest in sacramental absolution, they could hardly feel as they do.

When Catholic priests address their congregations as if religion were simply a matter of legalistic conformity, they fail in their primary task of preaching the gospel. As often as parishioners go to Mass and receive the sacraments without inner devotion, as a matter of mere obedience or custom, they belie the central meaning of their actions. Deprived of any close relationship to the Lord, they become easy prey to sectarian preachers who give evidence of a joyful encounter with the Word of Life.

When our Lord ascended into heaven, he did not leave us orphans. Christ continues to be present through the Holy Spirit in word and sacrament. He is present in those who minister in his name; he is present in the hearts and minds of all who believe in him. Drawing near to us in so many ways, Jesus seeks to enter into the sanctuary of every Christian heart. If we grant him that entrance, he will be a living, energetic reality and will take over the direction of our lives.

Cardinal John Henry Newman, in his *Grammar of Assent,* asked himself how Christianity so quickly became the dominant faith of the Roman Empire. After surveying scores of texts from the early church, he concluded that there was only one true explanation. The thought and image of Christ was the vivifying idea that made Christians so steadfast in their confession of the faith, so zealous in their practice of mutual love and so ardent in their hope of eternal life.

The power of the church today continues to rest on the living presence of the Lord, imprinted on the consciousness of the faithful. Everything in the life and worship of the church should be aimed at sharpening that consciousness.

In the final analysis it is not we ourselves who evangelize. The principal agent of evangelization, according to Paul VI, is the Holy Spirit, the divine witness par excellence. "It is not by chance," he wrote, "that the great inauguration of evangelization took place on the morning of Pentecost, under the inspiration of the Spirit" (*EN*, 75).

John Paul II agreed. "Missionary dynamism," he said, "is not born of the will of those who decide to become propagators of the faith. It is born of the Spirit, who moves the Church to expand, as it progresses in faith through God's love."[19] The Holy Spirit imparts the wisdom to seek out new and effective methods, the discretion to speak the appropriate words and the courage to bear witness with power.

Through the highest leadership of the church, we have received a call that is clearly inspired by the Holy Spirit. On hearing the call we may be tempted to respond, as Peter once did, "Master, we toiled all night and took nothing!" (Luke 5:5). John Paul II met this temptation by reminding us that evangelization does not rest on purely human logic. "Faced with the immensity of the tasks, we must repeat Peter's act of faith and trust in the Master: 'At your command I will lower the nets'" (Luke 5:5).[20]

The success of our efforts will not, of course, depend entirely on us. Our hearers must accept the grace to respond. The word of God sometimes falls on rocky soil, as Jesus himself experienced, but the possibility of failure and rejection cannot excuse us from our duty to bear witness. When the acceptable time arrives, the Lord is capable of bringing forth a harvest out of all proportion to our labor and talents.

If we faithfully take up our task, in a spirit of prayerful confidence, we can firmly hope that the church may be approaching a new springtime. We may yet be privileged to witness a new Catholic moment, a new Pentecost, the rebirth of a fresh and dynamic Catholicism.

CHAPTER 2

What Is Our Message?

Ralph Martin

In 1993 someone asked me why many Southern Baptists were so eager to share the good news with others, in comparison to the average Catholic's total disinterest. Several reasons came to mind. The chief one is that most Baptists have a clear understanding of the heart of the gospel message: that we are *saved by grace through faith.* Igniting this head knowledge is a personal appreciation for what Jesus has done for them. They also grasp the eternal consequences of faith, that there really is a heaven and a hell.

Unfortunately, I cannot say the same for most Catholics. Despite all the years of religious education and catechesis, there seem to be some astounding gaps in our grasp of the gospel message—at least enough to dampen our enthusiasm for sharing the Good News.

Dr. Peter Kreeft, a professor of philosophy at Boston College, has made similar observations through contact with his predominantly Catholic students. "The life of God comes into us by faith, through us by hope, and out of us by the works of love.... But many Catholics still have not learned this thoroughly Catholic and biblical doctrine. They think we're saved by good intentions, or being nice, or sincere, or trying a little harder, or doing a sufficient number of good deeds."[1]

Over the last twenty-five years Dr. Kreeft has asked hundreds of his students this pointed question: "If you should die tonight and God asks you why he should let you into heaven, what would you answer?" His findings? "The vast majority of them simply don't know the right answer to this, the most important of all questions, the very essence of Christianity. They usually don't even mention Jesus!"[2]

In our efforts toward evangelization, we must be clear on the content and substance of the gospel message, or else the means chosen and the results obtained will be quite ambiguous. While programs, plans and processes of evangelization are important, clarity of content is indispensable. What has been *revealed* to us about what it means to be a Christian? What is the *truth* that God wants us to communicate to others? In short, what is the gospel message?

SAVED BY GRACE

The Scriptures frequently summarize the most foundational elements of the gospel message. John 3:16 presents one such statement: "For God so loved the world that he gave his only Son, that whoever believes in him should not perish but have eternal life." Ephesians 1:7–8 is another: "In him we have redemption through his blood, the forgiveness of our trespasses, according to the riches of his grace which he lavished upon us."

When we read these brief summaries of the Good News, we are struck by the overwhelming love, mercy and generosity at the heart of the plan of salvation. The most foundational element of the gospel is not *our love for God* but *his love for us* (see 1 John 4:9–10). Just as his love initiated creation, his love initiates the chance for a renewal of creation. Scripture characterizes God's love and mercy as great, immeasurably generous, rich, kind and lavished upon us (see Ephesians 1:7–8; 2:1–10; Titus 3:3–8).

This saving gift of God's Son is totally undeserved and unmerited on our part. It is purely and entirely by God's free choice, by his favor, by his grace, that Jesus is given to us. "For by grace you have been saved through faith; and this is not your own doing, it is the gift of God—not because of works, lest any man should boast" (Ephesians 2:8–9).

What we deserve by nature is God's wrath, to die because of our sin. Apart from Christ we would be "slaves to various passions and pleasures," locked hopelessly in "malice and envy, hated by men and hating one another" (Titus 3:3). We would be "following the course of this world, following the prince of the power of the air,...following the desires of body and mind" (Ephesians 2:2–3).

God freely decided to give the human race another chance. And he chose a means designed to kill the root of pride at the origin of sin: Satan's lie that "you will be like God" (Genesis 3:5). At the heart of redemption is a profound act of humility, the self-offering of the Son of God as a sacrifice for us, and it must be met by an act of humility on our part, the acknowledgment of sin and the surrender of faith. We need humbly to receive rather than self-righteously try on our own strength to achieve salvation. Then pride can be broken, and no human being can boast of anything except the cross of Christ (see 1 Corinthians 1:27–31).

SAVED THROUGH FAITH

We also read in these scriptural summaries how we *receive* this great gift of God's saving love, his only Son, Jesus: we are *saved by grace through faith in Jesus.* "Whoever believes in him should not perish but have eternal life" (John 3:16). The baptism of new birth and renewal by the Holy Spirit both presuppose faith, which itself comes as a gift God offers to all people.

Faith normally comes from hearing the truth of the gospel preached, seeing or hearing about signs and evidence that confirm its truth and experiencing a direct work of the Holy Spirit in the soul (see John 14:10–11; Romans 10:8–15; 2 Corinthians 3:16–18; 1 Thessalonians 5:9). Faith and the conversion that flows from it are themselves gifts of God's grace and favor, the unmerited working of his Spirit. As John Paul II put it in *Redemptoris Missio:*

> The proclamation of the Word of God has *Christian conversion* as its aim: a complete and sincere adherence to Christ and his Gospel through faith. Conversion is a gift of God, a work of the Blessed Trinity. It is the Spirit who opens people's hearts so that they can believe in Christ and "confess him" (cf. 1 Cor 12:3); of those who draw near to him through faith Jesus says, "No one can come to me unless the Father who sent me draws him" (Jn 6:44). (*RM,* 46)

What then is faith? Faith is a way of knowing and seeing with our spiritual eyes invisible realities that are infinitely more important than the realities we can see with our biological eyes.

> Now faith is the assurance of things hoped for, the conviction of things not seen. For by it men of old received divine approval. By faith we understand that the world was created by the word of God, so that what is seen was made out of things which do not appear. (Hebrews 11:1–3)

Scripture invests the concept of faith with several different meanings. Second Timothy 1:13–14 (see also 2:2; Jude 3) speaks of the body of truths revealed by God, often called "the deposit of faith." This primary meaning of faith as a *knowledge of truth* is the one we have in mind when we talk about passing on "the faith" or teaching "the faith." Obviously, as essential as this kind of faith is, it is not enough. "Even the demons believe" (James 2:19), but they lack both obedience and trust.

Scripture also speaks of "the obedience of faith" (Romans 16:26). Faith in this sense means knowledge of truth that contains an implicit or explicit call to obedience. A well-known formulation of this concept would be "Faith by itself, if it has no works, is dead" (James 2:17). An aim and fruit of the gospel is a particular kind of human behavior that accords with the truth. Jesus said, "If you continue in my word, you are truly my disciples, and you will know the truth, and the truth will make you free" (John 8:31–32).

As we obey the truth that is revealed to us, we will understand still more of that truth and experience still more of its fruits in our lives. Real change becomes possible through the power of the gospel. Even years of habit, addictions and the influence of a pagan world can be overcome by a living relationship with God.

Yet this obedience, this sign of authentic saving faith, this manifestation of faith working through love, this growth in moral perfection, prayer, a life of love, fidelity and service, is itself brought about and perfected through the grace of God. Ephesians 2:10 tells us that "we are his workmanship, created in Christ Jesus for good works, which God prepared beforehand, that we should walk in them." We are once again humbled. The paths that we walk and the daily circumstances of our lives have been given to us for our transformation, that we may learn to serve and love God and others.

Even though salvation is a gift received through faith, Scripture exhorts us to "work out your own salvation with fear and trembling;

for God is at work in you, both to will and to work for his good pleasure" (Philippians 2:12–13). God's grace is at work to enable us to will and to do what he is calling us to do. He not only calls us to the obedience of faith but also enables us to obey. What grace!

Faith as *trust* is the third and perhaps most common use of this word in Scripture. "Blessed is she who believed that there would be a fulfilment of what was spoken to her from the Lord" (Luke 1:45). The basic thrust of Jesus' whole message is to trust in him and in the Father. He tells us to stop worrying about what we are to eat or drink and instead to seek out his kingship over us. The rest will follow in turn (see Luke 12:28–31).

Jesus calls us to faith in the goodness of God, the power of God, the truthfulness of God and, most of all, the personal love of God for each one of us in every aspect of our lives and needs. He calls us to the kind of surrender and abandonment possible only when we know who God is. This kind of faith is centered in a personal relationship with God, Father, Son and Holy Spirit.

Church leaders are recognizing that many Catholics are impoverished in their personal relationship with Jesus. While talking to a group of American bishops, Pope John Paul II stressed this point: "Sometimes even Catholics have lost or never had the chance to experience Christ personally: not Christ as a mere 'paradigm' or 'value,' but as the living Lord, 'the way, and the truth, and the life'" (John 14:6).[3]

We Catholics have tended to emphasize faith as propositional belief and moral obedience and not so much as a personal relationship of trust, surrender and abandonment to God. I believe that tendency has diminished the worship, life and mission of the church and has limited the experience and working of the Spirit. In any event, Scripture clearly presents faith as our lifeline to God. Faith is what inaugurates, sustains and deepens that relationship. It is as vital to our life with God as an oxygen line is to a deep-sea diver.

SAVED FROM HELL

The gospel is presented as a message with eternal consequences. Apart from Christ and faith in him, we are slaves to sin, to our own passions, "hated by men and hating one another," "foolish, disobedient" (Titus 3:3). Life apart from Christ amounts to hell on earth. Unless we are transferred, by grace through faith, from this kingdom of darkness and to the kingdom of the beloved Son of God, this state of hell becomes intensified and permanent.

Jesus had these grave consequences in mind when he commanded his disciples, "Go into all the world and preach the gospel to the whole creation. He who believes and is baptized will be saved; but he who does not believe will be condemned" (Mark 16:15–16).

Vatican II clearly spelled out the church's position on the necessity of Jesus for salvation in its Constitution on the Church, *Lumen Gentium* (17), and the document *Dominus Iesus* further develops this point. In summary, the Catholic church believes that salvation is impossible apart from Jesus but that those who "through no fault of their own" have never heard the Good News will be judged on the basis of the light God has given them in creation and in conscience (see Romans 1–2).

Despite this possibility, we should not be lax in preaching the gospel, since:

> rather often men, deceived by the Evil One, have become caught up in futile reasoning and have exchanged the truth of God for a lie, serving the creature rather than the Creator (cf. Rom. 11:21, 25). Or some there are who, living and dying in a world without God, are subject to utter hopelessness. Consequently, to promote the glory of God and procure the salvation of all such men, and mindful of the command of the Lord, "Preach the Gospel to every creature" (Mk. 16:16), the Church painstakingly fosters her missionary work. (*LG*, 16)

Jesus himself frequently spoke about the reality of hell (see Matthew 13:42, 50; 22:13; 25:46; Mark 9:43, 48; John 5:29). Despite all the debate about what is metaphorical and what is literal, one thing is undeniably clear: hell is real, unspeakably awful, and you really do not want to end up there. Jesus makes clear that hell is not exactly a long shot but is the way we all drift unless we cling to him. "Enter by the narrow gate; for the gate is wide and the way is easy, that leads to destruction, and those who enter by it are many. For the gate is narrow and the way is hard, that leads to life, and those who find it are few" (Matthew 7:13–14).

We have witnessed a virtual silence on the reality of hell as a consequence of people having rejected the gospel, not believing in it or disobeying it—even in some notable official documents of the church on evangelization, where an exposition on the reality of hell was virtually required by the subject matter. Certainly we should make an effort to present the Christian message in a positive and attractive way. We are not at liberty, however, to falsify it by silence where it conflicts with our increasingly secular and pagan culture. To do so is to diminish the gospel's power, distort its saving truth and remove an essential motivation for evangelization.

If everyone ultimately will be saved and there is no real possibility of hell for the "average person," why be concerned? Many Catholics are not. If it does not matter in the end whether someone repents, believes and is baptized, why bother to preach the Good News? Many Catholics do not.

SAVED FOR HEAVEN

God lavishes his love on all those who receive his gift of salvation through faith and baptism. Joined to Jesus, they are adopted as sons and daughters of God. The Holy Spirit makes his home in their hearts so that they begin to know the joy, peace and love of heaven right away—in an imperfect, limited but real way.

Scripture frequently speaks of the reality of heaven, which is described in various ways: eternal life (see Matthew 25:46); glory beyond compare (2 Corinthians 4:17); a place in which the redeemed participate in the life of God in glorified, immortal, incorruptible bodies (1 Corinthians 15:35–55); a dwelling in the heavens (2 Corinthians 5:1); the city of the living God, which is filled with angels in festal gathering (Hebrews 12:22). While we taste a bit of that heaven here on earth, we await a glorious inheritance far beyond our imagining: a new earth, a new heaven, the new Jerusalem, the Holy City, where God will personally wipe every tear from our eyes, where there will be no more death or mourning, crying or pain (see 2 Peter 3:13; Revelation 21:1–4, 10–11).

THE GOSPEL AND THE EUCHARIST

The gospel message is Good News beyond human comprehension: we are saved by love, for love, for all eternity. And yet there is more. God knows that this life of faith must be nurtured, like a tender shoot, lest it wither and die. Evangelization must lead to catechesis, to learning what Christ teaches.

An essential part of the Good News is that Jesus, through his cross and resurrection, is pouring out his Holy Spirit so we can become one body, a holy nation, a royal priesthood, the church, his very body and even his bride. He is gathering together his sons and daughters into a new family, the church. As part of the way of life of the redeemed community, Jesus has asked us to celebrate the Lord's Supper in memory of him.

In the Eucharist we remember and make present the central realities of our redemption—the sacrificial death of Jesus on the cross and his resurrection—and we look forward to his return in glory. We proclaim the Good News together: Christ has died, Christ has risen, Christ will come again. We are nourished through the sacramental presence of his Body and Blood. We worship the Father in Spirit and in truth.

Heaven is a *corporate* reality. Together we begin to learn what it means to live for the destiny for which we were created, to "live for the praise of his glory" (Ephesians 1:12). The church and the Eucharist are essential elements of the Good News. Christian initiation is not complete, and therefore evangelization is not complete, until the new convert becomes part of Christ's body, expressed in a local congregation, and is invited to participate in the Eucharistic feast.

Vatican II recognized the liturgy as the summit toward which the activity of the Church is directed, as well as the fount from which all her power flows: "For the goal of apostolic works is that all who are made sons of God by faith and baptism should come together to praise God in the midst of His Church, to take part in her sacrifice, and to eat the Lord's supper" (*SC,* 10).

Thus evangelization leads to incorporation into his body, the church, and is consummated and expresses itself in the liturgy, the formal, public worship of the church. In the Eucharist we remember that we are saved by grace, through faith, and we give thanks and praise to the Father for the immeasurably generous gift of his Son, Jesus. John Paul II spoke about this inseparable link between evangelization and the Eucharist in his first encyclical:

> The Church never ceases to relive his death on the Cross and his Resurrection, which constitute the content of the Church's daily life. Indeed, it is by the command of Christ himself, her Master, that the Church unceasingly celebrates the Eucharist, finding in it the "fountain of life and holiness" [Litany of the Sacred Heart], the efficacious sign of grace and reconciliation with God, and the pledge of eternal life. The Church lives his mystery, draws unwearyingly from it and continually seeks ways of bringing this mystery of her Master and Lord to humanity—to the peoples, the nations, the succeeding generations, and every individual human being—as if she were ever

repeating, as the Apostle did: "For I decided to know nothing among you except Jesus Christ and him crucified" [1 Corinthians 2:2]. The Church stays within the sphere of the mystery of the Redemption, which has become the fundamental principle of her life and mission. (*RH*, 7)

The Eucharist is a *representation* of the gospel in a very special way. As we gather at the table of the Lord, we remember the unmerited free gift of redemption through the sacrifice of Christ's life, death and resurrection and draw nourishment from his presence in the Eucharist according to our faith.

Eucharist in Greek means "thanksgiving." The liturgy is supposed to be characterized by a spirit of profound gratitude and praise for the awesome love demonstrated in the sacrifice of Christ. But how can we be grateful for something we do not know we have received or for something we think we deserve because of our own merits? How can we be grateful if we do not know what we have been saved from and saved for?

O foolish Galatians! Who has bewitched you, before whose eyes Jesus Christ was publicly portrayed as crucified? Let me ask you only this: Did you receive the Spirit by works of the law, or by hearing with faith? Are you so foolish? Having begun with the Spirit, are you now ending with the flesh? Did you experience so many things in vain?— if it really is in vain. Does he who supplies the Spirit to you and works miracles among you do so by works of the law, or by hearing with faith? (Galatians 3:1–5)

Faith in the crucified Christ is important not just initially; it is required daily if we are to follow the Lord, if the Spirit is to be continually poured out as we and the entire church desperately need. A "new Pentecost" must accompany the "new evangelization," and the key to both is the same: the basic gospel message. We are sinners saved by grace, through faith in Christ; saved from hell, for heaven, by Jesus Christ, our Savior and Lord.

Ralph Martin is president of Renewal Ministries, a Catholic ministry of renewal and evangelization. He is also assistant professor of theology and director of the graduate theology program in the new evangelization at Sacred Heart Major Seminary in the archdiocese of Detroit.

Renewal Ministries
P.O. Box 1426
Ann Arbor, MI 48106
734-662-1730
www.renewalministries.net
(www.SHMSonline.org)

CHAPTER 3

Why Should Catholics Evangelize?

Father Tom Forrest, C.SS.R.

The Holy Spirit gives us three excellent reasons why Catholics should evangelize: his supernatural gifts of faith, hope and charity. Concerning all God's gifts, Jesus commanded us, "You received without pay, give without pay" (Matthew 10:8).

In obeying this command, we have to give exactly the way Jesus gave to us. He shared with us the very best he had to give: his Father, his Spirit, his mother, his name, his life, his glory and inheritance. This means that we in turn have to share the very best we have to give: the faith, hope and love that enrich our lives and that we have in our hearts because of him.

Our Faith Unlocks the Gates of Heaven

I remember several years ago touring some of the ancient ruins of Rome with a pleasant priest. He talked with great excitement about his favorite therapeutic technique, "the primal scream." He spoke about it so much that I was tempted to let out a "scream" of my own, thinking how much good this exuberant priest could do if he were speaking with the same enthusiasm about Jesus.

If an angel were to suddenly announce that I had been granted one wish for the good of the church, my choice would be clear. I would wish for a new and unshakable faith conviction throughout the entire church regarding the incomparable value of knowing Jesus Christ. This conviction is the kind of faith for which martyrs give their lives and missionaries struggle at tremendous risk to implant in others.

Incomparable is a superlative, and superlatives, like absolutes, are out of style in this day and age. Even so, Jesus Christ *is* the supreme good. Nothing and no one can match him or even be compared. Jesus is in a class by himself! He is Emmanuel: God himself among us. Saint Paul wrote, "Indeed, I count everything as loss because of the surpassing worth of knowing Christ Jesus my Lord. For his sake I have suffered the loss of all things, and count them as refuse, in order that I may gain Christ,...that I may know him and the power of his resurrection" (Philippians 3:8–10).

In the opening scenes of the poignant film *The Mission,* a priest is martyred by Guarani Indians of Paraguay. Soon afterward another young priest sets out to bring Christ to these same Indians. When his companions express their concern that he is endangering his life, the future martyr (canonized by Pope John Paul II in 1988) responds with the simple words, "I *must* go." At any cost, he is saying, I *must* bring Jesus to those who do not know him.

This conviction about the absolute importance of knowing Christ leads us to the supreme charity of making him known to others. This faith, however, is being lost in an age of exaggerated egalitarianism that goes beyond the equal rights of individuals and gives equal value to all beliefs. A young woman once asked me about the hopes of Evangelization 2000 regarding good Hindus, Muslims and Buddhists. When I answered that our desire and prayer is to lead them gently and freely to Jesus, she responded in bewilderment, "But won't that do damage to their culture?"

I tried to explain some crucial distinctions that place this concern in proper perspective. Buddha is only a teacher; Jesus is the living Word of God. Mohammed is a prophet; Jesus is the fulfillment of all prophecy. Hindus at times worship a confusion of gods; Jesus is the one true God, King of heaven and earth. At Jesus' name—and at his name *only*—every knee must bend in the heavens, on the earth and under the earth, because "there is no other name under heaven given among men by which we must be saved" (Acts 4:12).

We perform a vast number of good deeds, but one is supreme: proclaiming Jesus Christ as the only Savior of the world. Those who do not know Christ have no guaranteed way of getting to heaven. *Only Jesus* reveals the Father (see Matthew 11:27). *Only Jesus* empowers us for godlike loving and godlike forgiving (Luke 15:31–32; John 15:9–12). *Only Jesus* gives us a totally new beginning by washing away our guilt and even the memory of our sins (Isaiah 53:11–12; Jeremiah 31:34; Micah 7:18–19; Hebrews 10:17–18). *Only Jesus* gives us his Holy Spirit to make us "the righteousness of God" (2 Corinthians 5:21).

A disciple of Christ enjoys a tremendous advantage, in regard to salvation, over the adherents of other religions. His Eminence Cardinal Francis Arinze expressed the understanding that, yes, it is true that Buddhists, Hindus and Muslims can be saved through a baptism of desire, but such a salvation involves many ifs, buts and maybes. It is certainly not the same as coming to explicitly know Jesus as the Way, Truth and Life.

Christ commissioned Saint Paul "to open their eyes, that they may turn from darkness to light and from the power of Satan to God, that they may receive forgiveness of sins and a place among those who are sanctified by faith in me" (Acts 26:18). The task of an evangelist is the delightful one of evacuating hell and populating heaven, a task that draws its power from a burning conviction that the very purpose of life and the measure of all human success are summed up in knowing Jesus Christ and being united with him.

OUR HOPE GIVES LIGHT TO A WORLD IN DARKNESS

In his great encyclical *Redemptoris Missio*, Pope John Paul II made this prophetic statement: "Today, as never before, the Church has the opportunity of bringing the Gospel, by witness and word, to all people and nations. I see the dawning of a new missionary age, which will become a radiant day bearing an abundant harvest, if all Christians...respond with generosity...to the calls and challenges of our times" (*RM*, 92).

If, indeed. If there were ever a time when sinners needed conversion, if there were ever a time when captives needed to be set free and mountains of pain and depression removed, if there were ever a time when the human race needed sanctification and salvation, if there were ever a time when the whole world needed to hear and follow Christ's teaching on love, mercy and forgiveness, that time is now!

So too, if there were ever a time when Christ held the only answer, if there were ever a time when Christian values needed to be proclaimed, if there were ever a time when our own faith needed to be renewed and activated, if there were ever a time when the church needed to be united in common and decisive efforts, if there were ever a time in history for dynamic evangelization, that time is now!

The pope was saying that if there were ever a time when the world was ready to listen and respond to the Christian message, our own moment in history is that time. We all know about the enormous problems in the world today: racial and ethnic hatreds fueling wars of unthinkable savagery; children who live in danger of abuse and violence even within their own homes; city streets too dangerous to walk that have become dormitories for the lost and homeless; self-doubts and chronic depression leading to "escape routes" of addiction and suicide; a planet threatened by global pollution and an overconsumption producing more garbage than we can handle.

Reporters and analysts talk endlessly about crime, poverty, economic recessions and global pollution, yet few claim to have any answers. Leaders have lost the confidence of the people, while scandals in palaces and rectories shake our loyalties and even our faith. That is why so many people are hungry to hear about something and someone in whom they can truly trust and believe.

Jesus is that Someone. He is Someone so good that he is called the spotless and innocent Lamb of God; Someone so wise that he is called the Wisdom come down from heaven, the Word of eternal life; Someone so faithful and merciful that he is called the Way, the Truth and the Life. He is Someone who promises his disciples an unbelievable destiny and who carries them as God's own children all the way to paradise.

Doctors need medicine before they can heal. Soldiers need arms before they can do battle. Cooks need ingredients before they can prepare a banquet. Farmers need seeds before they can reap a harvest. Cars need gasoline before they can run. Sailors need wind before they can sail. Orchestras need a musical score before they can enchant audiences with their symphonies. And the world needs Jesus, our *anchor of hope,* before we can find an answer to our problems and needs.

We are the "Easter people," God's own people of hope. Saint Peter told us to "always be prepared to make a defense to any one who calls you to account for the hope that is in you" (1 Peter 3:15). And the reason for our hope is Jesus Christ, the Lamb of God who washes away all our sins, who gives us a new heart, a new mind and a new and abundant life.

OUR LOVE BRINGS HEALING TO THE BROKENHEARTED

Only one word can fully describe the Christian life. That word is *love*. "If I have prophetic powers, and understand all mysteries and all knowledge, and if I have all faith, so as to remove mountains, but have not love, I am nothing" (1 Corinthians 13:2).

Two thousand years ago the invisible love that is God became visible by vesting himself with the flesh of a virgin and dying on a cross for the incredible reason that he loves each and every one of us. The fact that Christianity is a religion of love makes every evangelizer the teller of a love story, the singer of a love song. By example as well as by words, evangelizers must be teachers of love, calling others to love God above all else and to love their neighbors as they love themselves.

Too few Catholics realize that evangelization is the only adequate and convincing proof of their Christlike love for both God and neighbor. How can I say that I have learned from Jesus the Master how to love if I show no interest in continuing the mission he gave me after dying on the cross (see Matthew 28:19–20)? How can I claim to have found the pearl of great price (Matthew 13:45–46) yet share it with no one?

Learning how to love means helping others to find the path of righteousness, the green pastures that bring refreshment to the soul, the eucharistic bread that ends all hunger, the water that conquers thirst, the light that provides escape from the terror of the dark, the truth that sets us free. How can I claim to have learned that truth and yet not release a single prisoner from the slavery of spiritual selfishness—perhaps not even myself?

Christians possess the ultimate treasure! Christians know the name! Christians hold the answer! And until Jesus comes again, they have the finest of all opportunities for sharing that treasure, shouting that name and announcing that answer to all the world.

There is nothing more natural than wanting to share the Good News. When a man wins a million-dollar lottery, he almost falls from the window in his excitement to share that news with a neighbor. Jesus himself talks about shouting not from a window but from the housetops, shouting the Good News about all he has won for us by his cross (see Matthew 10:27). On another occasion he says that if Christians stayed silent with this kind of Good News, "the very stones would cry out" (Luke 19:40).

Paul explains that the love of Christ impels us (see 2 Corinthians 5:14). He expresses that fact in many ways: "Woe to me if I do not preach the gospel.... I have made myself a slave to all, that I might win the more. To the Jews I became as a Jew.... To the weak I became weak,...all things to all men, that I might by all means save some" (1 Corinthians 9:16, 19–20, 22).

The morning of the first Pentecost offers dramatic testimony to the power of love. A few minutes after the Holy Spirit had fallen upon them, all the disciples were down in the street proclaiming, converting and baptizing three thousand new believers (see Acts 2:40–41). Nor did their fervor cool off as the days and months went by. These first Christians continued to work with a sense of urgency. "Every day in the temple and at home they did not cease teaching and preaching Jesus as the Christ" (Acts 5:42).

Go QUICKLY!

Jesus never doubted the urgency of his mission. While still a small boy, he showed his determination: "I must be in my Father's house" (Luke 2:49). Using a parable, he tells us to "[go] out quickly to the streets and lanes of the city, and bring in the poor and maimed and blind and lame.... Go out to the highways and hedges, and compel people to come in, that my house may be filled" (Luke 14:21, 23).

An angel spoke with equal urgency to the women standing in astonishment at the sight of the empty tomb: "Go quickly and tell his disciples that he has risen" (Matthew 28:7). After the Ascension another angel indicated the same urgency when he said to the stupefied apostles: "Men of Galilee, why do you stand looking into heaven?" (Acts 1:11). In his own heavenly way, the angel seems to be saying, *"Get going!"*

Our task of love is so urgent that not even the most valid of excuses is acceptable. Jesus says bluntly, "Leave the dead to bury their own dead; but as for you, go and proclaim the kingdom of God" (Luke 9:60).

We respond with urgency when a baby falls down a well or when someone has a heart attack. If a house begins to rock with an earthquake, no one thinks about first taking a nap or paying the bills. When a father sees his home on fire with his children still inside, does he say, "Let's check the insurance to see if we have full coverage"? Does he procrastinate for a half hour before calling the fire department? Or when he calls, do the fire fighters respond, "We'll drop by right after our coffee break"? After they arrive at the blaze, do they chat with the father about the outside chance that the kids can find a way out on their own?

In urgent situations late responses are useless, and any postponement means a lost opportunity. Yet the church today is staying far too cool, seemingly oblivious that the world is blazing all around them and that people are dying for a drink of life-giving water. With participation at Sunday Mass melting away, some bishops still seem to be saying, "Don't disturb me! I have this important correspondence to finish." With few young people in sight, some priests are still busy only with routine services for the already converted.

With empty Catholic churches being torn down and Muslims flooding the world with new mosques, some theologians tell us to keep calm. They blithely explain that people just may find their way even if we fail to announce that Jesus is *the* Way. With the devil roaring around in search of someone to devour (see 1 Peter 5:8), many Christians are still using shyness as an excuse for not revealing the only name that saves—even to their own children, his most likely prey.

At least in some parts of the church, it is no exaggeration to say that the Father's house is on fire and that his beloved children are being trapped by flames. We are living in a time that calls for more than a quiet chat or another conference, dialogue or study paper. Faith, hope and love fuel our urgent mission to share the gospel.

Jesus commands us to "go…and make disciples of all nations" (Matthew 28:19).

Evangelization is a mission for all Christians, the highest expression of Christian love. It is a faith-filled response to the fact that the whole value of any human life depends upon hearing and putting into practice the Good News. An unresponsive church risks an awful consequence: "Because you are lukewarm, and neither cold nor hot, I will spew you out of my mouth" (Revelation 3:16).

Go now! Go with urgency! We are heralds of glad tidings (see Isaiah 41:27), messengers ready to run ourselves even to death in our determination to deliver the Good News of salvation as quickly as possible. We have only so much time. Tens of thousands die daily, many without ever hearing of Jesus. With so many in the world still waiting to be evangelized, we have to run hard and run to win, looking forward to the finish line, looking forward to meeting in glory, spending eternity with the church made perfect by the blood of the Lamb.

With offices in Rome and on all continents, Evangelization 2000 works through retreats, international prayer campaigns, conferences and LUMEN television to motivate and mobilize Catholics to share Christ and his love. For more information contact:

Evangelization 2000
3112 7th St., N.E.
Washington, DC 20017
202-526-2814
fax: 202-526-2871
E-mail: EV2000taf@aol.com

CHAPTER 4

How Must Catholics Evangelize? Evangelization and the Power of the Holy Spirit

Bishop Samuel Jacobs

The call to evangelize is not a new call, even though Pope John Paul II coined the term "new evangelization." What he said is that it must be new in method, new in expression and new in zeal. John Paul reiterated this call in 1991 in these words: "The new evangelization needs new witnesses,...people who have experienced an area of change in their lives because of their contact with Jesus Christ, and who are capable of passing on that experience to others."[1]

Jesus himself issued this call: "The time is fulfilled, and the kingdom of God is at hand; repent, and believe in the gospel"

(Mark 1:15). Before his ascension he commissioned the apostles to continue and extend his work of evangelization: "Go therefore and make disciples of all nations, baptizing them in the name of the Father and of the Son and of the Holy Spirit, teaching them to observe all that I have commanded you; and lo, I am with you always, to the close of the age" (Matthew 28:19–20).

John Paul II gave new emphasis to the call for evangelization and made us more aware of the urgency of our times. He exhorted us to a new zeal for unveiling the love of Christ toward all people. He called us to a new commitment to "sow Christian hope in hearts thirsting for the living God."[2] As Cardinal Thiandoum of Senegal put it, "Every person has a right to the good news, and we should leave no stone unturned to announce it to them."[3]

John Paul stressed the need for a new evangelization of society in a world torn asunder by war, so that "the liberating truth of the gospel will inspire the building of a new world of authentic peace and justice animated by love."[4] If the truth and life of the gospel were lived out more fully and proclaimed more effectively, then our society would reflect the values of the gospel more clearly.

The call is not just to evangelize but to evangelize *in the power of the Spirit with new boldness.* After commissioning the disciples to proclaim the Good News to all the nations, Jesus told them to wait for the coming of the Spirit promised by the Father. "You shall receive power when the Holy Spirit has come upon you; and you shall be my witnesses in Jerusalem and in all Judea and Samaria and to the end of the earth" (Acts 1:8).

BEING IN HARMONY WITH THE PLAN OF GOD

What does it mean to evangelize in the power of the Spirit? First of all, we must begin by acknowledging that evangelization is the plan of God and not simply a good idea. As such, our efforts to share the Good News will be effective to the extent that we are in harmony with that divine plan. We can design all the evangelistic programs and outreaches we wish, but if the power of the Spirit is not the soul of our efforts, then we will be exhausted very soon—just like all those batteries left in the dust by the pink Energizer rabbit.

Pope Paul VI summed up the central role of the Holy Spirit in his apostolic exhortation *Evangelii Nuntiandi:*

> It must be said that the Holy Spirit is the principal agent of evangelization: it is He who impels each individual to proclaim the Gospel, and it is He who in the depths of consciences causes the word of salvation to be accepted and understood. But it can equally be said that He is the goal of evangelization: He alone stirs up the new creation, the new humanity of which evangelization is to be the result, with that unity in variety which evangelization wishes to achieve within the Christian community. Through the Holy Spirit the Gospel penetrates to the heart of the world, for it is He who causes people to discern the signs of the times—signs willed by God—which evangelization reveals and puts to use within history. (*EN,* 75)

How important is it for us to follow the plan of God? Let me share a story.

After Jesus ascended to heaven there was a great party celebrating what he had accomplished on earth. The angel Gabriel asked Jesus a question. What recognition had the world given to his divine suffering for its sake? Jesus replied that only a few people in Palestine knew of it. Believing the whole world ought to know, Gabriel asked, "What is your plan, Master, for telling them of it?"

Jesus replied, "I have asked Peter, James, John, Andrew and a few others to make it the business of their lives to tell others, and those others to tell others, until the last person in the furthest circle has heard the story and has felt the power of it."

"But suppose they do not tell others. What then?" asked the angel.

Jesus answered quietly, "Gabriel, I have not made any other plans. I am counting on them."

To begin to grasp more clearly the plan of God, we need to look at the life of Jesus, the greatest of all evangelists. What we see is an intimate relationship with the Father. Jesus in his humanity was so in love with the Father that he committed his whole life to doing his will and his work. It was not enough for Jesus to know this in his heart; he wanted to make public his relationship and commitment. He wanted his life to be a public witness of his union with the Father, not just a private, vertical relationship. He wanted his deeds to be a witness of the love of the Father for all mankind.

This profound intimacy with the Father and the Spirit did not happen overnight. Jesus spent the first thirty years of his life being formed in the religious environment provided by Mary and Joseph and by his covenant with Yahweh. He heard the Scriptures in the synagogue every Sabbath and was immersed in God's saving deeds through the various religious celebrations. God's laws were not just words for Jesus but his rule of life.

When the time came for his public ministry, Jesus did not devise his own plan for evangelization. He was impelled by the Holy Spirit to go to the Jordan River and be baptized by John, not because of sin but because of his consuming love and desire to do the will of the Father. We read in Luke's Gospel: "Now when all the people were baptized, and when Jesus also had been baptized and was praying, the heaven was opened, and the Holy Spirit descended upon him in bodily form, as a dove, and a voice came from heaven, 'Thou art my beloved Son; with thee I am well pleased'" (Luke 3:21–22).

Observing the life of Jesus shows us that the effective evangelist must be rooted in a growing, personal love relationship with the Father, which is the call to holiness. Our relationship cannot be something that was experienced years ago as a child or as a young adult. It must be one that is alive and developing today, always open to the new gifts of God's personal love in the present moment. It must be nurtured daily in the quiet of prayer and intimacy, in word and sacraments, in the desert of purification and the valley of restoration.

This call to holiness is parallel and prerequisite to the call to evangelize. How can we effectively proclaim God's love if that love is not effectively visible in our lives? How can the Spirit empower us to evangelize if the life of the Spirit is dormant or stagnant within our hearts?

Evangelization and the Gifts of the Spirit

Jesus began his three years of public ministry following the visible Pentecostal experience at his baptism and the hidden temptations in the desert. The initial response was quite positive. Scripture tells us that "Jesus returned in the power of the Spirit into Galilee, and a report concerning him went out through all the surrounding country. And he taught in their synagogues, being glorified by all" (Luke 4:14–15).

Jesus knew, acknowledged and acted in the power of the Spirit. Peter later attested to this fact when he proclaimed, "Men of Israel, hear these words: Jesus of Nazareth, a man attested to you by God with mighty works and wonders and signs which God did through him in your midst, as you yourselves know" (Acts 2:22).

Peter later evangelized Cornelius by relating the works of Jesus:

You know the word which he sent to Israel, preaching good news of peace by Jesus Christ (he is Lord of all), the word which was proclaimed throughout all Judea, beginning from Galilee after the baptism which John preached: how God anointed Jesus of Nazareth with the Holy Spirit and with power; how he went about doing good and healing all that were oppressed by the devil, for God was with him. (Acts 10:36–38)

The Scriptures establish the direct relationship between evangelization and the gifts of the Spirit. Jesus evangelized and confirmed the words he was sharing with signs and wonders. Recall the encounter he had with the Samaritan woman at the well. As he led her from the external fact that he was a male Jew to the internal faith realization that he was the Messiah, Jesus exercised the gift of word of knowledge, telling the woman that the man she was living with was not her husband. The power of the Spirit was evident in bringing her to the grace of salvation (see John 4:4–26).

At other times Jesus would heal and then evangelize, bringing the person into an acceptance and response to God's gift of his saving love and freedom. His way of ministering to the man blind from birth demonstrated this approach. Jesus first healed him. As the grace of God continued to work, he was able to bring this man from physical blindness to physical sight, from spiritual blindness to spiritual sight (see John 9).

We see the power of the Spirit manifested in the process of evangelization both when a person experiences a miracle or sign of wonder and when he makes a proclamation of faith in the saving work of Jesus. For it is the Spirit who opens the heart of the unbeliever, or the heart of one who seeks the fullness of truth, or the heart of the sinner and backslider or the heart of the indifferent and inactive believer.

Whatever the case may be, it is the grace of the Spirit that triggers the response of faith and deeper commitment in the person who freely chooses to say yes to Jesus' call and plan. The evangelist is merely a chosen instrument in the hands of God, though an important one.

What was evidenced in the life of Jesus was taught, learned, experienced and imitated by the apostles after their own anointing by the Holy Spirit. The fire of Pentecost still glowed in Peter and John as they said to the crippled beggar at the temple gate, "In the name of

Jesus Christ of Nazareth, walk" (Acts 3:6). As the temple crowd rejoiced over the miracle, Peter proceeded to evangelize them, proclaiming that the healing was done in the name of Jesus.

Later, after receiving in a vision the message to go to the house of Cornelius, Peter addressed him and his household about God's plan of salvation, culminating with the birth, life, death and resurrection of Jesus. He concluded: "To him all the prophets bear witness that every one who believes in him receives forgiveness of sins through his name" (Acts 10:43). No sooner did Peter finish than the Holy Spirit descended on all who were listening, and they began "speaking in tongues and extolling God" (Acts 10:46).

We see this same process, which is the plan of God for evangelization, played out over and over in other New Testament accounts. "Philip went down to a city of Samaria, and proclaimed to them the Christ" (Acts 8:5). Because of the preaching and the miracles, many people accepted the word of God and were baptized in water and in the Spirit. Later, led by the Spirit, Philip was told to catch up with the carriage of the Ethiopian eunuch, who was passing by. Through the gift of interpretation, he proceeded to explain the passage from Isaiah fulfilled in the person of Jesus. The official asked for baptism in response to the grace of faith (see Acts 8:26–39).

Scripture tells us that Paul and Barnabas, "remained for a long time [in Iconium], speaking boldly for the Lord, who bore witness to the word of his grace, granting signs and wonders to be done by their hands" (Acts 14:3).

How Can We Respond to the Call for a New Evangelization?

I believe we can best respond to Pope John Paul's call for a "new evangelization" by understanding and submitting to God's plan as evidenced in the Scriptures. We do not have to reinvent the wheel or develop a new process. Our primary responsibilities are to be rooted in our relationship with God, to be formed in our faith, to accept the empowerment of the Spirit already given to us and to trust in God. As we try to be attuned to the lead of the Spirit and respond with obedience, we need to speak out fearlessly but faithfully the word of God and our own faith tradition, share the gospel message of salvation in simple terms and exercise the appropriate gifts of the Spirit as he inspires us.

Like Jesus and the apostles, we need to continue to seek the face of the Lord and to enter into greater intimacy with the living God. Like Jesus, we need to be obedient children of the Father of all. Like the apostles, we need to come under the lordship of Jesus, to live consciously in the presence of the One who is the beginning and the end.

Like Jesus, we need to be a people of prayer so that our witness and evangelization may flow from union with the Father in the power of the Spirit. An example of this is found in the healing of the paralytic (see Luke 5:17–26). Prior to this miracle Jesus had gone to the desert to pray (see Luke 4:1–13, 42); it is out of this context that the miracle occurred. Our witness and evangelization then need to be brought back to the Lord in thanksgiving and praise, as we see after the healing of Simon's mother-in-law (see Luke 4:38–39) as well as the many sick and possessed brought to Jesus that evening.

Like the apostles, we need to pray for the continual infilling of the Holy Spirit, so that we may boldly proclaim the Good News of Jesus. They beseeched the Lord in the Upper Room, "Now, Lord, look upon their threats, and grant to thy servants to speak thy word with all boldness, while thou stretchest out thy hand to heal, and signs and wonders are performed through the name of thy holy servant Jesus." God responded in a dramatic way. "When they had prayed, the place in which they were gathered together was shaken; and they were all filled with the Holy Spirit and spoke the word of God with boldness" (Acts 4:29–31).

Like Jesus and the apostles, we need to be open to the leading and power of the Spirit if our work of evangelization is to be authentic and fruitful. How many divine appointments have we already missed because of fear, laziness, a sense of inadequacy, an unwillingness to be a disciple of Jesus at the moment or any number of other excuses? How many people have not been given a chance to respond to God's invitation to a new life? How many have missed the grace of repentance, conversion and sanctification because we did not respond to the grace of evangelization?

Like the apostles, in the words of Paul VI, we must share "the name, the teaching, the life, the promises, the kingdom and the mystery of Jesus of Nazareth, the Son of God" (*EN*, 22). In all of this ours is a small part of the process, though by God's choice a necessary one. However, what the Spirit does through us and in the person being evangelized remains the heart of the matter, the essential part of the process of conversion.

We must always remember that the response of the person being evangelized is not the measuring stick God will use in judging *our* efforts. Whether someone comes to a saving relationship with Jesus and becomes a member of the community of faith is not our responsibility but that of the person evangelized. Our responsibility is to do the work of evangelization in the power of the Spirit.

To paraphrase a comment by Blessed Mother Teresa of Calcutta: God is not asking us to be *successful* but *faithful* to his command. We are not held accountable before the Lord for the number of people we actually evangelize but for how many times we obediently act on his lead and in his power to proclaim the Good News to others.

John Paul II saw the new evangelization as a sign of a new springtime coming for the church. "Despite the voices of the prophets of pessimism, I would like to repeat once again, with emphasis:…God is preparing a great Christian springtime, the beginnings of which can already be glimpsed."[5]

Having been blessed by the Lord and gifted by his holy and awesome presence, we need to hear his word to Isaiah uttered in our own hearts: "Whom shall I send?" The Lord is waiting to hear the fearless and generous response of Isaiah from our own lips: "Here am I! Send me" (Isaiah 6:8).

It is not enough for us to have our ears tickled, our minds instructed and illumined, our hearts challenged. God is looking for men and women who are committed to be evangelists in the power of the Spirit, who will pursue training if necessary, who will no longer be satisfied with being fed but who will seek to feed others the same Good News that brings them life.

To repeat Cardinal Thiandoum, "Every person has a right to the good news, and we should leave no stone unturned to announce it to them." Because we have heard and experienced the saving power and love of God in Jesus, we have the duty and responsibility to share it with others. The reward and the consequences are explicit in the Scriptures: "Every one who acknowledges me before men, I also will acknowledge before my Father who is in heaven; but whoever denies me before men, I also will deny before my Father who is in heaven" (Matthew 10:32–33). Consider these questions from the Letter to the Romans a personal challenge: "For, 'every one who calls upon the name of the Lord will be saved.' But how are men to call upon him in whom they have not believed? And how are they to believe in him of whom they have never heard? And how are they to hear without a preacher? And how can men preach unless they are sent?" (Romans 10:13–15).

If not you, who? If not now, when? If not the truth of the gospel, what? If not in the power of the Spirit, how? If not in your home or school or place of work, where? God needs us to do our part to help others to know his great love.

CHAPTER 5

The Fundamental Mission of Every Believer

Bishop William R. Houck

The word *evangelization* is still relatively new to so many of our Catholics. Some of them even consider it strictly a Protestant idea and activity. Cardinal Avery Dulles, in a lecture at Fordham University in December 1991 entitled "John Paul II and the New Evangelization," put it this way: "The majority of Catholics are not strongly inclined toward evangelization. The very term has for them a Protestant ring."

When I was a youngster growing up in Alabama, the prevailing attitude about the "work of the church," which we now call evangelization and which Pope Paul VI stated is "the essential mission of the church," relegated it to the business of priests and religious. Thus my own desire to spread the gospel led me to St. Mary's Seminary in Baltimore, where I prepared for the priesthood and studied theology from 1947 to 1951.

Being one of the native vocations for the mission diocese of Mobile, I had been advised by my bishop to prepare myself for doing mission work in the diocese. I prepared in part by joining the Catholic Evidence Guild at the seminary and doing street preaching in downtown Baltimore.

One afternoon, when a large crowd had gathered on the street corner, a woman asked, "Where are you guys from?" I told her we were students from St. Mary's Seminary and members of the Catholic Evidence Guild. She responded in a surprised tone of voice, "You mean you're Catholic?" I answered in the affirmative.

"Roman Catholic?" Again I said yes. I do not know if I ever fully convinced her or not, but she went on to exclaim, "I don't believe it. We Catholics don't do this kind of thing! Protestants do street preaching!"

Many in the church still hold the same view of evangelization, even years after the magnificent document of Pope Paul VI, *Evangelii Nuntiandi* (On Evangelization in the Modern World). But thankfully we now see a growing awareness of the fundamental mission given to every believer. The call for a renewed understanding of evangelization was set in motion by the Second Vatican Council. The Dogmatic Constitution on the Church, *Lumen Gentium*, calls all laity to holiness and to responsibility for the mission of the Church: "The obligation of spreading the faith is imposed on every disciple of Christ, according to his ability" (*LG*, 17).

EVANGELIZATION IN THE MODERN WORLD

The Roman Synod of Bishops was an outgrowth of the Second Vatican Council. The pope from time to time calls representative bishops from around the world together for consultation and input on a topic of concern for the church. Pope Paul VI was truly prophetic when he called for the Synod of Bishops in 1974 to be on the topic of evangelization. I believe the document produced, *Evangelii Nuntiandi*, will end up being recognized as one of the major church documents of the twentieth century.

Writing in 1974–1975, Pope Paul VI said the Roman Synod of Bishops on Evangelization faced three burning questions:

1. In our day, what has happened to that hidden energy of the Good News, which is able to have a powerful effect on a person's conscience?

2. To what extent and in what way is that evangelical force capable of really transforming the people of this century?

3. What method should be allowed in order that the power of the gospel may have its effect?

A year earlier Pope Paul VI had addressed the college of cardinals with these words: "The conditions of the society in which we live oblige all of us...to seek by every means to study how we can bring the Christian message to modern man. For it is only in the Christian message that modern man can find the answer to his questions and the energy for his commitment of human solidarity. The church has the duty of preserving the heritage of faith in its untouchable purity, and of presenting it to the people of our time in a way that is as understandable and persuasive as possible."[1]

In his synod document the pope set out the basics of what we understand by evangelization. One of the best known texts from that great document states it very clearly: "We wish to confirm once more that the task of evangelizing all people constitutes the essential mission of the Church.... Evangelizing is in fact the grace and vocation proper to the Church, her deepest identity" (*EN*, 14).

The Work of the Church

The church was born of the evangelizing activity of Jesus and the twelve apostles. That eucharistic, worshipping community of faith and love, small in the beginning, was sent out by Jesus, and it remains today the sign of a new presence of Jesus in the world. That community prolongs and continues the mission of Jesus. In a sense it is above all Christ's mission and his condition of being an evangelizer that the church is called upon to continue. The Christian community is never closed upon itself; it is sent out to make disciples. The church does not exist for itself; it exists for the building of the kingdom, and evangelization is this essential work.

In achieving this duty and task of evangelization, Pope Paul VI declared:

> There is thus a profound link between Christ, the Church and evangelization. During the period of the Church that we are living in, it is she who has the task of evangelizing. This mandate is not accomplished without her, and still less against her.
>
> It is certainly fitting to recall this fact at a moment like the present one when it happens that not without sorrow we can hear people—whom we wish to believe are well-intentioned but who are certainly misguided in their attitude—continually claiming to love Christ but without the Church, to listen to Christ but not the Church, to belong to Christ but outside the Church. (*EN*, 16)

Pope Paul went on to say, "And how can one wish to love Christ without loving the Church, if the finest witness to Christ is that of Saint Paul: 'Christ loved the Church and sacrificed himself for her'"? (*EN*, 16).

Jesus did not call us to follow him as rugged individualists. This is one of the many aspects of Jesus' life and teachings and criteria of discipleship that I love very much. We are made in God's image and likeness. When we pray the way Jesus taught us, we say *Our* Father and not *my* Father. One of the designations for the church coming from the Second Vatican Council is the biblical description of the church as the people of God. We are not called to be loners. We are called to know and love and care about one another, all of us brothers and sisters, children of a wonderful compassionate Father.

We, as church, are a eucharistic, worshipping community of faith and love who as individuals and as a community love God above all and love others as Jesus loves them and us—especially the poor, the needy, the marginalized and oppressed. Jesus raised the bar for discipleship when at the Last Supper he told his faithful disciples: "A new commandment I give to you, that you love one another; even as I have loved you, that you also love one another" (John 13:34). We are the church, and as disciples of Jesus Christ we are called to be genuine, enthusiastic evangelizers. We are the church, and we need the church. We are the sign of the presence of Jesus Christ our Savior in the world today. And indeed, we are also the church as an institution.

Pope Paul VI again put it quite succinctly:

For the Church, evangelizing means bringing the Good News into all the strata of humanity, and through its influence transforming humanity from within and making it new.... But there is no new humanity if there are not first of all new persons renewed by Baptism and by lives lived according to the Gospel. The purpose of evangelization is therefore precisely this interior change [conversion, continuing conversion for us Catholics], and if it had to be expressed in one sentence, the best way of stating it would be to say that the Church evangelizes when she seeks to convert, solely through the divine power of the message she proclaims, both the personal and collective consciences of people, the activities in which they engage, the lives and concrete milieu which are theirs. (*EN,* 18)

GOALS OF EVANGELIZATION

Today some Catholics who have become aware of evangelization look upon it primarily as "winning converts" or bringing back inactive or alienated Catholics to active participation in the life of the church. While those are certainly essential aspects of the concept of Catholic evangelization, they are only one part of a full understanding of evangelization. If we stop there we encounter what Pope Paul VI maintained, that the total understanding of evangelization is rich and complex and dynamic (see *EN*, 17). Flowing from this description and definition of Pope Paul VI, the three goals of Catholic evangelization as given in the United States Catholic Bishops' document of 1993, *Go and Make Disciples*, can help project the full picture of what evangelization is for us:

Goal I: To bring about in all Catholics such an enthusiasm for their faith that, in living their faith in Jesus, they freely share it with others (*GMD*, 46).

Goal II: To invite all people in the United States, whatever their social or cultural background, to hear the message of salvation in Jesus Christ so they may come to join us in the fullness of the Catholic faith (*GMD*, 53).

Goal III: To foster gospel values in our society, promoting the dignity of the human person, the importance of the family, and the common good of our society, so that our nation may continue to be transformed by the saving power of Jesus Christ (*GMD*, 56).

All three goals must be understood together for the true and full meaning of evangelization to be achieved. Note two examples, the church of Chicago and the church of Los Angeles, where these goals have been incorporated into the life of diocesan churches.

The archdiocese of Chicago has a plan for Catholics to evangelize entitled "Spreading the Holy Fire." It is built around three words: Believe, Share and Transform:

↦ Believe: Encourage all Catholics to experience conversion to a deeper holiness and a greater love of God.

↦ Share: Welcome and invite others to learn about and share in the Catholic faith and encounter Jesus Christ in the sacraments.

↦ Transform: Change society with the power of the gospel.

The Synod of the Archdiocese of Los Angeles issued its document *Gathered and Sent.* Their first of six pastoral initiatives is "Evangelization and the New Evangelization." In it they refer to three levels of evangelization:

1. Evangelization entails allowing one's own heart to be seized and saturated by the gospel, responding to the call to lifelong conversion to Christ by the gift of the Spirit.

2. Evangelization requires reaching out to others to proclaim in word and deed the reign of God.

3. Evangelization demands that the values of the reign of God—a reign of truth, holiness, justice, love and peace—permeate each and every culture, transforming every sphere of life.

NEW LIFE IN THE NEW MILLENNIUM

Pope John Paul II, from the early days of his Petrine ministry, called us to a new evangelization. Over and over he challenged the church to a new evangelization, a new attitude, a new way of living as Catholics—new in expression, methods and zeal. In his 1990 encyclical *The Mission of the Redeemer,* he spoke with urgency: "I sense that the moment has come to commit all of the Church's energies to a new evangelization and to the mission *ad gentes*. No believer in Christ, no institution of the Church can avoid this supreme duty: to proclaim Christ to all peoples" (*RM*, 3).

In his apostolic exhortation *Ecclesia in America* he said:

> The mission of evangelization today calls for a new program which can be defined overall as a "new evangelization."... I urgently desire to encourage all the members of God's People, particularly those living in America—where I first appealed for a commitment "new in its ardor, methods and expression"—to take up this project and to cooperate in carrying it out. In accepting this mission, everyone should keep in mind that the vital core of the new evangelization must be a clear and unequivocal proclamation of the person of Jesus Christ, that is, the preaching of his name, his teaching, his life, his promises and the Kingdom which he has gained for us by his Paschal Mystery. (*EA*, 66)

In his apostolic letter of 1994 entitled *Tertio Millennio Adveniente*, Pope John Paul II challenged all of us to prepare for the Jubilee Year 2000. He affirmed that the Second Vatican Council was a providential event whereby the church began the more immediate preparation for the Jubilee of the second millennium. He described the Second Vatican Council as a council "focused on the mystery of Christ and his Church and at the same time open to the world" (*TMA*, 18). That openness, he was convinced, was an evangelical response to changes in the world, including the terrible tragedies of the twentieth century.

Pope John Paul II again reminded us in *Tertio Millennio Adveniente* that the Second Vatican Council dealt with wonderful areas of life for us:

> The Church questioned herself about her own identity, and discovered anew the depth of her mystery as the Body of Christ and Bride of Christ. Humbly heeding the word of God, she reaffirmed the uni-

versal call to holiness; she made provision for the reform of the liturgy, the "origin and summit" of her life; she gave impetus to the renewal of many aspects of her life at the universal level and in the local Churches; she strove to promote the various Christian vocations from those of the laity to those of Religious, from the ministry of deacons to that of priests and Bishops; and in a particular way she rediscovered episcopal collegiality. On the basis of this profound renewal, the Council opened itself to Christians of other denominations, to the followers of other religions and to all the people of our time. (*TMA,* 19)

You will remember that Pope John Paul challenged us, as the best preparation for the new millennium, to apply as faithfully as possible the teachings of Vatican II to the life of every individual and to the whole church. He also pointed out that the series of Roman Synods begun after the Second Vatican Council were part of the preparation for our looking, hopefully, to a new life in the new millennium. The theme underlying them all was evangelization, or rather a new evangelization, the foundations of which, he said, were laid down in the apostolic exhortation *Evangelii Nuntiandi* of Pope Paul VI.

Pope John Paul II again shared his thoughts, as we completed the celebration of the Jubilee Year, and set us out on the course of the new millennium with his stirring expression *Duc in altum,* "Put out into the deep" (*NMI,* 1). It is helpful to recall several of the urgings of his apostolic letter *Novo Millennio Ineunte,* issued on the Feast of the Epiphany in 2001. In the mind of Pope John Paul II, the Jubilee Celebration of the Birth of Christ was not the end of a journey but simply a new beginning offering new challenges. He directed us to "the Word made Flesh" and the mystery of Christ as our Savior. With Christ as our foundation, he focused on the future and urged us to move afresh into the new millennium. Essentially the issues and challenges John Paul II brought to us constitute the elements of a full understanding of Catholic evangelization—fully living and freely sharing our Catholic faith.

We must, according to him, "gain *new impetus in Christian living,* making it the force which inspires our journey of faith" (*NMI,* 29). Catholic evangelization calls people to a lifelong journey to God, not a one time or once-for-all experience but a continuous process of conversion. For such pastoral revitalization, he indicated several priorities: the universal call to holiness; the need for prayer; participation in the Sunday Eucharist; the sacrament of reconciliation; a clear, honest dependence on God's help and grace and especially listening to the word and proclaiming the word. And the prerequisites for listening to the word and proclaiming the word are indeed holiness and prayer (see *NMI,* 30–40):

> To nourish ourselves with the word in order to be "servants of the word" in the work of evangelization: this is surely a priority for the Church at the dawn of the new millennium. Even in countries evangelized many centuries ago, the reality of a "Christian society" which, amid all the frailties which have always marked human life, measured itself explicitly on Gospel values, is now gone.... Over the years, I have often repeated the summons to the *new evangelization.* I do so again now, especially in order to insist that we must rekindle in ourselves the impetus of the beginnings and allow ourselves to be filled with the ardor of the apostolic preaching which followed Pentecost. We must revive in ourselves the burning conviction of Paul, who cried out: "Woe to me if I do not preach the Gospel" (1 Corinthians 9:16). (*NMI,* 40)

So we have the call. We have the urgency. We have the means. We have the challenge, and it stems indeed from the life and mission of Jesus Christ our Savior, who gave us the church. We are the church summoned today to a new evangelization. This evangelization is the responsibility of every member of the church. We are all involved by virtue of our baptism, which brings us dignity and responsibility.

The Spirit and Community

Our challenge today, in many ways, is to ignite the fire of enthusiasm in the hearts of our Catholics to realize that "there is a huge difference," as Cardinal Francis George of Chicago has indicated, "between belonging and conversion, truly being a disciple of Jesus Christ with all that means." We have come to a time in our society when many Catholics use secular values to critique the church's teachings instead of using gospel values and the teaching of the church to critique secular values.

Of course the question is, how do we create that kind of evangelizing Catholic community? It is first of all and truly the work of the Holy Spirit. "It must be said that the Holy Spirit is the principal agent of evangelization: it is He who impels each individual to proclaim the Gospel, and it is He who in the depths of consciences causes the word of salvation to be accepted and understood" (*EN*, 75). It certainly depends upon characteristics of each local community, but at the root, we have the same basic reality of the church, especially in the Eucharist, the priesthood, the sacraments and a worshipping community.

Catholics experience the faith on the parish level. It is in our parish community that we live and participate in worship, receive the sacraments, care for one another and reach out to the poor. We know, although many Catholics seemingly do not realize it, that in truth we are church as a diocese. Our ecclesiology is that we are gathered together around our local bishop. That means we care about one another on a diocesan level, each diocesan community with its own local bishop, building a sense of unity but not uniformity, all living in union with the Bishop of Rome, the successor of Saint Peter.

On the local parish level we look to our pastor and other parish ministers to inspire from the pulpit, to give leadership and motivation. But evangelization is truly the work of all the baptized. Rarely can all aspects of the three goals of Catholic evangelization be achieved simultaneously in every parish in an excellent manner. But all three goals need to be embraced and carried out for the full scope of Catholic evangelization. From time to time, one aspect or goal may be emphasized more than another.

Evangelization means living and sharing this great gift of faith with enthusiasm. It means truly accepting Jesus Christ and sharing him with others: sharing his life, his love, his truth, his goodness, his values, his compassion and his integrity. As we foster a deepening conversion to Christ in our own lives, we can joyfully promote a new mentality, an openness, a desire, a willingness to bring to all the world what we Catholic followers of Jesus Christ have to offer.

While we see the growing influence of secular values, there are signs of a spiritual hunger among many people in our society. All people want to experience "the good life." God wants to use us to make that colloquial expression become splendidly fulfilled through helping others know and accept Jesus as "the way, and the truth, and the life" (John 14:6). Catholic evangelization means "bringing the Good News of Jesus into every human situation and seeking to convert individuals and society by the divine power of the Gospel itself. At its essence are the proclamation of salvation in Jesus Christ and the response of a person in faith, which are both works of the Spirit of God" (*GMD*, 10).

We must be joyful and proud of our privilege and responsibility to be Catholic evangelizers. Our bishops call us "to reexamine our hearts and recommit our wills to the pursuit of evangelization." Our hope and vision is "to make evangelization a natural and normal part of Catholic life and to give evangelizers the tools and support they need to carry out this ministry today" (*GMD*, 64).

This new millennium is a time when we can experience the impact of the Holy Spirit acting in the church, generating enthusiasm and a new mentality for even the word *evangelization* but more especially for the meaning and activity of evangelization. What a joy to be alive in the beginning of this new Christian millennium, when we can help all members of the church to respond to the call for a new evangelization!

We must be about developing a new way of thinking, an enthusiasm that continues and grows. We are about deepening our realization of who we are as Catholics, of our commission by the Lord Jesus and of the power of the Holy Spirit, which enables us to live and share our faith.

Addressing youth in preparation for the Fourth World Youth Day, Pope John Paul II defined the whole church as missionary and evangelistic: "To be Christian means to be missionaries, to be apostles. It is not enough to discover Christ—you must bring him to others!…You must have the courage to speak about Christ, to bear witness to your faith through a lifestyle inspired by the gospel.…The harvest is great indeed for evangelization and so many workers are needed. Christ trusts you and counts on your collaboration."[2]

That message of Pope John Paul II still rings out to all Catholics. As we respond with generosity, the Holy Spirit will increase our awareness, deepen our commitment and strengthen our involvement in this ongoing mission of the church.

PART 2

PERSPECTIVES ON
EVANGELIZATION

Go and Make Disciples: The United States Bishops' National Plan for Catholic Evangelization

Father Kenneth Boyack, C.S.P.

It was groundbreaking. The bishops of the United States passed *Go and Make Disciples: A National Plan and Strategy for Catholic Evangelization in the United States* at their plenary assembly in Washington, D.C., on November 18, 1992, by an overwhelming vote of 229 to 2. All Catholics in this country would benefit from reading this national plan as a way of developing a common attitude and language about evangelization as the essential mission of the Catholic church.

Before publication of *Go and Make Disciples,* Catholics who wanted to create evangelizing parishes found inspiration by reading and studying Pope Paul VI's apostolic exhortation *Evangelii Nuntiandi* (On Evangelization in the Modern World). Written in 1975, it defined evangelization as the very mission of Christ and outlined the content, the methods, the beneficiaries, the workers and the spirit of evangelization.

While extremely instructive, *Evangelii Nuntiandi* was intended more as a meditation than an action document. It was written for a worldwide Catholic audience, not for people in any particular continent or nation. *Go and Make Disciples,* on the other hand, is a plan and strategy to lead Catholics in the United States to acquire new attitudes and behaviors for bringing the Good News of Jesus Christ to every person in our nation.

THE HISTORICAL SETTING: A NEW PERIOD OF EVANGELIZATION

Go and Make Disciples is the first major teaching on Catholic evangelization made by the United States bishops since Vatican II. Pope John XXIII called the Council in 1959 as a way to let the light of Christ shine more brightly in the modern world. The Dogmatic Constitution on the Church, *Lumen Gentium,* sets forth this primary goal of the council clearly: "Christ is the light of all nations. Hence this most sacred Synod, which has been gathered in the Holy Spirit, eagerly desires to shed on all men that radiance of His which brightens the countenance of the Church. This it will do by proclaiming the gospel to every creature (cf. Mk. 16:15)" (*LG,* 1). Vatican II equipped the church to live and proclaim the gospel more effectively.

Pope Paul VI called for the Third General Assembly of the Synod of Bishops to meet in the fall of 1974 to reflect on the topic of evangelization in light of the Council, which had ended some nine years earlier. After discussing evangelization from a worldwide perspective, the assembly "decided to remit to the Pastor of the universal

Church, with great trust and simplicity, the fruits of all their labors, stating that they awaited from him a fresh forward impulse, capable of creating within a Church still more firmly rooted in the undying power and strength of Pentecost a new period of evangelization" (*EN*, 2). *Evangelii Nuntiandi* was published in 1975 and set forth the elements of this new period.

The United States bishops, in *Go and Make Disciples,* acknowledged the historical roots of this new period of evangelization by referring to key church teachings that laid the necessary foundation, primarily *Evangelii Nuntiandi* and *Redemptoris Missio* (Mission of the Redeemer). In the United States this new period has been characterized by foundational teachings such as the *National Pastoral Plan for Hispanic Ministry*[1] and *Here I Am, Send Me: A Conference Response to the Evangelization of African Americans*[2] (*GMD*, 63).

The church teachings giving rise to this new period of evangelization guide Catholics into a new way of thinking and behaving. All the elements of the new evangelization have one aspect in common: they were produced under the guidance of the Holy Spirit working in the church. As Paul VI wrote, "Now if the Spirit of God has a pre-eminent place in the whole life of the Church, it is in her evangelizing mission that He is most active. It is not by chance that the great inauguration of evangelization took place on the morning of Pentecost, under the inspiration of the Spirit" (*EN*, 75).

It is under the same inspiration of the Spirit that Pope John Paul II wrote in *Redemptoris Missio,* "I sense that the moment has come to commit all of the Church's energies to a new evangelization" (*RM*, 3; cited in *GMD*, 62).

WHY WE NEED A PLAN AND STRATEGY NOW

We can only speculate about the reasons the bishops passed *Go and Make Disciples* in 1992, as opposed to 1985 or another date. Yet we know this plan meets a need. Large corporations, political groups and other institutions routinely develop strategic plans to chart their way into the future. Similarly, the bishops approved *Go and Make Disciples* to chart the evangelizing direction of the Catholic church in the United States.

The original idea for the national plan was presented in June 1989 by Archbishop Michael Sheehan (then bishop of the diocese of Lubbock, Texas) as the bishops gathered for their summer meeting at Seton Hall University. Archbishop Sheehan noted that since other churches, such as the Southern Baptists and the Assemblies of God, were developing plans for evangelism in the 1990s, the Catholic church should do the same. The Bishops' Committee on Evangelization, meeting at the same time under the leadership of Bishop William R. Houck, made creating a national plan one of their top priority agenda items.

The members of the Committee on Evangelization knew that the Catholic church has a unique and valuable contribution to make in developing a national plan and strategy for Catholic evangelization. The committee also recognized that a stronger and more defined Catholic evangelizing presence is needed as we experience the forces of a secularized culture, which threatens Catholic values and identity.

Sociologists give us insights into the realities behind the bishops' thinking. In his book *Christianity in the Twenty-First Century, Reflection on the Challenges Ahead,*[3] Robert Wuthnow comments that a Christian identity is no longer supported in our culture by the family or by the neighborhood. Dean R. Hoge, William D. Dinges, Sister Mary Johnson, S.N.D. de N. and Juan L. Gonzales, Jr., make this same point in their study, *Young Adult Catholics, Religion in the Culture of Choice.*[4]

As an immigrant church in the 1890s, Catholics experienced a strong ethnic identity as German, Italian or Irish Catholics. This experience was strengthened by other key elements of Catholic identity, such as not eating meat on Friday, studying from the

Baltimore Catechism and experiencing the same Latin Mass throughout the world. Not so today. Most Catholics no longer have an immigrant status but are "mainline," comprising about 23 percent of the United States population. Catholics today are affected by the cultural elements of consumerism, relativism and individualism and in most cases are indistinguishable in behavior from other Americans. These cultural changes make contemporary Catholic evangelization difficult.

Adding to this discussion, sociologist Wade Clark Roof found some revealing characteristics of Catholic baby boomers in his study *A Generation of Seekers: The Spiritual Journeys of the Baby Boom Generation.* Clark found, for instance, that of all Catholics born between the years 1946 and 1962, 33 percent remained loyal to the Church and 67 percent dropped out. Of the 67 percent who dropped out, 25 percent have returned to the church. The study showed that only 50 percent of baby boomers baptized Catholic are active in the Catholic church today, and another 8 percent are active in other churches.[5]

When interviewing these baby-boomer Catholics, Roof discovered that their definition of what constitutes a "good Catholic" diverged widely from church teaching on some key issues. For example, when asked if one could be a good Catholic without going to church every Sunday, 77 percent of the males and 90 percent of the females responded yes. Similarly, when asked if one could be a good Catholic without obeying the church's teaching on abortion, 67 percent of the males and 69 percent of the females said yes.[6]

Other sociologists have discovered similar trends in what constitutes a "good Catholic." William V. D'Antonio, James D. Davidson, Dean R. Hoge and Katherine Meyer, in their study *American Catholics, Gender, Generation, and Commitment,* found that 76 percent of the Catholics surveyed think that a person can be a good Catholic without going to church every Sunday, and 71 percent said they could be a good Catholic without obeying the church hierarchy's teaching on birth control.[7] These attitudes reveal the strong influence of secular American culture, a culture in which pluralism and personal opinion are prized.

Other research reveals that the number of American adults who are not active in any church is increasing. In the study *The Unchurched American*, the Gallup Organization found in a 1988 survey that 44 percent of American adults are "unchurched," as compared with 41 percent who were unchurched in 1978. Both studies defined an "unchurched adult" as one who was not a member of a church or who had not attended services in the previous six months other than for special religious holidays, weddings, funerals or the like.[8] Using the same definition, the Gallup Organization found in a 2005 survey that the number of unchurched had increased to 43 percent of American adults.[9]

In spite of the large number of individuals without a church family, the Gallup Organization in 1988, Wade Clark Roof in 1993 and Dean R. Hoge and his associates in 2001 all affirm from their research that many of the unchurched are seeking a spirituality that answers their questions and gives meaning to their lives.

In summary, we can point to three reasons why we need a national plan for Catholic evangelization now. First, we need a plan to enable Catholics to develop a renewed identity as an evangelizing people in an increasingly secular culture. Second, we need a plan to equip Catholics to share the gospel more effectively, especially with the large number of Americans who do not have a church family but who are open to an invitation. Third, we need a plan for Catholics to evangelize our society and culture, looking for ways we can transform our culture through the love and power of Jesus Christ.

MEETING THE NEEDS OF THE AGE

Go and Make Disciples is a short but powerful document that meets the needs of our age. The best way to capture the spirit of the national plan is to read this ten-thousand-word document yourself. The National Conference of Catholic Bishops Committee on Evangelization made the decision to write the plan for every Catholic and not specifically for Catholic leadership. Consequently, the language is engaging and easy to read.

Go and Make Disciples has two parts, "A Vision of Catholic Evangelization" and "Goals and Strategies." The vision section, making up over half the text, presents Catholic teachings on the topic and motivates and inspires the reader to action. The goals, objectives and strategies of part 2 form the heart of the document and present a process for planning and implementation.

PART 1: A VISION OF CATHOLIC EVANGELIZATION

The framework for part 1 is taken almost exclusively from Paul VI's *Evangelii Nuntiandi* and rightly so, because the bishops were taking the insights on evangelization from the universal church and applying them specifically to the situation in the United States. Number 18 of this apostolic exhortation provides a definition of evangelization that becomes the foundation for the three goals of *Go and Make Disciples:*

> Evangelizing means bringing the Good News into all the strata of humanity, and through its influence transforming humanity from within and making it new: "Now I am making the whole of creation new." But there is no new humanity if there are not first of all new persons renewed by Baptism and by lives lived according to the Gospel. The purpose of evangelization is therefore precisely this interior change, and if it had to be expressed in one sentence the best way of stating it would be to say that the Church evangelizes when she seeks to convert, solely through the divine power of the message she proclaims, both the personal and collective consciences of people, the activities in which they engage, and the lives and concrete milieu which are theirs. (*EN,* 18)

What does evangelization mean? The first part of *Go and Make Disciples* sets forth key Catholic teachings on being a disciple and making disciples. The bishops define evangelizing as "bringing the Good News of Jesus into every human situation and seeking to convert individuals and society by the divine power of the Gospel itself. At its essence are the proclamation of salvation in Jesus Christ and the response of a person in faith, which are both works of the Spirit of God" (*GMD*, 10). The language of this definition speaks to the heart of discipleship: proclaiming the gospel, responding in faith, relying on the power of the Holy Spirit and bringing the kingdom of God both to individuals and to society.

As teachers and shepherds, the bishops point out that Catholic evangelization casts a wide net; indeed, no one should be excluded. They identify five primary groups who benefit from the gospel: practicing Catholics, who are called to a renewal in faith and ongoing conversion; inactive and alienated Catholics, who are called to reconciliation; children, who are called to be formed as disciples through the efforts of their parents and religious educators; Christians from other traditions, who are called to the fullness of Christ's message; and those who have no faith in Jesus, who are called to know Christ through his church.

Primarily the Catholic church wants all people to know Jesus and experience the salvation and the new life only he can give. It is our love for Christ that calls us to evangelize, but evangelism is at the same time a duty. Jesus commands us to "go...and make disciples of all nations" (Matthew 28:19).

How does evangelization happen? Next comes an explanation of how evangelization happens. The bishops note that Catholics have done well as silent witnesses to their faith through living good lives. However, they also point out that in our society and culture more is needed. Catholics must learn to share their faith by speaking the gospel message clearly and by giving the reasons for their faith.

Throughout the vision section, the bishops' teaching is Christ-centered. The methods of Catholic evangelization involve inviting, welcoming, showing love for the unbeliever, entering into sincere dialogue with an inquirer and trying to discern the working of the Spirit in a person's life. These methods of evangelization reflect the methods and approaches that Jesus used, as revealed in the New Testament. By putting on the mind of Jesus, we are taught to be disciples, so that we, in turn, may make disciples of others.

Three goals of evangelization. A final section of part 1 presents the three goals that form the heart of the bishops' plan and strategy:

Goal I: To bring about in all Catholics such an enthusiasm for their faith that, in living their faith in Jesus, they freely share it with others (*GMD*, 46).

Goal II: To invite all people in the United States, whatever their social or cultural background, to hear the message of salvation in Jesus Christ so they may come to join us in the fullness of the Catholic faith (*GMD*, 53).

Goal III: To foster gospel values in our society, promoting the dignity of the human person, the importance of the family, and the common good of our society, so that our nation may continue to be transformed by the saving power of Jesus Christ (*GMD*, 56).

The three goals contain the essential elements of the definition of evangelization set forth by Pope Paul VI in number 18 of *Evangelii Nuntiandi*, thereby intricately connecting the teaching of the universal church with Christ's evangelizing mission in the United States. The presentation of these goals reveals that *Go and Make Disciples* is truly part of the new period of evangelization that the Third General Assembly of the Synod of Bishops spoke about in Rome in 1974. Under the guidance of the Holy Spirit, this new period of evangelization in the Catholic church can now move forward with even greater intensity in the United States through the insights of this plan and strategy.

PART 2: GOALS AND STRATEGIES

Before presenting the objectives and strategies for each goal, the bishops first offer suggestions about the ways in which all Catholics can use this plan. The objectives and strategies are not meant as a recipe to be applied by all people in exactly the same way in every situation. Rather, the bishops present a framework that individuals, parish staffs, parish councils, Catholic organizations and religious orders can apply to their own situations. All who read the plan are encouraged to affirm the ways in which they are already evangelizing, look for new areas to develop, discern the guidance of the Holy Spirit through the church and then engage in the process of evangelizing—going and making disciples.

Lest Catholics lose their perspective by being either too provincial or too zealous, the bishops offer a number of reflections that set the context for the three goals, a context that renders evangelization truly Catholic. The bishops teach that all Catholics are involved by virtue of their baptism; all evangelizing activity must be steeped in prayer; and evangelization is a ministry of the universal church: when one Catholic evangelizes, the entire church evangelizes.

The bishops also teach that evangelization is directly connected to the ebb and flow of everyday life. The parish is the most fitting location for living and sharing the gospel, since the goal of all evangelization culminates in the Eucharist—involving all people in the paschal mystery of Jesus Christ within a community of faith. Evangelization is a collaborative effort, a true partnership in Christ among laity, religious and clergy. Evangelization involves a consistent witness among all Catholics at each level of the church. And finally, the bishops teach that these goals will be difficult to attain in our secularized and modern culture.

Goal I: To bring about in all Catholics such an enthusiasm for their faith that, in living their faith in Jesus, they freely share it with others. The key elements of this goal include hearing the gospel at new and deeper levels, responding in faith and growing in holiness. Experiencing the love of God more profoundly enables each person to share the love of Christ more freely with others.

The strategy for achieving this goal centers on creating for people new encounters with Christ through the Scriptures and the sacraments of the church. As a result, Catholics will pray more intently, listen to Christ's call more clearly and live as disciples in the family and the workplace. Moreover, the strategy calls for being attentive to the physical, mental and cultural diversity among Catholics. All of these strategies enable Catholics to know, love and serve God at new levels, thereby becoming holier.

Of course, all of these objectives cannot possibly be realized at one time. The process of implementing this goal in a parish, for example, involves understanding the objectives, doing a pastoral analysis of one's parish, affirming areas in which the objectives and strategies are already being carried out, then selecting and implementing as many objectives and strategies as seem appropriate for the following year. After review and evaluation, the parish can celebrate what God has accomplished, then begin the planning process for the next year.

Goal II: To invite all people in the United States, whatever their social or cultural background, to hear the message of salvation in Jesus Christ so they may come to join us in the fullness of the Catholic faith. The bishops summarize the meaning of this goal by teaching that Catholics "are to invite effectively every person to come to know the Good News of Jesus proclaimed by the Catholic Church" (*GMD*, 104). Along with the invitation must come a welcoming spirit that draws others to Christ. Not only will individual Catholics invite and welcome but also parishes, organizations, hospitals, schools, chanceries—all Catholic organizations and institutions.

The strategy for achieving this goal is threefold: create a more welcoming attitude; develop new understanding and skills for sharing our faith; and actually undertake activities in which we can invite people to know Christ and our Catholic faith.

After a pastoral analysis, parishes can affirm the areas in which this goal is already being implemented. Then, through a process of discernment, parish leaders can engage in as many strategies as they choose to help the parish become more welcoming, train parishioners in the skills of sharing their faith and plan events to invite people to come to know Christ and the Catholic faith. Parishes are encouraged to celebrate what God is doing in their midst, evaluate the results and plan for the next year.

Goal III: To foster gospel values in our society, promoting the dignity of the human person, the importance of the family and the common good of our society, so that our nation may continue to be transformed by the saving power of Jesus Christ. The third goal draws on and incorporates Catholic teaching on social justice and the common good. It proclaims that the kingdom of God may be seen through signs in which the justice and healing presence of Christ transform individuals and all of society. Without these signs of God's kingdom, the first two goals will be weakened and incomplete.

The bishops' strategy for implementation involves being more attentive to showing the presence of Christ in our neighborhoods, fostering the importance of marriage and family and looking for areas in the workplace, the arts, economics, public policy and media in which Catholics can exercise influence for Christ.

After pastoral discernment, parishes can affirm their strengths and then choose to work on objectives and strategies in these areas: involving parishioners in their neighborhoods, fostering the importance of the family and working to transform all elements of society. After implementation, the process always involves reviewing the results, giving thanks to God and looking to further planning next year.

An Indispensable Catholic Framework

The three goals of *Go and Make Disciples* form an integral whole and are not to be viewed separately. One analogy is that of a tripod. Without all three legs rooted solidly on the ground, the tripod will fall. Similarly, the three goals form a solid tripod of Catholic evangelization. If we take away any one of them or allow one to lie dormant, we weaken the plan by not presenting the fullness of Catholic evangelization.

After presenting the three goals, the bishops appeal to all Catholics to implement this national plan as a way of being disciples of Jesus. They state boldly: "We invite you: Make this plan your plan" (*GMD*, 132). By virtue of baptism into the paschal mystery of Christ, no Catholic is exempt from carrying on Christ's evangelizing mission. This invitation is extended to all Catholics and to all levels of church structure, including families, parishes, Catholic institutions and local, diocesan and national organizations.

This plan and strategy is a distinctive contribution by the bishops of the United States to the new period of Catholic evangelization. *Go and Make Disciples* is rooted solidly in the vision of Vatican II and sets forth specific ways that Catholics can carry on the evangelizing mission of Christ in the church in our contemporary secular culture. An individual's participation in this plan and strategy is empowered by his or her baptism and confirmation and is sustained in the Eucharist.

Go and Make Disciples affirms a new way of being church, a new way of being disciples so that Catholics are better equipped to make disciples. Implementing this plan will enable Catholics to respond to the statement of the bishops who gathered for the Third General Assembly of the Synod of Bishops in 1974: "We wish to confirm once more that the task of evangelizing all people constitutes the essential mission of the Church" (*EN*, 14). Relying on the guidance of the Holy Spirit, which informs individuals as well as the institutional Church, Catholics will develop a stronger identity by living and proclaiming the gospel more effectively. Through this proclamation Catholics will come to love Christ and our Catholic faith more deeply.

As the Vicar of Christ, Pope John Paul II preached tirelessly on the new evangelization. His exhortation in *Redemptoris Missio* is beneficial to all Catholics reading *Go and Make Disciples*. He wrote:

> I wish to invite the Church to *renew her missionary commitment*. The [*Mission of the Redeemer*] has as its goal an interior renewal of faith and Christian life. For missionary activity renews the Church, revitalizes faith and Christian identity, and offers fresh enthusiasm and new incentive. *Faith is strengthened when it is given to others!* It is in commitment to the Church's universal mission that the new evangelization of Christian peoples will find inspiration and support. (*RM*, 2)

We pray that, under the guidance of the Holy Spirit, the implementation of *Go and Make Disciples* will enable Catholics to become holier, grow in missionary zeal and have an even greater impact in making all elements of American society new in Christ.

Father Kenneth Boyack is president of the Paulist National Catholic Evangelization Association, which publishes or distributes the resources listed below. For more information or to request a free copy of the PNCEA Evangelization Resource Catalogue, contact:

Paulist National Catholic Evangelization Association
3031 Fourth Street, NE
Washington, DC 20017
202-832-5022
E-mail:pncea@pncea.org;
www.pncea.org

Resources for Implementing *Go and Make Disciples:*

DeSiano, Frank, C.S.P., and Kenneth Boyack, C.S.P. *Commentary and Planning Guide for Go and Make Disciples: A National Plan and Strategy for Catholic Evangelization in the United States.* Washington: PNCEA, 1993.

DeSiano, Frank, C.S.P., and Kenneth Boyack, C.S.P. *Discovering My Experience of God: Awareness and Witness.* Mahwah, N.J.: Paulist, 1992.

Disciples in Mission: An Evangelization Experience (Washington: PNCEA) is a parish-wide, faith-filled experience that integrates personal prayer, the Lenten Sunday liturgies, small faith-sharing groups, catechesis, family activities, teen groups, pastoral reflection and follow-up activities into a coordinated parish-wide experience of evangelization. See www.disciplesinmission.org.

ENVISION: Planning Our Parish Future (Washington: PNCEA) is a comprehensive, results-driven parish planning process that fully engages parishioners in developing and implementing a faith-based vision for their parish based on *Go and Make Disciples.* See www.parishplanning.org.

Go and Make Disciples: A National Plan and Strategy for Catholic Evangelization in the United States, Tenth Anniversary English & Spanish Edition. Washington: PNCEA, 2002.

Rivers, Robert S., C.S.P. *From Maintenance to Mission, Evangelization and the Revitalization of the Parish.* Mahwah, N.J.: Paulist, 2005.

A Summary: Go and Make Disciples: A National Plan and Strategy for Catholic Evangelization in the United States. Washington: PNCEA, 1993.

CHAPTER 7

Evangelization and the Experience of Initiation in the Early Church

Father Kilian McDonnell, O.S.B.

What is the source of evangelization? Obviously evangelization is not just an academic process of imparting Christian information. It communicates life and power. Where do the evangelizer and the evangelized draw this life, this power? Where is the well from which the life-giving waters are drawn?

In my view the source is the rite of Christian initiation, as understood by the early church. This process could last as long as two or three years, culminating in the celebration of what we now recognize as baptism, confirmation and the Eucharist, all celebrated together on one night. What is primary is conversion, both individual and communal. Conversion effected by grace, born out of a personal religious experience, touches the entire community, always turning toward God, with a new way of thinking, a new way of living, embracing the whole of existence.

The rite of initiation, as well as the process of faith leading up to it, was highly diverse, with many local variations. No suggestion is made that everywhere the rite was the same.[1] Nevertheless, the theological and pastoral objective remained the same: to lead the catechumen into a living relationship with the Father, through the Son, Jesus Christ, in the Holy Spirit.

The Architecture of Initiation

A knowledge of the architectural setting in the early church helps one to grasp the theology of initiation. Though the arrangement was different in various parts of the West and in Syria, a widely used floor plan had the church divided into three basic rooms. (See the accompanying diagram.)

In the first room, the baptistery, the pit was filled with water so that if an adult stood up in it, the water might come to about the waist. There were three steps going down into the water and three steps ascending on the other side of the pit. Here the immersion in water (or the pouring of the water) took place.

In the second room was a chair for the bishop. In this room took place the imposition of hands and one of the anointings (what we would recognize now as confirmation).

The third, much larger room was the eucharistic room, which contained an altar and pulpit, or ambo, for the reading of the Scriptures. Here the Eucharist was celebrated with the local community as part of the rite of initiation.

At the beginning of the liturgy of initiation, the deacon led the men into the baptistery and told them to take off all their clothes.

Individually they were then led down three steps into the water, where they were immersed three times, in the name of the Father, Son and Holy Spirit. Going down into the water was a sign that being a Christian meant sharing in Christ's going down into death. After the third immersion the candidate rose up out of the water and ascended the three steps on the other side, where a white robe was placed on him or her, a sign of the Resurrection. To be a Christian, one must share in the resurrection of Christ.

The deacon then led the male catechumens into the second room, and the deaconess brought the female catechumens into the baptistery. Although the bishop was clearly the one administering the sacrament of baptism, calling on the three names in the baptismal invocation and anointing the head of each candidate, it was the deaconess who led the women catechumens into the water and completed the anointing.

When all the men and women candidates had received the imposition of hands and an anointing in the second room, they were led into the Eucharistic room, where the local Christian community was waiting, and together they celebrated the Eucharist. To become a Christian, one had to become a member of the church, a worshipping community. No isolated Christians existed, only Christians in community. This whole liturgy, not just the water bath, was called "baptism" or "Christian initiation." (See diagram on page 82.)

WHAT IS BAPTISM IN THE HOLY SPIRIT?

Research indicates that in the early church the passage of the candidates for baptism through these rites of initiation included what is today called baptism in the Holy Spirit. In fact, Justin Martyr,[2] Origen,[3] Didymus the Blind[4] and Cyril of Jerusalem,[5] writing from the second to the fourth century, all call the whole rite of Christian initiation baptism in the Holy Spirit. Baptism in the Holy Spirit was

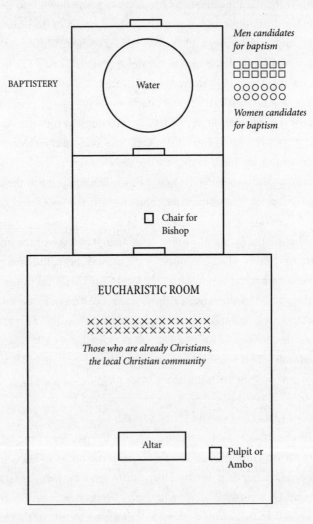

Candidates gather outside of church before liturgy begins

BAPTISTERY

Water

Men candidates for baptism

Women candidates for baptism

Chair for Bishop

EUCHARISTIC ROOM

× × × × × × × × × × × × × × ×
× × × × × × × × × × × × × × ×

Those who are already Christians, the local Christian community

Altar

Pulpit or Ambo

not a separate element but was integral to the grace and meaning of initiation.

Since the beginning of Pentecostalism around the turn of the century, baptism in the Spirit has referred to a contemporary experience of the power and charisms of the Spirit, which resembles what is described in various texts in Acts in conjunction with 1 Corinthians 12 and 14 and other New Testament texts. Such an understanding is found in various streams of classical Pentecostalism and the charismatic renewal in the historic churches. The same biblical texts cited in classical Pentecostalism for its teaching on the baptism in the Holy Spirit are cited by the authors from the earliest years of the church's life.

However, in referring to baptism in the Spirit, I am not talking about charismatic renewal. The two are separable. To accept baptism in the Spirit as integral to Christian initiation does not mean that one thereby joins a movement, charismatic or otherwise. One can accept baptism in the Holy Spirit without accepting charismatic renewal. The issue is not charismatic renewal but baptism in the Holy Spirit.

I will present only enough of the postbiblical texts to demonstrate the broad pattern.[6]

TERTULLIAN

When Tertullian (ca. 160–ca. 225) wrote his small treatise *On Baptism,* probably around 197, he was presenting the view on baptism held by the church of North Africa, not just his personal opinion, against the heretics who rejected baptism. His audience was the catechumens and neophytes, as well as those who believed in baptism without having examined the roots of the baptismal tradition.[7] Tertullian was preoccupied with the apostolic ministry in the church, the uninterrupted series of bishops who were a sign of apostolicity.[8] To this degree he wanted to retain the traditional doctrine.

Tertullian wrote in Latin in a situation where the baptism of adults was the general norm.[9]

At the end of his discourse, when he envisages the catechumens coming up from the water bath, passing through the rites of anointing, signing and imposition of hands, and walking into the eucharistic room, he addresses the catechumens (or, more precisely, the neophytes):

> You blessed ones, for whom the grace of God is waiting, when you come up from the most sacred bath of the new birth, when you spread out your hands for the first time in your mother's house with your brethren, ask your Father, ask your Lord, for the special gift of his inheritance, the distributed charisms, which form an additional, underlying feature [of baptism]. "Ask," he says, "and you shall receive." In fact, you have sought, and you have found: you have knocked, and it has been opened to you.[10]

The spreading out of the hands refers to the posture of standing with outstretched arms and palms open, customary when entering the prayer of praise. The expression "your mother's house" refers first to the Christian community and, secondly, to the church building. Tertullian encourages the catechumens to ask God the Father, and their Lord Jesus Christ, for the "special gift of his inheritance," which he names as the charisms that are found in the community. The imparting of the charisms forms "an underlying feature" of baptism. Tertullian, therefore, sees the imparting of the charisms as an integral part of the process of becoming a Christian, as part of the normal Christian equipment.[11]

ORIGEN

Like Tertullian, Origen presupposes his converts are adults, but he comes out of a Greek culture. At the beginning of a passage on Christian initiation, Origen writes of the great wonders Jesus performed, themselves "symbols of those delivered by the word of God in all ages from every kind of sickness and weakness."[12] These miracles are an appeal to faith.

"This [appeal to faith] is true of the water of baptism, symbol of the purification of the soul washed of every stain of sin, and it [baptism] is in itself the principle and source of the divine charisms for anyone who offers one's self to the divinity through the powerful invocation (epiclesis) of the adorable Trinity."[13] So baptism is the "principle" and "source" of the divine charisms. These two nouns have almost identical meanings of essential basis, origin, beginning and fountainhead. Placed next to one another, they are an intensive formulation.

This concentration of force is itself the object of a further intensive. The immediate context indicates that the charisms are those manifested in the Acts of the Apostles after the Pentecost experience.[14] For Origen, as for Tertullian, baptism is the normal locus for imparting the charisms.

Origen's witness is reinforced by the authority of Basil the Great, an important fourth-century witness and a doctor of the church, who quotes the passage with approval, the only time in the whole of Basil's writings that he quotes Origen.[15]

HILARY OF POITIERS

Hilary of Poitiers (ca. 314–367), apparently an adult convert to Christianity who was named bishop soon after his conversion, writes in Latin in a situation where adults are the usual candidates for baptism. Reflecting on his initiation later in life, he writes: "We who have been reborn through the sacrament of baptism experience intense joy when we feel within us the first stirrings of the Holy Spirit. We begin to have insight into the mysteries of faith, we are able to prophesy and to speak with wisdom. We become steadfast in hope and receive the gifts [plural] of healing."[16]

So Hilary writes of the intense joy he felt within the first movements of the Spirit during the rite of initiation as an adult. In another context he returns to the theme of experience: "Among us there is no one who, from time to time, does not feel the gift of the grace of the Spirit."[17] Care must be taken not to press the text, as though Hilary were saying that only what is felt is real or that the presence of the Spirit is always perceivable to the senses. Nonetheless, Hilary links the coming of the Spirit to experience.

He too specifically mentions the prophetic charisms that were imparted during initiation: word of knowledge, prophecy, word of wisdom, enduring hope, gifts of healing. Elsewhere he insists that the charisms "are profitable gifts."[18] If the charisms are effective, then "let us make use of such generous gifts."[19] Charisms are for the upbuilding of the church and should not be allowed to remain dormant.

CYRIL OF JERUSALEM

Cyril of Jerusalem has left the text of nineteen instructions for catechumens before the rites of initiation and five for the week after initiation. So we have good knowledge of how the catechumens were instructed. Cyril wrote in Greek for a group of adult catechumens.

Cyril is concerned to make these catechumens aware that the charisms belong to the normal functioning of the life of the community. "Great, omnipotent, and admirable is the Holy Spirit in the charisms."[20] Careful to avoid suggesting that the charisms are the property of the clergy, he maintains that "all the laity" are called to witness the power of the Spirit in the charisms.[21] Twice Cyril appeals to the list of charisms Paul gives in 1 Corinthians 12:7–11.[22] He views the Spirit as the dispenser of the charisms in "the whole Roman Empire" and then "in the whole world."[23] The Spirit is not a reluctant giver of gifts but pours them out "profusely."[24]

Looking upon the Pentecost experience as a baptismal event, he says that the grace given to the apostles "was not partial, but his [the Spirit's] in all fullness. For just as one immersed in the waters of baptism is completely encompassed by the water, so they were completely baptized by the Spirit."[25] Two other times he stresses the fullness and completeness of the baptism on Pentecost: "They were baptized without anything wanting, according to the promise"[26]; "They [the apostles] were baptized in all fullness."[27]

Toward the end of the baptismal instructions, Cyril, in referring to the gift of prophecy, says: "Only let each one prepare oneself to receive the heavenly gift."[28] And he repeats: "God grant that you may be worthy of the charism of prophecy."[29] "Those who are about to be baptized even now in the Holy Spirit" should bring an expanded expectation.[30] They need only make large their awareness, and "he will grant you charisms of every kind."[31] In the very last instruction before entering into the baptismal rite, he says: "My final words, beloved brethren, in this instruction, will be words of exhortation, urging all of you to prepare your souls for the reception of the heavenly charisms."[32]

BASIL OF CAESAREA AND GREGORY NAZIANZEN

Both Basil of Caesarea and Gregory Nazianzen (320–389), writing in Greek, situate the prophetic charisms within Christian initiation, though for historical reasons they are more reserved than Paul is in 1 Corinthians. Basil placed the charisms in relation to baptism: "The diversity of the charisms corresponds to the diversity of members, but all are baptized in one sole Spirit."[33] The Spirit is present in "prophecy, or healings, or other wonderful works," all of which are still to be found.[34] He refers specifically to "the distribution of wonderful charisms."[35]

Gregory refers to an inner transformation that can be accounted for only by the divinity of the Spirit: "If the Spirit is not to be adored, how can [the Spirit] divinize me in baptism?"[36] Writing of Paul's laying hands on the believers, imparting the Spirit, so that they spoke in tongues and prophesied (Acts 19:1–7), Gregory concludes: "This Spirit does all that God does: dividing into tongues of fire, distributing charisms, coming to expression in apostles, prophets, evangelists, pastors, and doctors."[37]

JOHN CHRYSOSTOM

John Chrysostom lived in Antioch. Though the capital of Syria, Greek was spoken in this seaboard city. Chrysostom finds the matter of the charisms in 1 Corinthians "very obscure."[38] The reason, he says, is "many of the wonders which then [in the time of the apostles] used to take place have now ceased."[39] Many of the charisms listed by Paul are no longer actualities in the life of the church.

But it was not so in the days of the apostles: "Whoever was baptized at once spoke in tongues, and not only in tongues, but many also prophesied; some performed many other wonderful works."[40] "All" who were baptized in the apostolic age received "certain excellent charisms."[41] Specifically with regard to prophecy, Chrysostom says, "This grace was poured out abundantly, and every church had many who prophesied."[42]

Chrysostom regrets the passing of many charisms from the life of the church. He tells of a beautiful woman who goes to her jewel box, opens it and finds it empty. "The present Church represents such a woman."[43]

Chrysostom's teaching is significant for three reasons. First, we begin to see the disappearance of some charisms from the broad pattern of the church's life in one part of the world. Second,

Chrysostom is aware of an earlier period in which an experience of the charisms was a normal part of initiation. Third, Chrysostom obviously considered the change a great loss for the church.

PHILOXENUS OF MABBUG AND THE SYRIANS

Tertullian and Hilary wrote in Latin, while Origen, Cyril, Basil, Gregory and John Chrysostom wrote in Greek. But Philoxenus and those of his tradition wrote in Syriac, a dialect of Aramaic. The previous authors all envisaged a situation in which adults were baptized, while in churches of the Syriac tradition, there was baptism of infants. So his situation was similar to that of many liturgical churches today.

We would criticize Philoxenus' view of the Christian life as too narrow. Like many of his contemporaries, he belittles the possibility of perfection within the married state. He and other Syrian theologians tie their theology too closely to monastic life. Yet they may preserve an ancient, indeed apostolic, theology, which only later was narrowed to monastic ideals.

Philoxenus speaks of two baptisms, one received in infancy and the second years later, when one gives oneself completely to the gospel by embracing the monastic ideals. His talk of two baptisms is deceptive, because he actually believes in only one, the first, given at infancy, which is fully actualized years later in adult life when one surrenders to the gospel. By living the gospel, by emptying oneself, "the sensation" of the divine life given at first baptism, but not then felt, blossoms into "the true experience of the knowledge of the Spirit" in the second baptism.[44] Philoxenus stumbles over himself excitedly when he writes of the second baptism: "You will only know that you experience happiness, but what that joy is you will not be able to express."[45] He does mention the charism of healing, but he implies there are more.[46]

One could mention other Syriac writers who place the charisms in relation to Christian initiation. John of Apamea (first half of the fifth century), like Philoxenus, writes of two baptisms, the second also a later actualization of the first. In the second baptism one takes possession perfectly "of the power of holy baptism."[47] In relation to the second baptism, he mentions prophecy, healing and miracles.[48]

Theodoret of Cyrrhus (ca. 393–ca. 466) witnesses to the abundant outpouring of charisms at initiation and mentions healing in particular.[49] Severus of Antioch (ca. 465–538), like John Chrysostom, acknowledges that "numerous charisms were bestowed on believers at that [apostolic] time, and those who were baptized by the apostles also received various favors."[50] Finally, Joseph Hazzaya (born ca. 710–713), one of the great Syrian mystics, after mentioning a variety of general gifts (love of God, kindness, illumination of the mind), mentions also the charisms of "the flow of spiritual speech," "word of knowledge" and "joy, jubilation, exultation, praise, glorification, songs, hymns, odes." Hazzaya concludes that these "are the signs by whose presence within you, you will realize that the Holy Spirit, which you received from holy baptism, is working within you."[51]

Commenting on these Syriac witnesses, Oxford scholar Sebastian Brock says the Syriac fathers "are well aware that the pentecostal effects of baptism do not necessarily manifest themselves at baptism itself, but may be delayed until later: the 'pledge of the Spirit.' The potential, however, is already present as a result of baptism."[52] Referring specifically to Philoxenus, Brock continues:

> What Philoxenus is saying here is something of great value. He is looking at the relationship between the personal experience of Pentecost, of the coming of the Holy Spirit upon an individual, and the actual rite of baptism, in a context where, because of the practice of infant baptism, the two events may be separated by many years of time.... The "two baptisms" are thus but two aspects of the one sacra-

ment, the first seen from the point of view of the Giver, the second, from that of the receiver.[53]

Baptism for the Syrians is not a one-time event. Rather, "baptism is seen as just the beginning which opens up all sorts of new possibilities, provided the baptized person responds with openness to the presence of the indwelling Spirit."[54]

Conclusions

These early authors view baptism in the Holy Spirit as being integral to Christian initiation, as belonging to the normal Christian life of the normal Christian community. The experience took place within the rites of initiation for adults or in a later actualization of what was received at initiation, in the case of someone baptized as an infant. The experience of Christian initiation was one of spiritual joy, issuing in praise and thanksgiving, and of the manifestation, either then or later, of the charisms (tongues, prophecy, knowledge, wisdom, discernment, healing). While classical Pentecostals and some streams of the charismatic movement see baptism in the Holy Spirit as a second (or third) subsequent work after conversion, the early authors saw it as belonging to the very making of a Christian—that is, to initiation.

From this evidence it must be clear that what is called baptism in the Holy Spirit was an integral part of becoming a Christian. There was, and could be, only one baptism, the celebration of which was prepared for over a long period of conversion and faith building. Unless conversion took place, the rites were empty gestures. The convert joined a converted community, living a converted life.

The charisms were expected and were imparted during initiation, which is seen in architectural terms in the diagram provided. If baptism in the Holy Spirit is integral to Christian initiation, then it does not belong to private piety but to public liturgy, to the official public worship of the church, and it is normative for all Christians. Baptism in the Holy Spirit clearly does not belong to the charismatic renewal but to the church.

Further, if the evidence I have placed before you is true, then baptism in the Spirit is not peripheral but central. Justin Martyr, Origen, Didymus the Blind and Cyril of Jerusalem all call Christian initiation baptism in the Holy Spirit. It is a synonym for baptism. The witnesses I have cited come from Latin, Greek and Syriac cultures, from almost the whole of the Mediterranean seaboard. The witnesses are not minor characters. Five are doctors of the church (Hilary, Cyril, Basil, Gregory, John Chrysostom), persons especially reliable in identifying the faith and practice of the church. Origen was the most influential theologian in the East during the first thousand years. Philoxenus was a major figure in Syria.

Classical Pentecostalism has not conceived of baptism in the Holy Spirit in relation to initiation. The research shows that, whatever disagreements there are over the exegesis of certain New Testament texts, the essential insight of classical Pentecostalism about the existence of something called baptism in the Holy Spirit is on target. They are also right in asserting that it is central rather than peripheral. The Christian world is indebted to classical Pentecostalism for its witness to the baptism in the Holy Spirit.

The evidence from the early church must be significant for evangelization. The intense joy to which Hilary of Poitiers and Joseph Hazzaya refer is a part of an inner transformation to which Basil and Gregory Nazianzen give witness, the dynamism of the charisms. All of this is a source for both evangelization and reevangelization. This is not fluff, not tinsel.

Once again, charismatic renewal and baptism in the Holy Spirit can be separated. In embracing the baptism in the Holy Spirit as integral to Christian initiation, one is not joining a movement. The issue is to embrace the fullness of Christian initiation and to utilize the total reality of initiation as the well from which we draw the water of life and power in the work of evangelization. Leading believers into a living experience of the baptism in the Holy Spirit as an integral part of Christian initiation should be the goal of the evangelizing church.

Kilian McDonnell, O.S.B.
St. John's Abbey
Collegeville, MN 56321
E-mail: kmcdonnell@csbsju.edu

CHAPTER 8

The New Evangelization in Africa

Cardinal Peter Turkson

By all practical reckoning, Catholic evangelization of Africa, south of the Sahara, did not precede by much the arrival of the Portuguese on the African coast in the fifteenth century. The case of the Ethiopian eunuch's encounter with Philip in apostolic times (see Acts 8:26–40) is an exception. The arrival of the Portuguese introduced the era of European exploration of and trade with Africa; and it was related to two principal factors:

✧ the Portuguese desire to expel the Saracens (Muslim Arabs) from Portugal and to protect Portugal from further Saracen incursions

↦ the search by Europe for new trade routes to the Far East

European traders, most of whom sailed under royal banners, and their chaplains would be the first missionaries and "evangelizers" of the African coastal settlements. The resultant evangelization of Africa would be very much a product of European Christian spirituality and a sense of being Christian in the fifteenth through seventeenth centuries, at the close of the Middle Ages.

EARLY MISSIONARY EVANGELIZATION: A PORTUGUESE INSTANCE IN WEST AFRICA[1]

Following the defeat and the expulsion from Portugal of the Saracens (Arab Muslims), the Portuguese, under Prince Henry, sought to ensure a total freedom from Saracen threat and invasion by pursuing them into North Africa (Morocco). There the Portuguese established their presence and a stronghold at Ceuta. As a sign thereof, they converted the mosque of Ceuta into a Catholic church; with the introduction of the statue of Mary, they dedicated the church and the continent on which it stood to "Santa Maria of Africa." This was the beginning of Catholic missionary presence and activity on the northwest coast of Africa, and by the end of 1460, the year of the death of Prince Henry, Portuguese explorers had reached as far south on the Guinea coast as Sierra Leone.

Under King Alfonso V, the Portuguese explored the West African coast further south, and in 1471 Portuguese traders on their way to the Far East berthed at Shama, where the River Pra entered the sea, on the Guinea coast. They came in search of fresh water, but they found gold and departed having discovered a "gold coast" (the former name of Ghana).

From 1471 to 1481, heavy trade was carried on with coastal villages on the Gold Coast, but all of this was from ships anchored offshore. In 1482 the need for a permanent trading post on land influenced the Portuguese under Prince João (later King João II) to build a fortress on the coast of the Gold Coast, at Edina, which the Portuguese called El Mina (the mine). And so, in January 1482, Diego D'Azambuja landed at El Mina to lay the foundation of a castle. His party, with arms concealed under their coats, chose a spot on a rocky promontory on the coast, hoisted the royal standard of Portugal upon a high tree, erected an altar beneath the tree and celebrated a solemn Mass.

They prayed for the success of their trade, the conversion of Africans and the endurance of the church they were about to found.[2] The church would operate from the castle that would later occupy the site. This castle church would be the first Catholic church in the Gold Coast (Ghana).

Indeed, an aspect of Diego D'Azambuja's mission was a fulfillment of an order that Pope Sixtus IV had given on August 21, 1471, to the archbishop of Lisbon. It was to see to it that churches were built all along Africa's coast. The same pope also granted the Knights of Christ spiritual jurisdiction over all churches in West Africa. Accordingly, these knights built a monastery in São Tomé, off the coast of Gabon, from which the vicar exercised jurisdiction over the Portuguese mission churches, which had developed in response to the order of the pope and as a result of the activities of chaplains of the Portuguese traders and forces.

One such mission church was the community that sprung up at El Mina following the arrival of the Portuguese in 1482. In 1505, twenty-three years after Diego D'Azambuga and his men had celebrated Mass on the El Mina coast, the first conversions and baptisms took place. The paramount chief of the Efutu, Nana Sasaxy, and six of his noblemen met with an official of the captain of the castle, Diego D'Alvarenga, and the vicar, and they received baptism.[3] The following day Nana Sasaxy erected a small shelter on a hill across from the castle. There the vicar, D'Alvarenga and members of the

Portuguese garrison met with the chief and his party and celebrated Mass. This shelter was the first Catholic church outside the castle in the Gold Coast, and it was named the Church of São Jago. As D'Alvarenga wrote to the king, the Portuguese sought to promote "God's glory and Your Highness' interests."[4]

In 1534 Pope Paul III created the new diocese of São Tomé, whose territory extended from the present-day Ivory Coast to the Cape of Good Hope. It included the missionary churches of El Mina (São Jago), São Tomé, Congo, Angola, Namibia and the western cape of South Africa. The first bishop of the new diocese was Diogo Ortiz de Vilhegas. In response to the increasing presence on the African coast of secular priests and chaplains, who were more interested in gold trade than missionary work, Bishop de Vilhegas brought in Augustinian priests in 1572 who would catechize the local population and teach them to read and write.

In support of their ministry, the Portuguese crown requested of Pope Urban VII in 1630 special faculties for the priests and chaplains in the land of Mina, on the Guinea coast:

> Most Blessed Father! Because the Island or rather the Land of Mina, under the Portuguese crown...does not have its own bishop, and since the one to whom recourse must be had in cases of necessity is far away and can be reached only with difficulty and great cost of time and money, the vicars and chaplains in that jurisdictional area beg Your Holiness to give them and their successors in perpetuity the faculties for confessions granted to bishops by the Council of Trent in Canon 6 of its twenty-fourth session, "de reformatione." They would like the faculties to be just like those which Your Holiness gave a short while ago to the discalced Carmelites in Arabia. They would like in addition the faculties to administer the Sacrament of Confirmation, bless vestments and other items necessary for mass.... His Divine Majesty will greatly profit by the granting of these faculties, and they will bring both spiritual and temporal consolation to the peoples in that area.[5]

In a well-considered response, the Congregation for the Propagation of the Faith[6] responded in 1632 to the request of the Portuguese king, granting only "personal faculties" for the blessing of vestments, corporals and palls to the vicar of El Mina. Such were the beginnings of the establishment of the Catholic church along the western coast of Africa.

For an evaluation of the character of this initial phase of Catholic evangelization on the Guinea coast, in El Mina and its environs, one may read the rather pessimistic report of the vicar of the São Jorge castle in El Mina to the Congregation for the Propagation of the Faith, as R. Wiltgen presents it:

He [the vicar] told how Diego da Azambuja had received from Caramansa [Kobena Ansah] the land on which the castle was built and how all the attempts to convert this Chief had been in vain. He told how churches had been built in Efutu and Komenda and the religious in charge there beaten to death, and all the church furnishings stolen.

The contemporary generation of Christians in Mina, he went on to say, were Christians in name only, going to confession only under pressure, and then not even knowing how to make a good confession, or what to confess. As far as he could see, the greatest good being accomplished in Mina was the baptism of infants who died before attaining the use of reason. As for the African women who lived with the Portuguese traders in the fort, they were the only ones considered well enough instructed and properly disposed to receive Holy Communion.

As for paganism, the village was rife with superstitious and magical rites of which the people were so fond that they allowed only every other child to be baptized...and those baptized were quickly corrupted by their pagan brothers and sisters.[7]

METHODS AND FRUITS OF EARLY MISSIONARY EVANGELIZATION
From what it is possible to glean from scattered references to church life and organization in the Portuguese period, missionary evange-

lization consisted in building churches, administering infant baptisms (initially to offspring of Portuguese and local women and later to children of willing parents), introducing pious devotional practices, such as devotion to the Blessed Virgin Mary and to Saint Anthony, catechesis and its close ally, education (the opening of schools). Access to and the use of Scriptures in this period were very restricted. Celebration of the Mass was the most common occasion for people to listen to Scriptures, not in its proclamation, which was in Latin, but in the sermons and homilies.

The era of Portuguese evangelization and missionary activities on the Guinea coast came to an end with the defeat of the Portuguese by the Calvinist Dutch in 1637 and the capture, in the Gold Coast, of the castle São Jorge of El Mina. The nascent Catholic faith of the people, which had been negatively presented to the Congregation for the Propagation of the Faith, suddenly showed itself noble and praiseworthy. For when it became clear that the castle was falling to the Dutch, the local Catholics hurtled away to safety the symbols of their religion and faith. "One after the other took something into custody, the missal, the vestments, the candlesticks, the statues and even the sacred vessels."[8] And as long as these symbols of the new faith remained with the people, the Portuguese Catholic missionaries nurtured and cherished hope in a return to the Guinea coast. Thus Father Colombin, the Portuguese vicar of El Mina who was banished by the Dutch to Brazil, wrote to Cardinal Antonio Barberini of St. Onofrio:

As for our Guinea Mission, it is not yet abandoned, not yet given up for lost. We still have hope! Yes, even though the mission has undergone persecution, even though eight of our Fathers have there laid down their lives, even though we have had to undergo such long and severe hardships, we still have hope. Some day the most merciful God will reap from out the evils that have befallen that unfortunate pagan land an abundant harvest that will redound to His own glory, to the salvation of souls, to the exaltation of the Church, and to our consolation.[9]

THE LATER PERIOD OF MISSIONARY EVANGELIZATION:
THE SOCIETY OF AFRICAN MISSION IN WEST AFRICA

The hope of Father Colombin for a return of Catholic missionaries to the Guinea coast would be fulfilled only two hundred years later; it would be a return of Catholicism to a Guinea coast now dominated by the Protestantism of the Dutch (Calvinism), the English (Anglicanism and Methodism), the Danes (Lutheranism) and the Swiss (Presbyterianism and Basel missionaries). The initial conduct and the experiences then, which Catholic missions and evangelization would make in this period, would depend largely on the type of openness and reception that the different colonial powers would fashion for them.[10]

In the nineteenth century the return of liberated slaves from Brazil to the coasts of Benin and Nigeria engendered lay Catholic evangelization among the populations there. Officially, however, the Congregation for the Propagation of the Faith had sought to maintain the missionary evangelization of the Guinea coast, after the departure of the Portuguese, by entrusting its mission to the French Dominicans, who already took pastoral care of the West Indies. This did not work out. Divisions and hostilities among the nations in Europe (for example, between the English and the French) affected the show of hospitality in the colonies.

Following this failure, the Congregation for the Propagation of the Faith divided the mission of the Guinea coast into two vicariates and entrusted them to two missionary congregations. The Vicariate of the Two Guineas, from the Senegambia to the Volta (in the Gold Coast), on one hand, was entrusted to the Holy Ghost Fathers, who were based in the Gambia. The Vicariate of Benin, from the Volta to the Niger (in Nigeria), was entrusted to the Society of African Mission (SMA).[11]

Accordingly, the SMA Fathers arrived in Ouidah (Benin) in 1861 to revive a mission outpost and a church, which the Portuguese had built in 1680. Soon the SMA Fathers were also to learn of the presence of a Catholic community in the Lagos area under the leadership of a lay preacher (catechist) called Padre Antonio. In response to this lay initiative, SMA missionaries, under Father Francesco Borghero, came into Lagos in 1868 to consolidate the work of the freed Brazilian slaves and to promote Catholic evangelization. The subsequent spread of Catholic missionary activities in Nigeria would be affected by the presence or the lack thereof of tribal and cultural openness to the new religion and by British colonial government orders, such as that which stalled missionary advances into northern Nigeria.

In the Vicariate of the Two Guineas, administered by the Holy Ghost Fathers, however, another former Portuguese mission, and now a British colony, languished from the lack of missionary attention. This was the Gold Coast. After the Dutch ceded all their holdings on the Guinea coast to Britain in the Treaty of the Hague in 1871, the British created the Gold Coast Colony in 1874, made up of the Gold Coast (Ghana) and Nigeria. This political and administrative circumscription, however, did not coincide with the ecclesiastical definitions of the Guinea coast. While Nigeria (Lagos) belonged to the Vicariate of Benin and was administered by the SMA Fathers, the Gold Coast belonged to the Vicariate of the Two Guineas and had to be administered by the Holy Ghost Fathers from Senegambia (Senegal-Gambia). As a result, nobody paid attention to the Gold Coast mission.

It was not until 1877 that Sir William Marshall's letter to *The Tablet* in England awakened the Congregation for the Propagation of the Faith to the situation in the Gold Coast.[12] Sir William Marshall had written to the editor: "I write from a part of the world, the West Coast of Africa, in which England now has almost exclusive interest and power, but for which the Catholics of England, clerical and lay, have as yet done nothing.... On the whole of the Gold Coast there is not a single Catholic priest or mission of any nation."[13]

In response to Marshall's letter, the Congregation for the Propagation of the Faith asked the Holy Ghost Fathers to comment on the advisability and the chances of success of a mission in the Gold Coast. By way of communicating a response, Father Gommenginger, a Holy Ghost Father, visited the Gold Coast and wrote the following to the Congregation for the Propagation of the Faith:

> Think of it, we Catholics were the very first ones...to take root in the Gold Coast, and yet now we have not even a single missionary in the land! The Protestants themselves cannot figure it out. When they saw me arrive, they felt surely the sole purpose of my coming was to open a Catholic Mission. Personally I am convinced that the opportune moment has arrived. It is time for us to take up again the work begun so propitiously by our missionaries of the...fifteenth century, and then interrupted so inexorably by the ascendancy of the Dutch. Conditions have changed and obstacles have in part been removed. God and souls are calling us back to the Gold Coast.[14]

There would indeed be a response to the "call of God and souls" for a return of Catholic mission to the Gold Coast, but Father Gommenginger and the Holy Ghost Fathers would not be the ones to make the response. The SMA Fathers would make it, with a mandate from the Congregation for the Propagation of the Faith.

In the wake of Father Gommenginger's report, the Congregation for the Propagation of the Faith decreed on April 28, 1879, the erection of a Prefecture Apostolic of the Gold Coast, separating it from the Vicariate of the Two Guineas and entrusting it to the SMA

Fathers. It extended from the River Volta to the River Cavally in the Ivory Coast.

On May 7, 1879, Pope Leo XIII approved of the decree, confirmed it and ordered it published. On September 27 the decree was published, and the Prefecture Apostolic of the Gold Coast was official. Father Planque, the successor of Bishop Bresillac, and the SMA Missionaries were put in charge; the former Portuguese mission post of El Mina was to serve as the central station. From there Catholic missionary evangelization would spread; and the method, from the start, was the development of schools and the use of an intensive educational program. As the missionaries believed, "a mission without schools is a mission without a future."[15]

Accordingly, the SMA missionaries (Father Moreau, joined by Father Michon after the death of Father Murat) rented a house for a mission house and a school. Mass was celebrated on the veranda, and Father Moreau prepared a *Fante* catechism for religious instruction.[16]

In 1881, at Christmas, five pupils of the school were baptized. As interest in the school grew, the number of children seeking education increased, and other children followed to receive baptism. Soon some adults, parents of the pupils, followed their children to embrace the new faith. These would become the first catechists and lay apostles of the faith.

The spread of the Catholic faith outside El Mina was the work of these past students of the mission schools. They took the faith beyond El Mina and formed Catholic communities, which would host the trekking priests and prepare to become new mission posts. The former students also served as the interpreters of the missionaries and taught catechism in the communities. The founding of the church in Cape Coast, the present see of the archdiocese of Cape Coast, located about nine kilometers east of El Mina, was greatly facilitated by the labors of one such lay catechist, Francis William Hazel Cobbinah.

Not long after the development of the schools for boys, the SMA Fathers introduced schools for girls. They believed too that lasting results for their mission required that girls also be trained and instructed in the faith because, they said, prayers must be learned at the mother's knee and religion practiced at home if it is to establish strong roots. Accordingly, they arranged for the assistance of some female collaborators of the SMA Fathers, the Sisters of Our Lady of Apostles (O.L.A.), to educate the girls.

On December 26, 1883, the first two O.L.A. Sisters arrived in El Mina; and on March 31, 1884, they opened the first Catholic girls' school in the Gold Coast with twenty-six pupils. In a matter of months the sisters also began to run a clinic alongside the school.

THE METHOD OF LATER MISSIONARY EVANGELIZATION

The method of evangelization of the later missionaries was, to a large extent, heir to the methods of the early missionaries. It was a method centered on the celebration of the sacraments, such as baptism, Eucharist and penance, and on the teachings (catechesis) that preceded and accompanied their administration. Catechism books and rudimentary books of hymns and prayers were developed with the help of converts from the mission schools. Later, in 1903, the SMA Fathers would establish a printing press in Cape Coast to help distribute their catechetical material.

Devotional practices and paraliturgical activities, which had been part of the Portuguese evangelization, continued to play vital roles in the people's practice of their faith. Serving a population that until lately had been largely illiterate, the church made good use of such popular acts of piety as devotion to the Blessed Virgin Mary, the praying of rosaries, devotion to the Sacred Heart, devotion to Saint Anthony, the stations of the cross and so on to teach her faith and to express her life.

The rituals and the symbolisms of Catholic celebrations and worship may also have struck a sympathetic chord with the people, coming as they were from a culture with traditional forms of worship, which made use of rituals and symbols. While this affinity might have disposed the people generously toward Catholicism, it certainly was also a temptation to syncretism, as the vicar at El Mina had observed.

The use of schools and educational institutions as tools for evangelization was characteristic of all missionary groups in the Gold Coast and elsewhere on the Guinea coast. The schools drew people and created for them situations of experience with the new religion. The schools also prepared people to place their talents and endowments at the service of the new faith. They made people catechists and interpreters of the message of the new missionary faith. Properly done, this would have marked and traced out useful beginnings and pathways for enculturating the new faith.

But that was not all. Perhaps the most important thing that schools did for evangelization and for the spread of the new faith was the access that they fashioned for the new believers to the basis of their faith. Schools educated people and enabled them to face life's challenges and to hold positions of leadership in society, but they also put people in touch with the roots of their religion. They enabled people to read the Scriptures on which their religion was based.[17]

Schools certainly were great assets to the missionary enterprise, but their existence also brought the risk of reducing the missionary communication of faith by replacing evangelization with catechesis (teaching) and conversion and faith experience with acquired knowledge. Since reception into the church was marked by catechetical instruction, the possibility was real that people learned about articles of faith without basing their lives on them.[18] This, indeed, may be the greatest weakness of missionary evangelization and of the foundation it laid for the African church. It continues, unfortunately, to characterize modern-day evangelization and pastoral praxis.[19] Teaching and learning "catechism" is still the most adhered to means of entry and admission into the church.

THE RESULTANT CHURCHES OF MISSIONARY EVANGELIZATION

Both methods of missionary evangelization, that of the early period and that of the later period, may constitute what Cardinal Ratzinger (now Pope Benedict XVI) once referred to as "classic evangelization."[20] It communicated the gospel of salvation in Christ—celebrating the Eucharistic mystery, administering the sacraments, preaching the word and seeking human promotion through education and health care services. It established most of the local churches on the continent and determined their lives as churches.

A fruit of such evangelization was superficial conversions, which the missionaries themselves observed and which continues to manifest itself occasionally in distressing instances of ethnic intolerance, syncretism, attachment to deleterious customs and cultural practices. The local churches in Africa have long desired a deep, "permanent and uninterrupted and never to be interrupted evangelization, a new evangelization, capable of being heard by that world that does not find access to classic evangelization."[21]

The "classic evangelization" of one or both waves of missionary evangelization on the continent did, however, lead to the establishment of local Catholic churches of various ages, sizes and strengths.[22] Exceptions to this were the churches on the north coast of Africa, which dated from Christian missionary travels of the first century but were practically wiped out by Islamic Arab expansionism.

Although numbers and statistics do not matter much and are not determinative in matters of the kingdom of God, [23] available statistics concur to describe the African church generally as a fast-growing church. According to the Congregation for the Propagation of the Faith, out of a total continental population of about 719,257,499 people, about 146,207,178 are Catholic.[24] This represents 20.3 percent of the population of the continent.[25]

This Catholic population is distributed among eighty-three archdioceses, 367 dioceses, fifteen apostolic vicariates, seven apostolic prefectures, one apostolic administrator, three military ordinariates and one *Missio sui Iuris* or mission church. The growth can be described only about churches in countries between the two African deserts, Sahara and the Kalahari. North of the Sahara are Arab Islamic countries, where the Catholic church is practically a church of migrants. South of the Kalahari the Catholic population thins to 4.7 percent in Botswana, 5.3 percent in Swaziland and 7.5 percent in the Republic of South Africa.

THE AFRICAN SYNOD AND A VISION OF NEW EVANGELIZATION

As a reality, however, that was born from the various methods of missionary evangelization we have observed, the fast-growing African church must become a deeply renewed and a permanently evangelized church. It must become all these with due regard for and an appreciation of:

⬦ the plurality of faiths and the pluriformity of Christian confessions, which now crisscross the terrain of missionary evangelization

⬦ the cultures of the new "home" of the gospel and the Christian faith

⬦ the distinction between evangelization (proclamation) and catechesis and the priority of evangelization

⬦ the relationship between faith and life, between conversion and Christian living (social action)

These were some of the concerns that inspired the convocation of the African Synod; and by way of responding to them, the African

Synod invited the African church first to be more deeply evangelized and renewed and then to understand evangelization as:

- a proclamation, in all its senses and by all, of the Good News of salvation in Christ
- calling for enculturation
- engendering an openness to dialogue with other Christians and religions
- leading to social action and a commitment to justice and peace
- a response to the mandate to "go…make disciples of all nations" (Matthew 28:19) and to the need, therefore, to ceaselessly seek out ways of sharing (communicating) the gospel effectively

The desired result, as Pope John Paul II prayed, was that "the Synod may result in a deep renewal of the Church in Africa, so that Christians on that continent may be filled with zeal to live the Gospel fully and to share Christ's salvation and liberation with humanity."[26] This, since the conclusion of the African Synod and the promulgation of the post-synodal exhortation, *Ecclesia in Africa,* has translated into a fundamental pastoral program for the African church.[27] A tool that has distinguished itself in the execution of the program has been the formation of such lay renewal groups and movements as the Cursillo, New Catechumenate, Focolari and the charismatic renewal.

Due to their Spanish and Italian origins respectively, the Cursillo and the New Catechumenate have had very slow starts in the English-speaking countries of the Guinea coast (Nigeria, Ghana, Sierra Leone, Liberia and Gambia). In Ghana the Cursillo movement and the New Catechumenate are hardly known. By far the most popular movement, which has spearheaded the new evangelization program of the church, is the charismatic renewal and, in places, its attendant School of Evangelization.

THE CHARISMATIC RENEWAL AS A TOOL OF NEW EVANGELIZATION

Long before the African Synod could convene the African church, in the context of the universal church, to consider her particular situation and to assess her evangelizing resources before the challenges of modernity, several local churches had noticed the inadequacy of aspects of classic missionary evangelization. Several local churches, as a whole (clergy, religious and laity) or in part (clergy alone, religious alone or laity alone), had begun to seek out and to adopt several initiatives to surmount the deficiencies of missionary evangelization and to make Catholic evangelization deep and permanent.

In Ghana in the early twentieth century, the Catholic church had an arduous uphill climb against the superficiality of missionary evangelization and against Protestantism. The missions of the latter had a head start under the British. They had access to and were familiar with the Scriptures, in which Catholics believed their faith was rooted but with which they were not familiar. The iconoclasm and reductionism of the Protestants dismissed much of Catholic sacramental worship and ridiculed the images and symbols of traditional Catholic devotions. Protestant pietism, which made regular mention of the Holy Spirit and his gifts, appeared to be what true biblical religion had to be.

Sacramental worship, the traditional devotions and the ministries of the priests still did well to make Catholics and to maintain them in their faith; but the advent of the charismatic renewal movement in the 1970s did much by way of challenging traditional Catholics to genuine conversions and dismantling some of the exclusive claims that Protestants made to the use and knowledge of Scriptures, to the exercise of the gifts of the Spirit and even to prayer.

It was a Holy Ghost missionary, the director of a retreat center, who introduced the charismatic renewal in Ghana. By October 1984 the movement had become so popular, having spread throughout parishes in Ghana, that a good contingent of priests would travel to Rome to participate in the Worldwide Retreat for Priests. With a supply of literature from covenant communities in the United States, well-formed leadership teams emerged to take care of the "charismatics" in the parishes and institutions. It was from these leadership teams that promising individuals would be sent to the I.C.P.E. School of Evangelization in Alleheiligen, Germany, to the SION School of Evangelization in Surrey-Essex, England, and in Africa to the relatively better established EMMAUS School of Evangelization at Katikamu, Uganda. From these schools a group would form, as staff, to begin the KNOW-and-TELL (K&T) School of Evangelization at Takoradi, Ghana.

The charismatic renewal, as observed above, helped to dismantle Protestant prejudices about Catholics and the Catholic church. It helped fashion for the faithful a familiarity with Scriptures and a habit of reading the Word of God. It also introduced them to the world of the experience and the exercise of the spiritual gifts. This, however, has not been without problems. There have been cases where some, in the experience of the spiritual gifts, have become in fact Protestants within the Catholic church, denying any use for the sacraments. Others, in their newly discovered hunger for prayer, the Word of God and morality, have become very judgmental, considering everybody else less holy, their parish priests included.

By way of helping to deal with such exceptional situations, and for the general ongoing formation of the groups and their leaderships, the Ghana Bishops' Conference has supported the development of a National Catholic Charismatic Centre at Kumasi, which gives regular leadership and organizational training programs. This centre and other archdiocesan and diocesan offices of the renewal receive teams from Renewal Ministries in Ann Arbor, Michigan, from the Gulf Region Alliance of Catholic Evangelism (G.R.A.C.E.) in Florida and from groups like Isaiah II of California, which support and encourage them in their call to discipleship and to holiness.

CONCLUSION

At the end of the day, the charismatic renewal is a tool for a deeper and a more permanent evangelization. Like any tool, it can be mishandled and used poorly. But it can also be used efficaciously and properly. Most importantly, as a movement in the church with papal recognition, the charismatic renewal must be recognized more and more as an instrument of God to be utilized for the growth of his church!

CHAPTER 9

Which Churches Are Growing and Why?

Vinson Synan, PH.D.

Evangelization enlarges the community of faith. Although the term "church growth" represents a specific movement among Protestants, it refers in the broadest sense to what all Christians desire: sharing with the non-Christian world the Good News of Jesus Christ as the only Savior.

Simply put, churches that evangelize tend to grow in membership, while those that do not evangelize tend to stagnate or even decline. As a rule, churches that are not experiencing growth tend to speak in terms of "quality" rather than quantity. For example, on a trip to Malaysia I met with a group of local bishops and pastors representing most of the churches in that largely Muslim nation. I asked them, "Which churches are growing the fastest in Malaysia and Kuala Lumpur?"

The dozen or so leaders looked sheepishly at each other before replying, "Well, if you are talking about quality and depth, the mainline churches are growing the fastest. But if you are speaking of numbers alone, the Pentecostals and charismatics are growing the fastest."

As the conversation continued, it became clear that indeed the Pentecostals were growing the fastest. But the largest actual increase in membership during the previous months was among the Roman Catholics, who had experienced dramatic breakthroughs in certain areas of the nation. The Catholics and the Pentecostals! How striking that the greatest growth was taking place at opposite ends of the liturgical and sacramental spectrum, from the oldest to the youngest of the world's churches.

We can learn a lot about evangelization from examining which churches in the world are growing and why. Let's review the major researchers who have made it their business to track the growth and size of the churches of the world. Their findings may help us understand the paradox of the Malaysian situation as well as the role of evangelization in expanding the worldwide body of Christ.

THE CHURCH-GROWTH MOVEMENT

The increasingly popular church-growth movement was pioneered by Donald McGavran, a venerable missiologist who first became interested in the principles of church growth as a missionary to India in the 1930s. He could not help but notice that some congregations and parishes grew rapidly while others did not.

McGavran's research caused a great stir among missiologists. Due to high demand, he founded in 1961 a new Institute of Church Growth on the campus of Northwest Christian College in Eugene,

Oregon. This institute drew so much attention that it soon outgrew its facilities and moved to Fuller Theological Seminary in Pasadena, California, becoming part of the Fuller School of World Missions.

Here McGavran gathered a group of brilliant students and faculty, including C. Peter Wagner, Win Arn and John Wimber. Almost all of McGavran's previous research had centered on Third World nations. By the mid-sixties, however, church leaders in the United States demanded that the same research and principles be applied to the American scene. Thus a booming church-growth industry emanated from Pasadena, affecting churches in America as well as the rest of the world.

Succeeding McGavran as the leading exponent and popularizer of this influential movement was the prolific researcher, lecturer and writer C. Peter Wagner, a man who spread the gospel of church growth to the four corners of the earth. From Wagner we learned the "pathologies of dying churches" as well as how to do "autopsies" on dead and dying congregations to find out why they died. Here are some of the Fuller findings on why particular congregations die:[1]

↔ *Ethnikitis.* The ethnic changing of a neighborhood—for example, from white to black or Hispanic—often kills the older church, whose members flee to the suburbs.

↔ *Old age.* The "ghost town" disease kills congregations. When small towns die, the churches die with them.

↔ *People blindness.* The controversial "homogeneous unit principle" states that "people prefer to worship with other people who are like themselves." That would include racial, ethnic, linguistic, social and economic groupings.

↔ *Hyper-cooperativeness.* With too much ecumenical cooperation, efforts toward Christian unity can hinder evangelism.

↬ *Koinonitis.* "Spiritual navel gazers"—that is, churches that are too ingrown—fail to welcome new people who are a little different from the "in group."

↬ *Sociological strangulation.* Healthy churches are choked to death by limited facilities such as small buildings, inadequate parking space and so on.

↬ *St. John's syndrome.* The lukewarm church is neither cold nor hot, the kind that Saint John said would be vomited out of the mouth of God (see Revelation 3:14–18).

Wagner also describes traits that characterize a growing congregation: a gifted pastor; a well-mobilized laity; churches that are "big enough" to serve the whole family; "celebration plus congregation plus cell equals church"; the homogeneous unit principle—that is, "mostly one kind of people"; churches that use effective evangelistic tools; churches that have their priorities straight—that is, their most important function in the community is religious rather than merely social or economic.[2]

Wagner's emphasis on the purely religious factor in church growth was influenced by Dean Kelley, a sociologist related to the liberal-leaning National Council of Churches. He published his groundbreaking book in 1972, *Why Conservative Churches Are Growing,* which simply stated the results of his research: "conservative" churches were growing, while "liberal" churches were declining.

Kelley attributed this situation to the fact that most people are more interested in answers to the "ultimate" question of salvation than in social questions. He said that liberal churches often offer "art or music appreciation, instruction in women's liberation, guidelines to politically correct causes, and dialogues with important local leaders," while most people are generally uninterested in such affairs. Instead, they are "hungry for God" and for the assurance of salvation.[3]

In addition to these insights, church-growth researchers discovered the importance of "church planting" as a major evangelistic tool. The movement also developed a method of tracking church growth through a system known as the "decadal growth rate." Through this objective method churches could estimate their growth or death rates and compare them to the biological growth rates.

Other research introduced us to the "life cycle of churches," which showed that the typical American Protestant church followed a life cycle that looked like the bell curve. New churches tended to grow for ten years, began to plateau at about twenty years and began a decline after about thirty years. Much of this research appeared in Wagner's best-selling books *Your Church Can Grow*, published in 1976, and *Leading Your Church to Growth*, published in 1984. In these books Wagner assured us that "church growth is a science," with theories that can be tested and proven.[4]

Further research by Carl George, head of the Charles E. Fuller Institute for Evangelism and Church Growth, also located in Pasadena, centered on the crucial role of pastoral leadership in church growth. From research in the business world, George taught us the differences between the "catalyzers," the "organizers" and the "operators."

Each of these leaders has specific gifts. The catalyzer is a charismatic individual who attracts a "pile" of people. This person is disorganized but attractive. The catalyzer is usually succeeded by the organizer, who organizes the "pile" and puts it in logical order. This second person is usually quite critical of the disorganized predecessor. Third, the operator comes on the scene and operates the church that was created by the catalyzer and then organized by the organizer. Afterward the succeeding operators need only oil the machinery they have inherited from the catalyzer and organizer. So much for church-growth theory![5]

The main blind spot in the research by McGavran, Wagner and

George, however, was that they never applied their methods to Roman Catholic and Eastern Orthodox churches. They focused solely on the Protestant churches of the world, with a heavy emphasis on mainline denominations in the United States. Surely Catholic churches face the same demographic pressures as urban Protestant churches. Why then were Catholics not studied by the church-growth researchers? Moreover, why did Catholics not study their own situation in America and the world using church-growth methods? Would the results be similar?

ASTONISHING SURVEY RESULTS

In 1982 David Barrett and Oxford University Press published his monumental *World Christian Encyclopedia,*[6] the most complete survey of Christianity and other world religions ever attempted. In a major review of the book, *Time* magazine said that Barrett had "counted every soul on earth." After the publication of the *Encyclopedia,* Phillip Hogan, world missions director of the Assemblies of God, quipped, "Only God and David Barrett know how many Assemblies of God members there are in the world." In 2001 Barrett revised the encyclopedia.[7]

What Barrett revealed in 1980 astonished people. Based on his research, the Roman Catholic church was by far the largest religious organization in the world in 1980, with some 809,157,029 members. Next came the Orthodox Christian churches, with 124,419,230 members. To the amazement of many, the largest Protestant family of churches in the world was no longer the Reformation churches, such as the Lutherans, Anglicans, Presbyterians and Baptists, but the Pentecostals with 51,000,000 members. And the Pentecostal movement had begun only eighty years before.[8]

By 2000 Pentecostals and charismatics had grown to be the second largest family in the world after the Roman Catholic church family. The following figures indicate the growth of these movements in the last century:

The Global Number of Roman Catholics

1900	1970	2000	2005	2025 (projected)
266,546,000	665,475,000	1,055,651,000	1,118,992,000	1,336,338,000

The Global Number of Pentecostals and Charismatics

1900	1970	2000	2005	2025 (projected)
981,000	72,223,000	526,916,000	588,502,000	798,320,000 [9]

Unlike most evangelical Protestant statisticians, who tended to count only "born again" believers or "Bible believers" as true Christians, Barrett also counted all baptized Catholics as Christians. He also counted such groups as Mormons and Jehovah's Witnesses as "marginal Christians." Furthermore, he used demographic techniques that counted entire families as members of churches and movements rather than official church records alone.

The results of Barrett's massive research demonstrated that, in general, Western churches from Europe and North America were declining, while Third World churches were growing. His figures for 1980 were startling. For instance, in that year 7,600 Christians per day dropped out of the Western churches, both Protestant and Catholic, while in an average day 16,000 Africans became Christians. Indeed, Barrett estimated that somewhere around 1980, the number of nonwhite Christians exceeded the number of white Christians for the first time in history.[10]

Barrett also estimated and projected the numbers and percentages of all churches for the entire twentieth century, beginning in 1900 and ending in the year 2000. The figures were illuminating as far as the growth of the Roman Catholic church was concerned. His research revealed that in 1900, Roman Catholics totaled 271,990,786, making up 16.8 percent of the world's population. By the year 2000 that number reached 1,055,651,000 members, accounting for 18.7 percent of the world's population. Barrett's findings indicated a growth of almost one billion Catholic souls in one century![11]

If church-growth theory resulted in larger churches, then research was needed to track the largest congregations in the world and to see why they had grown. This project was taken on in 1985 by John Vaughn, a professor of church growth and founder of the Church Growth and World Missions Center at Southwest Baptist University in Bolivar, Missouri.

Vaughn first became interested in fundamentalist Baptist congregations in America, which were far larger than those in any denominations during the 1950s and 1960s. For years his records showed that the "ten largest churches" in America were indeed Baptist churches, like the ones that sponsored Vaughn's university.

By the middle 1980s his research took him to the nations of the world, resulting in *The World's Twenty Largest Churches* (1984) and *The Large Church: A Twentieth-Century Expression of the First-Century Church* (1985). By the time these books appeared, the largest Protestant churches in the world were no longer conservative Baptist congregations but Pentecostal ones, which soon outgrew all others in scope and size.

By 1990 all ten of the largest congregations in the world were either classical Pentecostal or charismatic Protestant. These "megachurches" grew to astonishing proportions. For instance, in the early 1990s in Seoul, Korea, the Yoido Full Gospel Church, pastored by Yonggi Cho, counted no less than 800,000 members. Other Pentecostal and charismatic churches around the world completed an impressive roster of super-churches.

BIOLOGICAL OR CONVERSION GROWTH?

A survey of the foregoing research reveals two major ways that churches grow: by biological (demographic) growth and by conversion growth. The two largest families of Christians on earth, the Catholics and Pentecostals, owe their growth to both factors—the former primarily through biological means and the latter primarily by conversion.

Many church leaders are still trying to find the reasons for such rapid growth among Pentecostal and charismatic churches around the world. When asked this question, most Pentecostal leaders would answer simply, "The baptism in the Holy Spirit with the accompanying manifestations of charismatic gifts." Many researchers tend to overlook this answer as being too simplistic, looking rather for more sophisticated sociological or economic causes. At some point they may be forced to face the truth of these Pentecostal claims.[12]

Pentecostals seem to grow in most places because of aggressive evangelism accompanied by such "signs and wonders" as healing, speaking in tongues, casting out of demons and prophesying. In his book *Power Evangelism,* the late John Wimber pointed to "power encounters" as the most significant points of dramatic breakthrough into non-Christian cultures.[13]

Many other factors could be cited for the growth of Pentecostalism in this century: the renewal of expressive worship and spontaneous public prayer, a love of Scripture, the use of cell groups, massive church planting and cultural adaptability. Yet it seems that the Pentecostals' dynamic and expressive worship coupled with an expectant faith that miracles could happen at any time go far to explain their explosive growth.[14]

OF PENTECOSTALS, CATHOLICS AND LIBERAL PROTESTANTS

Not surprisingly, Pentecostal churches are growing in Africa. The cultural freedom of Pentecostals to dance, shout, sing and exercise the gifts of the Spirit constitutes an undeniable attraction to Africans as well as other Third World peoples, most of whom remain unmoved by the more conventional church life represented by most Western Protestant churches.

On the other hand, the Roman Catholic church is also growing explosively in Africa, faster than it is growing anywhere else in the world. Some of my African friends explained that Africans not only are attracted to the spiritual freedom of worship that is found in Pentecostal worship but are equally attracted by the liturgical pageantry of Roman Catholicism. Imagine the growth potential in Africa of a church life that combined these qualities in a Pentecostal Catholicism!

A factor balancing Roman Catholic growth in Africa, however, is the problem of massive defections in the West for various reasons. In Europe and North America, millions of Catholics have left the church for the same reasons that Protestants have dropped out. It has been commonly stated that in America lapsed Catholics, which number some sixteen million persons, would make the second largest denomination in the nation if they were organized into one body. Millions of other Catholics have left to join Evangelical and charismatic churches.

While Roman Catholics have increased their percentage of world population since 1900, the figures for mainline Protestants show an overall decline. In 1900 all Reformation Protestants numbered 103,056,655 persons, making up 6.4 percent of the world population. By the turn of the century that number had grown to 347,762,000, but this figure accounted for only 5.5 percent of the world population.

These trends mean that, for reasons already explained by Dean Kelley, mainline liberal Protestant churches will not play as significant a role in this century as they did in the past. This marked decline among mainline Protestants stands in stark contrast to the burgeoning growth of the Pentecostal and independent charismatic churches during the twentieth century.[15]

The growth among Evangelical churches not associated with the Pentecostal/charismatic movement proves to be an exception to the losses among the mainline Protestant churches. The best example is the Southern Baptist church, which is now the largest Protestant denomination in the United States, with over fifteen billion members. Added to these numbers are the African-American Baptist churches—for example, the National Baptist Convention—with over eight million members. These evangelistic churches send thousands of missionaries around the world.

To summarize the most recent findings about which churches are growing and why, I offer the following scheme suggested by Michael Jaffarian, assistant researcher to David Barrett. Looking at it *denominationally*, Pentecostals, charismatics, Evangelical Protestants and Roman Catholics are growing. Looking at it *regionally*, Third World churches are growing, especially in Africa and Korea; Eastern European churches are growing, due to the vacuum left by the fall of communism; Chinese house churches are growing, 85 percent of them charismatic; the greatest growth in the world is in the southern hemisphere. Looking at it *ethnically*, nonwhite churches are growing.

Looking at it according to *internal church life*, churches are growing that have gifted leadership; a genuine spirituality, such as the baptism in the Holy Spirit; an emphasis on missions and church planting; an emphasis on Bible study and teaching; an emphasis on worship and community life; an emphasis on signs and wonders; an emphasis on evangelization by *doing it, not just saying it!*

In the end Peter Wagner makes the important point that despite all the research and techniques of church growth, the ultimate reasons churches grow is "God at work through the Holy Spirit."[16]

PART 3
HOW *YOU* CAN EVANGELIZE!

CHAPTER 10

Six Steps to Effective Evangelization

Susan Blum Gerding, Ed.D.

The thought of doing evangelization intimidates most of us, yet it simply means loving people into the kingdom. This responsibility is not an optional contribution on the part of Catholics, not something we have decided to do in the last fifteen years because we had nothing else to do, because we thought it might be fun or because we thought the Protestants were doing it better. Bringing people into the kingdom is the very reason for the church's existence.

My favorite definition of evangelization is based on Henri Nouwen's widely accepted theology of humility, which indicates that none of us is superior to another: we are all broken, we are all wounded, we are all scarred. We have sorrows, disappointments and disillusionments. We also have joys, successes and dreams for the future. The crucial point is that we are all in this together, and so the Catholic evangelizer's approach is one of gentleness and service.

Likening ourselves to beggars reaching out to help other beggars implies a spirit of mutuality and respect between us and those whom we are evangelizing. Effective messengers of the Good News do not operate out of a position of power or superiority, feeling that they have all the answers and are going to set others straight whether they want it or not. If we truly desire to bring people into the kingdom, we need to start looking at evangelization inside out and upside down—not the way we always have in the past.

CALLED TO EVANGELIZE WHOM?

We are called to evangelize five major groups: the active Catholics, the inactive Catholics, the unchurched, the Protestants and the non-Christians. We certainly want to evangelize this last group, but they usually account for only a small number of the people we actually encounter during the course of our daily lives. And while we want to share our faith with practicing Protestants, Catholics are not into "pew-snatching." We should praise Protestants and respect them for their beliefs and not attempt to actively proselytize Christians committed to Protestant denominations.

So I suggest that we look at three major populations as primary targets for Catholic evangelization: the active Catholics, the inactive Catholics and the unchurched. It is fairly obvious why we want to evangelize those who say they have no church affiliation, who may account for up to 40 percent of any given community. Inactive Catholics are also obvious targets for evangelization. Current estimates indicate that one out of every four baptized Catholics becomes inactive at some time during his life. So of course, as

Catholic evangelizers, we want to invite anyone in this group to return to the church.

I have seen many instances in which the inactive Catholic is looked down upon. The very term "fallen away Catholic" automatically implies some degree of inferiority, that something is wrong with such a person. I would invite all of us to change this viewpoint by acknowledging that inactive Catholics have made their decision to leave the institutional church for a reason, whatever it may be. We need to respect and esteem such people, assuming that they have been hurt or had some sort of experience that has led them away from the church. They must have a good reason. We may not know what it is, but we would like to hear it. While some may leave the church out of sheer laziness or lethargy, most have left after a great deal of pain and soul-searching.

I was an inactive Catholic for four years, and believe me, I spent more time on my knees during that part of my spiritual journey than when I was attending Mass regularly. I also read more Scripture because I was searching for the truth. After seeking long and hard, I found a loving community that did not put me down but instead welcomed me back as a worthwhile person whose spirituality and morality had not gone out the window. They even told me they needed me and invited me to use my teaching skills in a first-grade C.C.D. class.

The need to evangelize the unchurched and those who have left the church may seem obvious, but why are we called to evangelize active Catholics? One day in my own parish I was sitting over on one side of the church, where I could see the faces of all the people in the center section and on the opposite side. We were at the point of singing the responsorial psalm, one that says, "This is the day that the Lord has made. Let us rejoice and be glad in it." I happened to look around, and I have never seen such sad-looking Christians in my life! It was just shattering to me. I thought, "My dear brothers and sisters in Christ, if you really believe that 'this is the day that the Lord has made, let us rejoice and be glad,' would you please inform your faces?"

So I am convinced that we need to zero in on the active Catholics. All five of these groups need evangelization, but if we could *reevangelize* the active Catholics among us, the rest would be a piece of cake. Our parishes would be so dynamic, so exciting and so magnetic that we might need to schedule ten Masses every Sunday. We might have waiting lines outside of church and have to build five-story parking lots! So I say, "Let's focus on the active Catholics!"

George Gallup published a study in 1984 called *Religion in America*,[1] in which he looked at two populations across all Christian denominations, the "churched" and the "unchurched." The "churched" were those who attended Mass or church services at least two times a year other than Christmas, Easter, weddings or funerals. The "unchurched" were those who attended church even less often or not at all. Gallup made a further distinction within the category of the "churched" Christians. Based on responses to various questions regarding spiritual commitment (such as believing in the divinity of Jesus, seeking God's will in prayer, trying hard to put one's faith into practice and so on), Gallup identified 12 percent of the "churched" as "highly spiritual" Christians and 88 percent as "nominal" Christians.

After quizzing the "churched" and the "unchurched" on all kinds of ethical and spiritual issues, Gallup then compared the responses of the 88 percent of the "churched" with the responses of the "unchurched." The only statistically significant difference between these two groups was that one went to church and the other did not! He found absolutely no significant difference between most "churched" Christians and the "unchurched" in terms of cheating on income tax, infidelity in marriage, lying, pilfering in business and all kinds of things.

However, Gallup's survey revealed enormous differences between the 12 percent he called "highly spiritual" Christians and both the "nominal" Christians and the "unchurched." To mention only a few, he concluded that this committed group was more satisfied with their lot in life and far happier, placed a greater importance on family life, were more tolerant of other races and religions and were vitally concerned about the betterment of society.

I believe this 12 percent figure holds true for the approximately fifty-nine million active Catholics as well. In your parish do you not find a handful of people who do the bulk of the work? They regularly attend Mass, they are committed in time and money, they are members of the prayer group or the C.C.D. program or some other volunteer service. If anywhere close to 88 percent of active Catholics are still sitting on the sidelines, so to speak, then we have plenty of need to evangelize Catholics in today's society.

One of our first tasks as evangelizers reflects the first goal stated in the American bishops' document *Go and Make Disciples:* creating a new enthusiasm in active Catholics so that they will go out and share their faith. Our faith is a free gift that is far more valuable than any material possession in our lives and one that will outlast any human relationship. If we are excited about that Good News, should we not be sharing it with our relatives, our neighbors, even total strangers? We should be shouting it from the rooftops. Given the enormous hunger for the Bread of Life, how can we become more effective evangelizers?

Step 1: Becoming Disciples

Discipleship is both the beginning and the end of evangelization. In order for us to be effective messengers of the Good News, we first have to be sure of what we believe. We need to be steeped in prayer, we need to be rooted in Scripture, we need to belong to a worshipping community, and we need to be active in serving others.

Those four basic marks of the church, which are related in the early chapters of Acts, are extremely critical to this whole sense of discipleship. You cannot *make* a disciple unless you *are* a disciple. Have you ever thought about that?

Do cows make sheep? No, sheep make sheep. In the same way, disciples make disciples. You cannot share something unless you possess it yourself. Most people quickly see through a façade, just mouthing the words, "talking the talk but not walking the walk." Your faith must be genuine.

STEP 2: BEFRIENDING PEOPLE

I use another definition of evangelization that I borrowed from Dr. M. Scott Peck, psychiatrist and author. In *The Road Less Traveled* he gives a wonderful definition of love that serves equally well in terms of evangelization: "to extend one's self for the purpose of nurturing…another's spiritual growth."[2]

I especially like the word *extending*. Evangelization is a very active ministry, rather than a passive one. You cannot pray all day long and evangelize. It just does not happen that way. Prayer is an absolutely necessary *foundation* for effective evangelization, but eventually you have got to get out of your prayer chair and move! "*Go* and make disciples." After becoming disciples ourselves, we begin to practice this second step of evangelization by reaching out and befriending people.

My own spiritual journey includes being raised in the Presbyterian church, where I experienced an enormous amount of hospitality. This was partly the natural result of belonging to a small community. The average Protestant church may number two hundred members, while the average Catholic parish may have two thousand members. It is difficult to establish a sense of community when you are one of thousands. But extending hospitality and being a welcoming community is absolutely essential to loving people into the kingdom.

I attended a national conference several years ago put on by a well-known Catholic organization. Their official welcome of myself and the eleven other newcomers impressed me a great deal. We were given "newcomer" ribbons and wore pink badges while everybody else had blue. The program listed a special luncheon where they would introduce each newcomer, so that the other folks would know who we were and be able to welcome us, plus a special cocktail reception for us one evening. I thought, "Wow, this is real hospitality. I don't think I've ever seen the welcome mat extended like this."

All of this looked good on paper, but what actually happened was quite different. This conference turned out to be what Southerners call "a good old boys' club," where the veterans did not want to meet or talk to newcomers. The twelve of us got together and made some new friends among ourselves, but everyone else at the reception had his or her own little group. At the luncheon the veterans had their own tables. I am a fairly gregarious person, and I like to meet new people, so I tried. And I was given a cold shoulder. I left that conference early the next morning because of it.

Visitors or newcomers can experience this sort of "negative hospitality" when they visit a parish for the first time. You may have a welcoming committee that greets people at the door and serves coffee and doughnuts afterward, but any such efforts will fail miserably if the people in the pews do not want to extend hospitality to visitors.

I am talking about *sincerely* befriending people, not approaching someone with the thought, "Aha! There's a prospect. She'd make a good Catholic!" Evangelizing does not mean looking at people as prospects from a sales point of view but putting into practice the Scripture passage that tells us always to put the needs of others before our own. Become genuinely concerned about the people who visit your parish, the people you visit in their homes or those you encounter in your daily life. Always approach others out of mutual respect, never with an attitude of "one-ups-manship" or feeling "holier than thou." We always want to extend a warm welcome to people, whether we are inviting them into the whole community or into our homes for a cup of coffee.

A wonderful experience of getting to know people in church happened in a parish in Albany. We were a marriage-encounter community of ten to fifteen couples. We decided on our own that whatever Sunday Mass we went to, we would find somebody we did not know—maybe a family with children the ages of ours—and invite them home for breakfast. And we just did it.

The first thing that happened was that people nearly passed out cold when we invited them, and we would have to explain what we were doing. "No, we're just having coffee and doughnuts and juice for the kids. Come on, we'd love to get to know you." And then before they would leave our homes that morning, we would encourage them to do the same thing the following Sunday. Pretty soon that whole parish really got to know each other.

STEP 3: SHARING YOUR FAITH

After focusing on the first step of becoming disciples and then extending ourselves in order to nurture the spiritual well-being of others, we come to the third step of sharing our faith. Most Catholics are pretty good at what Pope Paul VI called "the silent witness of our lives." We go to Mass on Sundays. We may send our children to Catholic schools. We may show up at work with the sign of the cross smudged on our foreheads on Ash Wednesday, or visitors may see sacred pictures or religious artwork in our homes.

I grew up in a very anti-Catholic family and was not allowed to have any Catholic friends. I did manage to sneak one in, however, an Irish Catholic named Maggie. When I would go over to her house, I was absolutely fascinated by the twenty-seven different statues her mother kept on top of their upright piano. To me they looked like little dolls, especially the Infant of Prague. This simple witness of faith was my introduction to the Catholic faith.

One day I went into Maggie's parlor and said, "What's wrong? All the statues are turned around and facing the wall!" And Maggie's mother vehemently told me, "Until my prayers are answered, they're all going to face the corner!"

I always wear a crucifix, one of the silent witnesses in my life that often attracts people when I am on an airplane. Complete strangers will look at me and say, "Oh, you're Catholic." And then they will say, "I was Catholic too." We do many such things that reveal our faith without saying a word.

However, we are not nearly as comfortable in terms of verbal witnessing. We all have many faith stories to share that offer evidence of ongoing conversion in our lives. You may have entered into this continual process by being baptized as an infant, being confirmed as a child, being raised in a Catholic family or entering into holy matrimony. In your middle years you may have attended a powerful retreat and come alive in the Spirit. The fact that your whole life changed at that moment in no way negates everything that went before.

We always should be growing spiritually, constantly coming closer to Jesus. If Mother Teresa or Pope John Paul II were sitting here right now, I would be the first to tell them that God wants them to draw even closer. Jesus himself might say, "Mother, there are a few things you still need to do. I have some other things in store for you. Have you ever thought about…?" And I believe that Mother Teresa would agree, "Yes. I want to come even closer."

This is what evangelization is all about: ongoing conversion. Sometimes we experience a more profound moment of conversion,

like Saint Paul falling to the ground or in less dramatic circumstances, like Elijah hearing God not in the earthquake, not in the
storm, but in the gentle whisper of the wind. When Jesus touched
me, the Holy Spirit came into my life in a gentle way—healing, perfecting, forming, molding and melting. We all have these whisper-
in-the-wind stories. And we need to tell one another how God has
touched our lives in a powerful way.

STEP 4: PROCLAIMING THE GOSPEL

If we have trouble telling faith stories, proclaiming the Good News
of Jesus Christ is usually even more challenging. Many of us do not
know what we believe, or if we do know, we cannot articulate it. Two
reasons may account for this inability. One, we have never been
expected to verbalize our beliefs; and two, we have never been
trained to do so.

Growing up in the Presbyterian church, I was taught how to proclaim the four central truths of the gospel. Most Protestant children
learn how to do this by eight or nine years of age—certainly not in
its entirety but in a brief and simple statement of faith that would
make sense to someone else. I do not know many Catholic children
who could do that. In fact, I do not know a whole lot of Catholic
adults who could do that!

You need to be able to proclaim what you believe. You do not have
to be a theologian. You do not have to be a professional evangelizer.
You do not have to be an ordained member of the clergy. You do not
have to have a master's degree in religious studies. But you do have
to know what you believe.

Remember that the best gift you have to offer may not be your
theological knowledge but yourself. *You* are your best ammunition
in terms of proclaiming the gospel. People can argue with your theology; they cannot argue with your personal experience.

Step 5: Inviting Others to Conversion

Let's say we have befriended people, shared a faith story (and invited them to tell their own faith stories in a mutual sharing) and explained what we call "the Christ story"—the proclamation step. It would be absolutely horrible if after all of that we just dropped them like a hot potato and said, "Well, I've told you all this Good News. Hope it helps. Bye!"

The next step in leading people into the kingdom is extending an invitation to conversion. What does this mean?

Again, the goal of evangelization is ongoing conversion. We ourselves, of course, cannot convert anyone—even ourselves. Only the Holy Spirit can change the hearts and minds of people. So I define the role of evangelizers as facilitators of conversion.

We can help conversion along by creating a setting or an atmosphere conducive to drawing closer to God. We can organize an evangelistic event or bring someone to a prayer meeting, a Sunday Mass or a healing service. Facilitating conversion is sometimes only a matter of listening to people—really listening with your heart—and then inviting them to take that step of coming closer to Jesus, committing their lives to Jesus or recommitting their lives, as the case my be.

The invitation to conversion might mean asking a simple question. I might say, "Would you like us to pray with you or for you and your family?" Always ask for permission. Only one or two people have said no to such an invitation in the course of all the home visits I have made over the years. Remember that this might be the first time they have ever prayed together in a small group or prayed out loud, so make it as nonthreatening as possible.

If they answer yes, then I always tell them exactly what we are going to do. I might say, "What I'm going to do is just say a short prayer, just to quiet us down a little bit. Do you mind if we hold hands in a circle? And then I'm going to lead a prayer for your family. Is there anybody special you'd like to pray for? Oh, your son? We'll make sure that we pray for him. And if you're comfortable with this, maybe at the end, if you'd like to offer a prayer, fine. Or we can close by saying the Our Father together."

Then they know what to expect. They're not sitting on pins and needles, worrying about what's coming next. They can relax and really enjoy the prayer as communication with God, inviting God more fully into their lives and into their families. This invitation to conversion brings us back to discipleship, which makes us all brothers and sisters and also means inviting others into our own lives, into our families and into the community of faith.

STEP 6: INTEGRATING NEW PEOPLE INTO COMMUNITY

Integration into community is the phase where catechesis or sacramentalization takes place, depending on the person's situation. Inactive Catholics may need to sign up for an RCIA program and be updated in the Vatican II church. Non-Catholics may need something else. Our aim is to involve newcomers on an individual level in the faith community.

This final step in the evangelization process might include formation of ministers within the parish, pastoring or discipling people, setting up Bible studies or support groups. It would involve the whole communal life or family spirituality in a particular parish. Our hope is that these new converts will become disciples, who will go out and start the whole cycle over again: befriending people, witnessing to their faith, proclaiming the gospel, inviting others into conversion, integrating newcomers into the community, making them disciples, who then will go out....

This ongoing, cyclical process reflects the order that Pope Paul VI suggests in his document *Evangelii Nuntiandi*. And I think it makes all the sense in the world. But in reality I think we miss the mark here somewhere. It seems to me that we often put the cart before the horse. Many of us tend to jump right into step 6, integration into the community, long before we have laid the necessary foundation.

These six steps can be applied to both *relational evangelization* and *institutional evangelization*. All of the formal programs or ministries in your parish—the RCIA, prayer groups, "Re-membering Church," "Come Home for Christmas"—are forms of institutional evangelization. Relational evangelization refers to the level of interpersonal relationships. How do you share your faith with your daughter-in-law over a cup of coffee at the kitchen table? I call it the "hedgerow ministry" because it is through our one-on-one efforts that we invite folks to come to the larger, formal programs that are being offered in the parish.

No matter how well trained we are in theology and evangelization, we must always remember that only the Holy Spirit can convert others to Christ. And we often run into the most stubborn roadblocks with members of our own families.

I tried every way I could think of to bring my atheist mother to Jesus. To my knowledge she never set foot into a church except on two occasions: my wedding and my brother's wedding. And my being converted to the Catholic faith and then becoming so strongly involved in Catholic evangelization made matters much worse.

Several years after my parents retired to Tucson, Arizona, my mother was placed in a nursing facility because of Alzheimer's disease. Many times when I would be visiting, she would not recognize me. But one day I went in and my mother greeted me by name. And then she asked me about my four children by name—for the first time in three or four years. She knew what day it was, what year it was. We had a wonderful visit.

When I got up to leave, Mom said, "No, I have to tell you something first. Last night my mother and my father and that other person came and stood at the foot of my bed."

My mother was eighty-six years old, and I knew that it is not unusual for elderly people to see long-departed loved ones. Maybe she had dreamed about them, but I could not figure out who she meant by "that other person." I asked her if it was one of her two brothers.

She said, "No, Susan, it was that *other* person."

I said, "Mom, I just don't know who you're talking about."

Mom was so exasperated with me. She said, "Susan, you've just got to help me. You know, it's that 'separate person.'" I still could not figure out who she was talking about. She kept struggling to explain it. "That *separate* person. That *savior* person."

And I said, "Mom, do you mean Jesus?"

And she said, "Yes, *that's* who it was! My mother and father and Jesus came and stood at the foot of my bed last night. And they told me I could come home now."

I almost fell off the chair. My mother told me that this experience was so strong and so real that she felt that she was now ready to go home. And for the first time in my life I was able to pray with her. We sat and held hands, she in her wheelchair and I in a little folding chair, and we invited Jesus to come into her life and thanked him for coming in the way that he chose.

I have often wondered why Jesus did not come sooner. It could have been so much easier, but I will let God be God for this one. The most wonderful gift was that we were able to pray together, and I was able to leave my mother that day filled with joy. As it turned out, it was the last time I would ever see her. Shortly after I returned to Florida, my mother died peacefully in her sleep. Saint Paul tells us that "neither death, nor life, nor angels, nor principalities, nor things present, nor things to come, nor powers, nor height, nor depth, nor anything else in all creation, will be able to separate us from the love of God in Christ Jesus our Lord" (Romans 8:38–39). I can add a few more things to that list: not alcoholism, not old age, not Alzheimer's, not agnosticism and not even atheism. Our God is a faithful God. As Mother

Teresa said we're not called to be successful; we're called to be faithful. And that, I believe, is the essence of Catholic evangelization.

Dr. Susan Blum Gerding is the executive director of Isaiah Ministries, which promotes renewal and evangelization through parish missions. Her publications include *The Ministry of Evangelization* and *Text, Study Guide, and Implementation Process for Go and Make Disciples*. For more information, contact

Susan Blum Gerding
Isaiah Ministries, Inc.
5840 Wind Drift Lane
Boca Raton, FL 33433
561-368-2322
E-mail: Jeremiahpr@aol.com
www.jeremiahpress.com

CHAPTER 11

Employing Charisms in Evangelization

Peter Herbeck

"They went forth and preached everywhere, while the Lord worked with them and confirmed the message by the signs that attended it" (Mark 16:20). As the disciples went forth to preach the gospel after Jesus' resurrection and ascension, the Lord "worked with them" by demonstrating his presence through confirming signs.

These signs are "manifestations of the Spirit" (1 Corinthians 12:7), works of power through which God communicates his life and truth to men and women. Throughout the New Testament we see evidence of the important role these signs or works of power play in bringing people to Christ. In Acts 9:40–42 Peter raised Tabitha from the dead. "And it became known throughout all Joppa, and many believed in the Lord." On another occasion Peter healed Aeneas, a paralytic, "and all the residents of Lydda and Sharon saw him, and they turned to the Lord" (Acts 9:35).

Jesus' mission was to reveal and establish his Father's kingdom (see Luke 4:43). When the disciples performed signs and wonders, they experienced Jesus' carrying on his ministry through them. He had told his disciples that visible signs would accompany their preaching (see Mark 16:17–18). These extraordinary works of power, such as healing the sick and driving out demons (see Matthew 12:28), were an indication to many that God's kingdom was present.

Works play an essential role in establishing God's kingdom in the world. If a new evangelization is to succeed in our day, we must rediscover the indispensable role these signs play in evangelization and conversion. It is important to see clearly that the disciples were able to communicate effectively the life of the kingdom because Jesus had given them the power to do so. He gave them *charisms*— spiritual gifts that enabled them to do his work (see 1 Corinthians 12), something they could not do on their own power.

That is why a resurgence of the sign-gifts in our day is so important for the work of evangelism. We cannot reveal the kingdom of God by our own strength or eloquent words. Like the disciples, our proclamation of the gospel needs to be accompanied by the confirming signs, making clear to all who will hear and see that God himself stands behind the message.

THE FORGOTTEN GIFTS

The charisms the Spirit bestows upon the church are many and varied. All of them contribute to the building up of the body, and many are exercised in the church today. Paul enumerates many spiritual gifts but reminds us that "the greatest of these is love" (1 Corinthians 13:13).

Our particular focus here is on what is often referred to in the Scriptures as "signs and wonders," the many miracles of healing and deliverance performed by Jesus and his disciples. Unfortunately, many Catholics forget or ignore the sign-gifts when discussing and practicing evangelism. For some the use of these gifts is not an acceptable part of Catholic culture. Their operation is viewed from a distance, outside the church and often associated with Protestant faith healers such as Benny Hinn or Oral Roberts. For others these gifts are viewed as part of Catholic experience yet limited to the miraculous deeds performed by the saints, those who were exceptionally holy and favored by God.

Secular society often ridicules and disparages outward signs of God's power. As a result, some Catholics shy away from anything that may cast them in a negative light. Most of contemporary culture is steeped in skepticism, uncomfortable with the supernatural. Simple unbelief or lack of faith is a significant reason why many Catholics no longer employ these charisms.

In addition to all these considerations, perhaps the one that most stifles the use of these gifts is a prevalent understanding of "personal faith." Many Catholics view Christianity as a higher morality whose duties are fulfilled through strength of will and personal discipline. Catholics do not typically regard their faith as a new life empowered by the Holy Spirit. Few are conscious of possessing spiritual power; therefore, the particular gifts bestowed on them through baptism lie dormant.

The New Testament is characterized not only by signs and wonders but also by the disciples' *awareness* of the spiritual powers they possess. The third chapter of Acts recounts the story of Peter's healing the crippled man at the Gate Beautiful. Strongly conscious of possessing spiritual power, Peter spontaneously responds to the man's appeal by saying, "I give you what I have; in the name of Jesus Christ of Nazareth, walk" (Acts 3:6).

We are witnessing a fresh awakening to the importance of these spiritual gifts and the role they must play in the revitalization of the church. Paul VI prayed, "God grant that the Lord would increase the rain of charisms to make the Church fruitful, beautiful, marvelous, and capable of inspiring respect, even the attention and amazement of the profane world, the secular world."[1] These charisms capture the imagination by communicating the transcendent dimension of the church.

John Paul II also acknowledged the role of different charisms: "At the beginning of the Christian era extraordinary things were accomplished under the influence of charisms…. This has always been the case in the Church and is so in our own era as well."[2]

WE NEED TO DO IT GOD'S WAY

Jesus promised his disciples that "these signs will accompany those who believe" (Mark 16:17). Even though they had witnessed Jesus as he performed many miracles, they were nonetheless often surprised that the power of God was working through them. When Jesus sent out the seventy to minister, they returned to him joyful yet incredulous: "Lord, even the demons are subject to us in your name!" (Luke 10:17).

We are similar to the disciples in this way. Even though Jesus told us it would happen, we rarely *expect* signs to follow the preaching of the gospel. This lack of expectation and faith often hinders the release of these gifts. We can define and limit God's action through a human and rational understanding of how we "think" he should work. Yet throughout creation and salvation history, God has often expressed his presence through both words and deeds. Vatican II's Dogmatic Constitution on Divine Revelation states, "In His goodness and wisdom, God chose to reveal Himself and to make known to us the purpose of His will.... This plan of revelation is realized by deeds and words having an inner unity" (*DV*, 2).

At the summit of revelation God spoke his word to the world in Christ Jesus, the Word of God who became incarnate. This taking on of human flesh was a specific act, a deed, a sign, a wonder. The Council fathers point out that God reveals himself through both the words and works of Jesus. He speaks to human beings in the language of words and deeds.

We must realize that God's message to us is incomplete without the deeds—not only those of love and kindness but the deeds of power. When the word is communicated in its fullest measure (in both speech and deeds), then people will know God and understand that a transcendent kingdom has come into the world.

THE KINGDOM OF GOD IS AT HAND

John Paul II reminded us in *Redemptoris Missio* that the proclamation and establishment of God's kingdom are the purpose of Jesus' mission (*RM*, 13). In his coming Jesus brings the kingdom of God. Jesus said, "The kingdom of God is at hand; repent, and believe in the gospel" (Mark 1:15). The kingdom of God is the dynamic rule and reign of God. It is "the manifestation and the realization of God's plan of salvation in all its fullness" (*RM*, 15).

This heavenly kingdom is characteristically revealed through Jesus' words, his actions and his own person. It includes healing, miracles and deliverance. "If it is by the Spirit of God that I cast out demons, then the kingdom of God has come upon you" (Matthew 12:28). Jesus instructs his disciples and interprets for them the meaning of his actions.

Signs are important because these extraordinary works of power point to and confirm the reality of God's kingdom. "The deeds wrought by God in the history of salvation manifest and confirm the teaching and realities signified by the words" (*DV*, 2). The greatness of

God and the wonder and nature of his kingdom are made manifest through powerful signs. Evangelization is essentially a continuation of this work of revealing the kingdom of God.

We need charisms to carry on Jesus' work. "To each is given the manifestation of the Spirit for the common good" (1 Corinthians 12:7). Jesus gives us his power to do his work: the task of revealing his Father's kingdom. Therefore the apostle Paul emphasizes that "the kingdom of God does not consist in talk but in power" (1 Corinthians 4:20).

The contemporary world awaits a fuller revelation of the kingdom of God. For too many the kingdom consists only in words. Yet words alone will not capture the hearts and imaginations of millions of Chinese yet to hear the gospel. Neither will they penetrate the ever-growing world of Islamic fundamentalism. It is time for the world to see God's power and glory manifest in the life of his people.

How can we minister in these gifts? We must begin by praying for a greater understanding of the power of God already within us. Paul earnestly prays for the Ephesians that "having the eyes of your hearts enlightened,…you may know…the immeasurable greatness of his power in us who believe" (Ephesians 1:18–19). We must keep asking God, like the persistent widow (see Luke 18:1–8), to open up these treasures and to help us overcome our fear in using them.

Secondly, Scripture instructs us to "earnestly desire the spiritual gifts" (1 Corinthians 14:1). We cannot pick and choose, but we need to accept the gifts *God* wants to give us, even if what he gives us shakes us out of our comfort zones.

Finally, "just do it!" Like Peter in the boat, we need to step out with expectant faith and act on God's promise to us, believing that "signs will accompany those who believe" (Mark 16:17). The Catholic church boasts a wonderful collection of documents that speak of the value and necessity of gifts and charisms, yet few people actually exercise them. We must move from theory to practice.

WE LEARN BEST BY PERSONAL EXPERIENCE

Because most of us feel awkward when trying to pray with someone, it can be helpful first to find others in your parish or town with some experience in exercising these gifts. We have learned a great deal of practical wisdom from listening to and praying alongside others who are more experienced.

It was precisely that kind of "hands on" mentoring that I received at a leaders' conference many years ago, which helped open up the whole area of exercising spiritual gifts in my own life. Up to that point I had read quite a bit about this topic, and I had gained some experience in praying with people for the baptism in the Holy Spirit, yet I usually felt a bit intimidated when praying for healing or deliverance. Most of my anxiety was due to a lack of experience and a fear of failure.

In order to gain some firsthand experience, I asked a conference leader if I could pray alongside one of the team members. He obliged. I spent the next three days praying with a team of people who had years of experience in praying with others. I watched how they did it and asked them questions, and by the end of the three days I was leading some of the prayer under their guidance. My confidence level grew tremendously as I saw the Lord working through our prayers.

Receiving this kind of training can be helpful in terms of getting beyond initial fears and awkwardness, but it can also provide additional discernment and a deeper understanding of the kind of gifts God has given to you personally. As I prayed with the small team at the conference, I could see there were different kinds of gifts present as well as different levels of gifting.

That conference experience also enabled me to see that praying with people is often a relatively simple thing. You do not have to be a theologian or a ministry expert to ask the Lord to touch a person's life in a particular way. It is easy to think this kind of prayer is complicated or needs to follow a certain preset form. It does not. Look closely at the ministry of Jesus or the disciples, and you will not find set formulas. What you will find is an expectant faith that enabled them to follow the leading of the Holy Spirit in a given situation.

Jesus claimed a direct connection between his deeds and the Father's. He said, "My Father is working still, and I am working.... The Son can do nothing of his own accord, but only what he sees the Father doing" (John 5:17, 19). God is still at work today, healing the sick, setting captives free and drawing men and women to himself. Like Jesus, we simply need to do what we see the Father doing.

How can we know what the Father is doing in a given situation? Ask him. Expect a response. Is that presumptuous? I do not think so. It is simply a matter of obedience. Jesus commands all the baptized to carry on his work. His work was to do what he saw the Father doing. Our charge is to do the same.

God has given us his own Spirit, who "will not speak on his own authority, but whatever he hears he will speak, and he will declare to you the things that are to come" (John 16:13). The Holy Spirit is our helper, our counselor. He will enable us to carry on this work. Jesus' word to us is clear: "The Holy Spirit, whom the Father will send in my name,...will teach you all things, and bring to your remembrance all that I have said to you" (John 14:26).

When an opportunity arises to pray with someone, we can begin by simply asking the Holy Spirit to show us how to pray. A friend told me about a number of experiences he had had praying with people he was evangelizing. This man is a professor at a Midwestern university. On one occasion a Chinese graduate student came to his office to discuss a research project he had been working on. During their discussion, my friend noticed that the student was experiencing back pain. He then asked the Holy Spirit if he ought to do anything or say anything to the student. He felt the Spirit prompting him to pray for him.

When my friend asked about the back pain, the student told him he suffered from chronic back trouble, which caused him a great deal of pain and discomfort. My friend then asked if the student would like him to pray that Jesus would heal his back. The student agreed. My friend simply reached out and touched the point where the pain was the sharpest and prayed a simple prayer: "Lord Jesus, I ask you to heal this man's back problem."

After a few minutes the young Chinese man began to experience complete relief from the pain. He was overjoyed and amazed. Not long after their meeting, this man gave his life to Christ. Now, one year later, he is leading a Bible study with other students.

My friend's prayer was simple and powerful. He did not use any preset formula. He simply responded with compassion and expectant faith to what he believed God was doing in that situation. Like Jesus, he knew his Father is always at work. Living in a posture of active faith equipped him with this readiness to recognize the needs of others and respond. As a result, the Chinese student has an experiential knowledge of God's love for him that does "not rest in the wisdom of men but in the power of God" (1 Corinthians 2:5).

EXPECT THE UNEXPECTED

I would like to relate some of my own experiences of learning how to minister to others with gifts of power. Some years ago I spoke at a large evangelization rally in a new diocese in Ghana, Africa. At one point I sensed the Lord's showing me that we should pray for those in the audience who had gone to the voodoo masters and witch doctors to receive power over some difficulty in their lives.

When I stood up and addressed anyone who fit this description, about sixty people came forward. I spoke quietly and calmly about Jesus' presence and the need for repentance. We prayed, "Come,

Holy Spirit," and asked Jesus to free them from the domination of various demons.

Almost immediately there were signs and manifestations of the working of the Holy Spirit. One woman's head jerked back, her eyelids flipped open, exposing only the whites of her eyes, and she fell backward like a board. To my amazement, her body then began to flip back and forth, like a fish on a dock, at an incredible and humanly impossible speed. There was a clear resistance raging within her, an encounter between two opposing powers.

Watching from the stage, I was stunned. Although I had prayed for her, I honestly had not expected anything that dramatic to occur! A priest bent down over her and prayed a simple prayer of deliverance. Immediately the woman's body went limp, and she lay there peacefully. When someone helped her up fifteen minutes later, she was totally free.

Just a few months after the Africa mission, I was part of a team preaching at an evangelistic conference in Lithuania. During a time of ministry I began to experience an intense pain in my right ear. I tried to ignore it, thinking I must have caught a cold the night before. As the pain persisted, I sensed that the Lord wanted us to pray for people with right inner ear problems. A number of people came forward to be healed.

One of our team members, an architect who believes that God commands us to pray for the sick, prayed over a twenty-three-year-old man. This young Lithuanian had lost his hearing three years earlier during the struggle for independence in Vilnius, when a tank cannon went off nearby and blew out his right ear drum. As they prayed he was able to hear, first faintly and then more clearly. The young man was ecstatic, as were many around him. People were stunned and awed by the power and grace of God at work.

Because we are human, we all experience a risk factor when we step out in faith to exercise these gifts. We are afraid of being wrong:

"Is God really speaking to me?" Or of embarrassment and losing our reputation: "What if I look strange or it doesn't work?" We are called to be obedient and not necessarily successful. God has freed us to follow and obey him. "Where the Spirit of the Lord is, there is freedom" (2 Corinthians 3:17).

In this new age of evangelization, God wants to reveal his presence and the glory of his kingdom in a renewed way through the manifestation of signs and wonders. The Lord is sending forth his word through us, his church, not only as we preach the gospel but also as we do the works that Jesus did.

As Catholics, we must respond to the challenge of these times by freely employing the gifts and charisms God has given us. We must also learn how to train and help others to use their gifts so that evangelization will move ahead with greater power and effectiveness. Let us be like the apostles Paul and Barnabas, who "remained for a long time [in Iconium], speaking boldly for the Lord, who bore witness to the word of his grace, granting signs and wonders to be done by their hands" (Acts 14:3).

Peter Herbeck is mission director and vice president of Renewal Ministries, a Catholic organization that promotes renewal and evangelization through television, radio, publications and conferences. For more information contact:

Renewal Ministries
P.O. Box 1426
Ann Arbor, MI 48106
734-662-1730
www.renewalministries.net

CHAPTER 12

Catholic Street Evangelism Today

Leonard Sullivan

Some years ago a small group of Catholics enthusiastically told their parish priest about a meeting in a nearby city. They had witnessed healing and heard prophecy, seen people raising their arms and heard them praising God in words and in song, in their own and unknown languages.

The priest listened patiently and asked a few questions about the last detail. Then he observed, "I see. You call it 'praying in tongues.' So *that's* what I've been doing for so many years! I often wondered what it was."

I had the same experience when I read the extracts of the sermon Pope John Paul II delivered at Denver on August 15, 1993. When he challenged Catholics to go out and proclaim the Good News on the streets and in public places, I thought, "That's what I've been doing since 1950." I belong to the Westminster Catholic Evidence Guild, which has been doing street evangelization in London for seventy-five years. So the new evangelization is not quite so new to me.

If evangelization is new to you, you may be wondering where to start and how to go about it. I would like to share some of the knowledge and experience I have gained through the Catholic Evidence Guild. My hope is that it might pave the way for you to participate more actively in sharing the Good News with the people around you.

THE NUTS AND BOLTS OF EVANGELIZATION

The word *evangelization* means different things to different people, and this has caused a lot of confusion. Here is the best definition I have found: *Evangelization is the Lord Jesus Christ's proclaiming his Good News, through the members of his body, which is the church, to those who are not so fortunate as to hold the one true faith.*

Some people have questioned me about the last part. It simply means the "haves" sharing with the "have-nots." This definition excludes the idea of Catholics being evangelized. Catholics can be instructed, retreaded, recycled, rejuvenated, rehabilitated, resuscitated, revitalized, renewed, enriched and many other things. But once people direct the spotlight of evangelization toward Catholics, they can easily lose sight of the call to reach out to those who do not know Jesus Christ.

We can spread the Good News in many ways. Priests can preach sermons expressly aimed at non-Catholics. Trained evangelizers can participate in an organized door-to-door campaign. Radio and television offer other avenues. In brief, we street talkers are not the only workers trying to gather in the harvest as Jesus builds his kingdom.

While the street evangelist may reach only a few people, this personal contact can build a mutual rapport often missing when a speaker is talking *at* people in an auditorium or on the radio. Street evangelization can also be conducted in different ways, perhaps by pushing a wheelbarrow full of literature, free or for sale, with people available to talk about the church.

Not all of us are commissioned *evangelists,* called to take the initiative in seeking out lost sheep. But by the privilege of our baptism, we all have the responsibility to do *evangelization* when the opportunity arises. Scripture says, "In your hearts reverence Christ as Lord. Always be prepared to make a defense to any one who calls you to account for the hope that is in you, yet do it with gentleness and reverence; and keep your conscience clear" (1 Peter 3:15–16).

This verse should raise a few questions in your mind. *What in my life radiates the hope I have? What will lead people to ask what it is that makes me tick? What answers can I give for the questions that come my way? My answer may fit the question, but will it fit the questioner? How could my answer be improved or varied?*

Consider a simple example. A man might comment, "I read the newspaper every day from cover to cover. The world is a mess." A Christian might reply with a question: "Have you tried reading the *Good* News?" This response would leave the field open for the man to ask about the Good News.

From my experience in England, I suggest that any Catholics wanting to work in evangelization need to consider the following three points:

1. Do you know Catholic teaching accurately? In practice I have met a lot of Catholics who thought they did but in fact held ideas that were not true to Catholic teaching. For example, someone recently said to me that it did not matter to which denomination you belong.

2. Can you explain the teaching in a clear way, one that the listener can understand? Thinking over the ways in which I have heard some Catholic teachers of children and adults trying to do this, I have seen some dismal results.

3. Have you considered the questions a listener might ask, and will your answers be clear—especially if a listener belongs to a different religion and knows something about that religion?

In brief, we may do our best to evangelize, but without some thought or further instruction, we may not get very far. In these instances, keep in mind that we are sharing our faith as individuals and not as commissioned teachers proclaiming the Good News in the name of the church.

IF I CAN DO IT, SO CAN YOU!

I see my task as an evangelistic speaker as quite simple: somehow or other, the Lord Jesus Christ is trying to introduce himself, even through me, to those who do not know him. This is a variation of Jesus' statement in Luke 10:16: "He who hears you hears me, and he who rejects you rejects me, and he who rejects me rejects him who sent me."

If you read the *beginning* of Luke 10, you should get a shock: Jesus was not speaking to the twelve apostles but to the seventy others who suddenly popped up from nowhere. They had not had Catholic parents, they had not been to Catholic schools, and they were probably not trained as teachers—yet these seventy were called to be evangelists. If they could do it, so can I. And if I can do it, so can you!

Before you start thinking of excuses, I will give you three of them: (1) *I don't know my faith* (in London, this is usually put to me by people who *have* been to Catholic schools); (2) *I don't know anything about public speaking*; and (3) *I might do more harm than good*. If these were valid reasons, then how did somebody like me ever become an evangelistic speaker? I had the good fortune of stumbling into the Catholic Evidence Guild.

Let me provide a little bit of history. In 1917, during World War I, a New Zealander traveling through London noticed the Speakers' Corner at Marble Arch and thought that the church ought to be there having her say as well. After a discussion with the cardinal archbishop of Westminster, a meeting of those interested was held in January 1918. In April the Catholic Evidence Guild was formed. After some training by the clergy, these few brave souls started speaking in public on August 4, 1918.

The system of qualification that had evolved by 1921 is still in use today. When men and women decide to be trained as Guild speakers, they choose one subject from the many listed as "junior subjects" in the *Catholic Evidence Training Outlines* by Maisie Ward and Frank Sheed, published by Catholic Evidence Guild in Ann Arbor, Michigan. Those who are wise select an easy subject and then study it, ignoring all the rest of theology. After preparing a fifteen-minute talk on this topic, they then deliver it at an indoor practice class, where others ask awkward questions. The instructor sums up the effort with constructive criticism.

This practice is repeated until candidates have satisfied the instructor that their presentation and technique are adequate and that they know enough theology *on this one subject* to be tested. The test is private before two persons: one is a priest appointed as "examining chaplain" by the bishop; the other is an experienced speaker of the Guild. The test follows the same pattern as the practice class.

If both examiners are satisfied, the beginner is licensed to speak for the Catholic Evidence Guild on that *one subject* and to answer questions *only* on that subject and *only* in the presence of a chairman speaker. With those safety catches in place, the beginner is let loose on the public. The point to note here is that within a couple of months or less, a would-be speaker can be doing street evangelism.

Speakers extend their repertoire by studying and passing tests on other subjects. A major step is the test on the divinity of Christ. Later on speakers may be encouraged to go before a priest and senior Guild members to take the chairman's test, a question-and-answer exam on the general knowledge of dogmatic theology. Those who pass this exam can lecture on specific subjects according to their ordinary license but may also field other questions and run outdoor meetings, which include supervising and training less experienced speakers.

TARGETING THOSE TO BE EVANGELIZED

A few public places in London are recognized as speakers' areas where, subject to a few rules, people can stand and say whatever they like. The best known is the Speakers' Corner at Marble Arch in Hyde Park. If you have such a designated area in your locality, you may not have to look farther. If you have to find somewhere to speak, what you want is a place suitable for a public meeting where many people pass by who might have time to stop and listen.

Four considerations need to be kept in mind in determining a location: avoid noisy traffic; make sure that the meeting will not seriously inconvenience other people; find out whether you need permission to hold a meeting from the owners of the property, the local civil authority or the police; and find out how the local Catholic clergy view your intentions (they may have to pick up the pieces).

Identifying potential listeners can be even more difficult. As a rough guide, you will likely encounter three varieties of people: those who come deliberately to listen to a speaker on a matter of religion; those who come hoping for a bit of free entertainment; and those who are passing by and stop to listen, even for a minute or two.

What may potential listeners be thinking, especially on matters of religion? This question is vitally important, because we need to know something on which to build our proclamation. Our Lord's listeners were almost exclusively Jews, which made life simple. When Saint Paul evangelized the Jews in synagogues, he used the truths of Judaism on which to build the Christian message. He used an entirely different approach with the pagans in Athens.

In practice, listeners usually turn up with no indication as to what makes them tick, so the speaker may have to try various approaches before noticing a change in facial expression to indicate that some remark is on target. A few months ago at Tower Hill in London, I had two listeners with whom *nothing* seemed to register. I finally learned that they were tourists who did not understand English! Remember that when one attempts the study of mankind, nine-tenths of the training is done in the hard school of practical experience.

Our Lord often started his teaching with some common item that was under the noses of his listeners, like a shepherd who had lost a sheep or a rich man meeting a poor man. You would also be wise to start with something that is already in the minds of your listeners. You must try tuning in on their wavelength on a subject that may hold their interest and from there lead into the proclamation of the gospel.

Keep in mind that the listeners at an outdoor platform usually have to stand and are free to come and go as they please. Some will actively listen, indicating by their facial expressions that they understand the message even if they do not ask questions or comment. Some will passively listen, just standing and staring blankly. You should also watch for listeners who know practically nothing about the Catholic faith. Especially watch for those who *do* know something about the Catholic church and don't like the look of it.

My experience suggests that listeners tend to belong to one of two general groups: the minority, who accept and read the Bible as the words of God, and the majority, who have not read and do not read the Bible, which they regard as a collection of myths now disproved by science. An evangelistic speaker can often use biblical ideas with effect, without saying where they come from.

Many people believe in some parts of the Catholic faith, and they are willing to accept Scripture as evidence for an extended understanding of the truths revealed by Jesus Christ. You can often discern the attitude of listeners by their reply to a touchstone question, "Do you believe and accept as true that Jesus Christ rose from the dead?"

How to Conduct an Outdoor Meeting

In theory, the first step is to grab the listeners' attention with a story related to your subject, in which you should state clearly and briefly what the church teaches. You then provide evidence to support this teaching, show the richness of the doctrine as it stands and then perhaps show its relationship to allied teachings. Finally, you may say something about why this teaching is valuable to you personally. (You usually have to improvise and try variations of this approach, especially when the listeners decide that they do not want to hear that particular subject and begin to drift away from the meeting.)

The result is that listeners receive a fragmented presentation of the Catholic faith. It is perfectly possible to start a talk with one set of listeners and to finish it with a different set. This is a typical scenario: a man (or woman) with no thought of religion pays a casual visit to Marble Arch. Pausing near the speaker's platform in hope of a bit of free entertainment, he may hear something that starts him thinking. He then returns, perhaps weeks later, and is further stimulated, so he starts to come regularly.

This man is learning about the Catholic faith in bits and pieces, but he is beginning to see how they interconnect. Eventually he sees an overall picture, albeit with significant gaps. He may approach a speaker who had climbed down from the platform and ask questions about becoming a Catholic, or he may remember a distant relative whom he knows to be a Catholic. Either way, this man finally decides to take instruction and is received into the church. In many such cases the Guild speaker knows nothing about this conversion. He has tilled the soil, and God has planted the seed of faith. That is what matters, not vanity for the speaker.

Our meetings in England are usually quite lively, since many listeners respond with comments and questions. Guild speakers work at producing a *constructive* dialogue rather than getting into an abusive, verbal slinging match. If the audience happens to be too polite and reserved on matters of religion, I would suggest challenging them along these lines:

> This is the proclamation of Jesus Christ. The stakes are high: either life in the friendship of God or death in sin. You have heard something of the truth which God wants you to have. You may need to know more before you are in a position to accept or to reject what he wants you to have. Deliberate ignorance is the same as rejection. Each one of you must make your own decision, and this can decide where you will spend your life after you die.

If this sounds too strong for your taste, I suggest you read Mark 16:15–18. Further study of the Gospels and the Acts of the Apostles shows a pattern of demonstration, proclamation and demonstration. Thus far the Westminster Catholic Evidence Guild has concentrated on the proclamation of the truth and has hardly touched on the possibility of employing signs and wonders in this effort. I consider this an important subject for the present time and for the future.

I believe signs and wonders are Jesus Christ at work through the members of his body, to attract attention and to confirm the truth of the Good News. Street-corner evangelists or everyday evangelizers need to resolve two basic questions in their own minds:

↦ First, how much does the Lord Jesus Christ want to use signs and wonders now and in the future in his work of building the kingdom? In other words, are signs and wonders intended to be used on a wide scale or only on rare occasions?

✧ Second, how willing are the evangelists themselves to be used by the Lord in working signs and wonders?

You will need to pray with a listening heart to learn how God wants you to participate in the new evangelization. He will provide the necessary gifts, but he can use only those who are willing to be used. So whatever he tells you to do, do it. I would suggest that you prayerfully consider joining any evangelistic efforts being made in your area. On the other hand, the Lord may have other ideas as to how he wants you to participate in building his kingdom. Pray.

If you are interested in starting a local Catholic Evidence Guild, I suggest you gather a group of lay enthusiasts and find a friendly priest. Then discuss the idea and determine how to get started in a way that fits in with the church's work of evangelization. You also need to consult with your diocesan bishop about the use of the word *Catholic* in proclaiming the Good News.

If the bishop agrees, formally set up a local Guild with a constitution and leaders. Under the guidance of the bishop, organize the training and qualification of lay speakers. You should also link up with other Guilds to share information and for mutual support. Then go out and proclaim the Good News, ready to take those who seek the Lord farther into the kingdom.

Even though Jesus commands us to go out and proclaim the Good News (see Mark 16:15–18), at times we may face "no-go" areas, as did Paul in his attempt to enter Asia and Bithynia (see Acts 16:6–7). We do not know the Lord's detailed plan for the building up of his kingdom in the world today. All we can do is to ask him, with listening hearts, to guide us step-by-step in his work, doing whatever he tells us to do.

WHAT ROLE CAN THE LAITY PLAY IN EVANGELIZATION?

The prevailing view during the early days of the Guild in England was that priests could teach and preach but that the laity should refrain from "preaching" on the outdoor platform. In hindsight, I believe this attitude resulted in weakening the effectiveness of lay speakers. They had contact with the *minds* but not the *hearts* of listeners, which left the listeners to ask, "You have explained this teaching—so what?"

Explaining the value of a truth is still a long way from inviting the listeners to pray for the special gift of acceptance and to offer a prayer to this effect from the platform. Our goal today in the new evangelization is to proclaim the Good News—with teaching and preaching—and to make potential disciples whom God can enrich by whatever means he chooses.

Recent papal teaching has also stressed the importance of personal example and witness in evangelization. Some reduce this concept to "Just be a good example to your neighbor," which could apply equally well to paganism. Frank Sheed, a well-known Guild speaker, writer and publisher, pointed out some years ago in a talk I heard, "You will not proclaim that adultery is wrong just by not practicing it in public."

Speakers can witness to Christ by being courteous to their listeners, especially the awkward ones, and by telling from their own experience the value of the particular teaching they are giving and the riches they have in being a Catholic. Telling your personal story first tends to put the emphasis on the speaker rather than on Jesus Christ. I have heard speakers from other Christian groups begin by saying, in effect, "I was once a sinner, and now I am saved." Their listeners could offer a reasonable rebuttal: "Your Christianity may suit you, but I don't think it will fit me."

Even though personal witness can be quite convincing, without the teaching of Jesus Christ, there is nothing much about which to be convinced. A teacher passes on the definitive truths of Jesus Christ and the church. Teaching does not require us to be theologians, whose role is to clarify statements of truth, develop a fuller understanding of these truths and extend the present limits of the truths so far defined. Theology can enrich those who already accept the truth but is usually too deep for those who do not. In fact, apart from the clarifiers, I try to keep theologians *off* the outdoor platform, since they can distract listeners from the basic truths I am trying to communicate to the have-nots.

Those who already profess faith in the gospel are known corporately as the body of Christ, which has two basic dimensions.

- ✧ First, the church is the continued life on earth of the Lord Jesus Christ. We are members of his body, and he is the Head. Most people outside the church know nothing about this "insider" dimension, and so we need to enrich them with this truth and its implications.

- ✧ Second, the church is an institution of human beings, which is how "outsiders" see her. Their questions and comments focus on the *people* in the church, especially the well-known sinners.

These two dimensions are connected by the fact that Jesus Christ came to save sinners, not those who thought they were good. The church is Jesus Christ trying to turn sinners into saints fit for heaven as individuals, while the Lord is simultaneously trying to build up his body as a whole.

TEMPTATIONS FOR THE EVANGELIST
We have to recognize that Satan does not like evangelization and will target evangelists and would-be evangelists for special attention. Here is a recently intercepted memo from Satan to his demons:

1. The half-truth or innuendo can usually do more damage than a lie.

2. Tempt people to do good—in the wrong place at the wrong time. For example, someone with an unused talent for outreach in a parish should be encouraged to take on the flower arrangements around the altar. Those already using their talents in outreach should be guided to take on another good work so as to make them almost useless in both.

3. Tempt people to admire the view of the Christian horizon, especially of the past (tinted glasses can be provided), so that they will be mesmerized, stay put and do nothing.

4. As it is often worse than useless to tempt active Christians to sin seriously, suggest minor sins. When they descend to the level where they say, "Venial sins don't matter," then leave them to their own inertia. They will drift so far from Jesus Christ that they won't want him even at the hour of death, as they will have forgotten him.

5. Encourage people to promote peace in a pompous, self-opinionated way. Use the fact (but don't remind them of it) that in spite of the crucifixion and in spite of being baptized, people are still prone to sin. This tactic can result in quite a lot of infighting for the cause of peace.

6. Get people to talk, write, discuss and argue about evangelization—a clear way to make sure that little or nothing is done.

7. Remind them that an actively evangelistic church may cause offense to other Christian churches. Better to do nothing or to offer a watered-down, lowest-common-denominator Christianity—the kind that wouldn't make a self-respecting cat open one eye.

8. Get bishops and clergy to preach, "Just be a decent sort of person and set a good example." On the assumption that they're already doing that, the congregation will turn off mentally and ignore

anything else that may be said. The result will be to leave Jesus Christ out of their Christianity.

9. Encourage new religious societies and groups so as to duplicate what is already being done. This will make active Christians think they're busy and in fact steer them away from what Jesus Christ actually wants them to be doing.

10. Pay special attention to the Catholic Evidence Guild platform. When a speaker is answering a question, get listeners to interrupt with another, so that the full answer to the first question is never given.

11. Distract leaders with irrelevant issues so as to waste their efforts.

12. Encourage humility (false, of course) so that Christians will underrate their value to Jesus Christ in the building up of his kingdom. Make them feel so useless that they will want to do nothing.

It is important to say a few things in light of the current scandals in the church. There have always been scandals in the church. When the Catholic Evidence Guild began in 1918, listeners harped back to the notoriously corrupt Pope Alexander VI of the sixteenth century. It is still possible for an individual to accept Jesus Christ and live a life of growth in the friendship of God when those around him in the world, even in the higher levels of the clergy, are in a state of habitual, serious, unrepented sin.

The church is often attacked on the grounds that it is impossible to live up to its code of morality. The answer is that the church stands by Jesus' instructions on his terms. Many times in the past, governments, claiming to be Christian, have changed their laws to suit the level of the fallen human race. Some examples are the acceptance of divorce and remarriage, euthanasia and homosexuality. But the church is something more than just a collection of human beings with common ideals; if it were this, it would have changed the rules long ago. Non-Christians who hear about Christianity will have to decide sooner or later whether they want Jesus Christ on his terms or theirs.

OUR RESPONSE TO GOD'S CALL

God spoke the words to the prophet Jeremiah: "Before I formed you in the womb I knew you, / and before you were born I consecrated you; / I appointed you a prophet to the nations."

Jeremiah immediately made excuses: "Ah, Lord GOD! Behold, I do not know how to speak, for I am only a youth."

The Lord replied, "Do not say, 'I am only a youth'; / for to all to whom I send you you shall go, / and whatever I command you you shall speak....Behold, I have put my words in your mouth" (Jeremiah 1:5–9). Jeremiah heard and obeyed. And so should we.

Leonard Sullivan is currently the vice-master of the Catholic Evidence Guild in London, England. This diocesan organization promotes training for street evangelism in the Catholic church. For more information contact:

The Catholic Evidence Guild   or   The Catholic Evidence Guild
25 Banstead Road   84 Grove Green Road
Purley-Surrey CR8 3EB   Leytonstone
United Kingdom   London E11 4EL
                                               United Kingdom

CHAPTER 13

Preaching Evangelistic Homilies

Father Bruce Nieli, C.S.P.

Evangelistic preaching, as the name implies, is a proclamation of Jesus Christ designed to convert people to the life of the gospel. It is, in the words of Pope Paul VI, a living preaching that "leads to belief" (*EN*, 42).

Scripture tells us that "faith comes from what is heard, and what is heard comes by the preaching of Christ" (Romans 10:17). Thus the aim of evangelistic preaching is to inspire people to fall in love with Jesus, to embrace him and to imitate him in his body, the church.

Since evangelistic preaching is directed specifically to touching the heart, it can be a highly emotional experience, yet not necessarily nor exclusively. Evangelistic preachers like Jonathan Edwards and

Phoebe Palmer were learned theologians who appealed to the mind as well as to the heart. Cardinal Archbishop Stephen Langton of Canterbury, an evangelistic preacher and one of the greatest theologians and teachers of the Middle Ages, composed the *Veni Sancte Spiritus*, divided the Bible into the contemporary chapters and authored the *Magna Carta*, the document leading up to the United States Constitution and modern democracy.

Moreover, periods of great evangelistic preaching and related activities produced much-needed social change and reform in the history of the United States. During the eighteenth-century era known as the Great Awakening, the labors of people such as Jonathan Edwards and George Whitefield not only helped convert individual hearts but also helped form the heart of a nation. Evangelistic preaching helped inspire the unification of the thirteen colonies just prior to the American Revolution as well as the birth of some of our country's earliest institutions of higher learning. In fact, Jonathan Edwards served as an early president of one such institution, Princeton University.

The nineteenth century began with a period of intense evangelistic preaching known as the Second Great Awakening. Charles Finney and others helped mobilize social and political reform as diverse as abolition, higher education and women's rights. Ohio's Oberlin College, the first institution of higher learning in the United States to admit women and African Americans, was launched by a team of well-known and respected evangelists.

Like-minded women evangelists also made significant contributions to social reform. A remarkable woman by the name of Sojourner Truth, a slave until 1827, went on to preach emancipation and women's rights. Lucretia Mott, Elizabeth Cady Stanton and Julia Ward Howe (author of "The Battle Hymn of the Republic") would follow in this tradition.

The evangelistic movement also brought forth enduring literary works, such as Harriet Beecher Stowe's *Uncle Tom's Cabin.* Abraham Lincoln, famous for his stirring oratory, often incorporated an evangelistic style in his speeches. His second inaugural address serves as a primary example.

Throughout the twentieth century, evangelistic ministry inspired such efforts at social transformation and justice for the poor as the twelve-step programs, the civil rights movement and the pro-life movement. Few people have had as great an impact on our sociopolitical structure as Dr. Martin Luther King, Jr., a master of evangelical preaching. Even American music has been touched profoundly by evangelistic activity, especially in forms like spirituals, gospel, the blues, soul and jazz. As Pope Paul VI wrote, true evangelization brings the Good News "into all the strata of humanity" (*EN,* 18).

In this country evangelistic preaching is usually associated with our brothers and sisters who belong to Protestant churches. Probably the most famous evangelical preacher of our time is Billy Graham. This gifted and fearless evangelist appeals to a broad spectrum of the American people across denominational boundaries. Dr. Graham clearly and simply proclaims Jesus Christ as Lord and Savior, with the urgent need for each of us to acknowledge our sinfulness and make a decision to turn our lives over to Jesus. Thousands have accepted the altar call at the end of his crusades and become followers of Christ.

A CATHOLIC TRADITION

It is important to remember that evangelistic preaching has been an integral part of Catholicism for centuries. Great Catholic evangelists such as Saint Augustine, Saint Bernard of Clairvaux, Saint Peter Damien, Saint Bernardine of Siena, Saint Catherine of Siena and Saint Catherine of Genoa transformed the hearts of their listeners and readers by speaking and teaching of the dying and rising of Jesus Christ. Mendicants like Saint Francis of Assisi spoke of the sacred humanity of Jesus in such vivid word-pictures that their hearers were mystically drawn to respond.

In fact, the earliest missionary preaching conducted in what is now the United States of America was performed by Franciscan Friars. A famous modern disciple of Saint Francis, Sister Thea Bowman, granddaughter of a slave, effectively incorporated the artistic and musical traditions of her ancestors in her own lively and holistic method of evangelization.

Perhaps the most articulate of all American evangelistic preachers was the unforgettable Archbishop Fulton Sheen, the very first television evangelist. He proclaimed the word of God so powerfully that he drew overflow crowds of people (including me). In fact, so many gathered to hear him conduct the seven last words service at St. Agnes Church on Good Friday that they stopped traffic around Grand Central Station in New York City.

This brings us to the techniques of evangelistic preaching in the unique Catholic style. If we keep in mind our focus on conversion and reconversion and ongoing conversion to Jesus Christ, things fall more clearly into place. We must also remember that Catholic evangelization speaks of the whole Christ, or the *totus Christus*, as Saint Augustine would say, of Jesus as the head of the church in intimate and unbreakable union with his body (see *EN*, 16).

We seek not only to draw people into ever deeper communion with Jesus in his church but also to call ourselves as members of the church to daily reform and renewal. We are called to pray and work for our own growth in holiness as well as to work one day at a time for the ongoing reform and renewal of our country. With this overall vision before us, I offer the following suggested techniques for Catholic evangelistic preaching, flowing from the spirituality of Paulist founder Father Isaac Thomas Hecker, America's leading nineteenth-century Catholic apologist:

1. *Invoke the Holy Spirit.* Ask the Holy Spirit, Jesus' "living water" (John 7:38), to quench the transcendental thirsts of the soul for unity (intimate love), truth (endless love), goodness (sacrificial love) and beauty (universal love).

2. *Prayerfully read the Scripture passage to be preached upon, particularly the Gospel, as an encounter with the living Jesus.* Assume, for example, that we are to preach on the following passage: "I am the good shepherd; I know my own and my own know me, as the Father knows me and I know the Father; and I lay down my life for the sheep. And I have other sheep, that are not of this fold; I must bring them also, and they will heed my voice. So there shall be one flock, one shepherd" (John 10:14–16).

   The idea in evangelistic preaching is to read this passage several times, pray over it and visualize Jesus shepherding and nurturing you, calling you by name and bringing you home when you are lost. You might even see yourself in the arms of Jesus, with your head on his bosom, like the beloved disciple at the Last Supper.

3. *Discern the impact of this encounter on you personally.* What is Jesus saying to you? In this passage from John, for example, Jesus is saying that he calls me by name, and I am his (see Isaiah 43:1) (truth). I am important to him. I can never be far away from him, even if I try to hide or flee (unity). He died for me, so that I and others might live (goodness). "He leads me beside still waters" and "makes me lie down in green pastures" (Psalm 23:2) (beauty).

   I have a Father who loves me and knows me, even if my earthly father and mother have gone on to eternal life. I need not compare myself with anyone else, because Jesus calls me by my name. I am free. I am at peace.

4. *Summarize this personal encounter in a simple declarative sentence, at least for yourself.* This is the message you want to communicate.

I would summarize the above in these words: Jesus shepherds me so that I may shepherd others.

5. *Illustrate this message with a contemporary person or event.* Be sensitive to the cultural situation of the people to whom you are preaching.

What a marvelous example of a good shepherd to the people of our time was Pope John Paul II! His own prayerful, even mystical union with Jesus flowed into his unifying mission to the church and to the world. (Leaders of practically every world religion and heads of state of even conflicting nations experienced the Exchange of Peace at his funeral Mass.) He was a forthright preacher of the truth, perhaps the greatest teaching pope in history.

His sacrificial love for his flock came within a fraction of an inch of making him a good shepherd in the ultimate sense of laying down his life for his sheep. Indeed, his illness made him in his final days a holy witness of redemptive suffering and the defense of life from conception to natural death. And his love for the Eucharist and his entrance into eternal life on a Saturday (Our Lady's day), the vigil of Divine Mercy Sunday, in his own proclaimed Eucharistic year, were personally enriched by the love of beauty of an experienced artist. How rightfully did Billy Graham declare: "Pope John Paul II was unquestionably the most influential voice for morality and peace in the world during the last 100 years."[1]

6. *Connect this contemporary example to the life of Mary, or a saint or holy person in history who has made an impact on the church and whose life gives witness to your central idea.* Passages from a great spiritual writer and images from tradition may also help to illustrate and further develop your message.

A good example here would be Saint Paul the apostle, whose evangelizing mission throughout his contemporary world made him "all things to all" (1 Corinthians 9:22). Pope John Paul heroically followed in this multicultural, multinational, multiethnic, ecumenical and interreligious spirit. Read his *Redemptoris Missio* (The Mission of the Redeemer) and *Ecclesia in America* (The Church in America) for more of his evangelizing and reconciling spirit.

Also helpful might be to mention the figure of the Good Shepherd as perhaps the earliest artistic image of Jesus.

7. *Connect your central theme to a church teaching, document or council.* This will communicate the catholicity of your message— how your preaching relates to the church universal.

Paragraph 754 of the *Catechism of the Catholic Church* provides a beautiful description of the church as the flock of Jesus the Good Shepherd. Other documents, like the Second Vatican Council's *Lumen Gentium* and Pope John Paul's *Pastores Dabo Vobis* ("I Will Give You Shepherds"), are also most appropriate to quote from, among many others.

8. *Communicate the impact of this message on your own life.* I could tell of how humbled and honored I was to be asked to write the draft of a talk Pope John Paul II would give at Plaza Guadalupe in San Antonio, Texas, in September 1987, on the parish as family of families.

Or I could tell about how my mother nurtured me while I suffered as a child from asthma, often singing to me the reassuring hymn, "Yes, Jesus loves me, the Bible tells me so." I could go on to share how I was privileged to do the same for my mother as she lay dying of a brain tumor and how earlier, by God's grace and the intercession of Our Lady of Guadalupe, I was able to receive her into the Catholic church.

I am also reminded of Mary nurturing her son Jesus. Was not she the holiest shepherd to the Good Shepherd!

9. *Always connect everything to Jesus.* Be succinct, yet preach with passion. Show your listeners that you are in love with Jesus and with the fullness of his body, the Catholic church.

I am a Catholic priest because I am in love with Jesus and his church. He has been shepherding me all of my life through precious people who have nurtured me, inspiring me to do the same in my own weak way for others.

THE PRIMARY FOCUS OF EVANGELISTIC PREACHING

Notice that evangelistic preaching, more than any other form of public speaking, represents the fruit of prayer and meditation on the Word of God and on one's own spiritual life. Those who preach do not have to wonder if their message is effective or what others think of their sermons. They will be the first to know, since they themselves will be listening and feeling the impact of the proclamation while it is being delivered.

Evangelistic preaching is particularly focused on the *kerygma,* the initial proclamation of the gospel. To put it another way, the primary goal of missionary preaching is "to arouse faith" (*CT,* 18). With this in mind, we as preachers must be aware of our own ongoing conversion to faith in Jesus as we call others and our society to such conversion.

This particular focus of evangelistic preaching goes hand in hand with the first goal of *Go and Make Disciples: A National Plan and Strategy for Catholic Evangelization in the United States,* promulgated in 1992 by the United States Conference of Catholic Bishops. Goal I states: "To bring about in all Catholics such an enthusiasm for their faith that, in living their faith in Jesus, they freely share it with others" (*GMD,* 46).

Enthusiasm comes from two Greek words: *en* ("in") and *theos* ("God"). To be "enthusiastic" means to be "in God," to be filled with the Holy Spirit. This first goal is thus directed to forming holy and Spirit-filled Catholic Christians.

Evangelistic preaching can help instill this kind of enthusiasm for the Catholic faith and the desire for daily conversion to Jesus. It can also encourage Catholics so renewed and converted to develop a welcoming attitude toward everyone, as a fulfillment of Goal II of the bishops' plan: "To invite all people in the United States, whatever their social or cultural background, to hear the message of salvation in Jesus Christ so they may come to join us in the fullness of the Catholic faith" (*GMD*, 53).

Finally, evangelistic preaching can challenge the Catholic community, so spiritually reformed and more welcoming, to offer Catholicism as a *spirituality for America*, a leaven for the spiritual reform of our country and a renewal in her guiding principles. This will result in a living out of the third goal of *Go and Make Disciples:* "To foster gospel values in our society, promoting the dignity of the human person, the importance of the family, and the common good of our society, so that our nation may continue to be transformed by the saving power of Jesus Christ" (*GMD*, 56).

May our evangelistic preaching flow from a renewed soul and, in imitation of Our Lady, serve to magnify the Lord (see Luke 1:46). May our proclamation of the Good News of Jesus Christ draw others into communion with her Son, particularly in the Eucharist. And may our constant calling of ourselves and of our nation to increased discipleship serve ultimately to make disciples of all nations (Matthew 28:19).

Father Bruce Nieli, C.S.P., is former director for evangelization of the National (now United States) Conference of Catholic Bishops. Father Nieli travels throughout America giving parish missions, retreats and conferences as a full-time evangelist and missionary assigned to the Paulist Preaching Apostolate. For more information contact:

Father Bruce Nieli, C.S.P.
St. Patrick Church
277 South Fourth Street
Memphis, TN 38126
901-527-2542 (office)
901-292-9112 (cellular phone)
E-mail: dbrucecsp@aol.com
or dbrucecsp@paulist.org

PART 4

BRINGING THE GOOD NEWS TO ALL PEOPLE

CHAPTER 14

Evangelizing the Poor

Sister Linda Koontz, S.N.J.M.

Many Catholics say to me, "I just don't know what my ministry is. I'm so confused. I've been praying for ten years to know what God wants me to do."

I tell them to stop praying. God has already given us our mission and ministry in this world: it is the mission and ministry of Jesus. When Jesus returned to Nazareth in the power of the Spirit, he went into the synagogue and stood up to read the Scripture:

> The Spirit of the Lord is upon me,
>   because he has anointed me to
>   preach good news to the poor.

He has sent me to proclaim release
    to the captives
and recovering of sight to the blind,
to set at liberty those who are oppressed,
to proclaim the acceptable year of the Lord.
(Luke 4:18–19)

Then Jesus closed the book and sat down. With all eyes fixed on him, he said, "Today this scripture has been fulfilled in your hearing." (Luke 4:21)

When he read this passage from Isaiah 61, Jesus was talking about himself. But later on he said that he was giving that same Holy Spirit to us. Jesus came into the world not only to proclaim liberty to the captives but also to anoint each person who believes in him and who follows him with that same Holy Spirit. The Spirit of the Lord is upon us so that we too can bring glad tidings to the poor.

God generously gives his Holy Spirit to his sons and his daughters. He does not ration it or hold back the best gift of all. We can ask him today, "Lord, give me a double dose of the Holy Ghost. Give me the Holy Spirit so I can become the person that you meant me to be, a person who carries your Good News, a person who is filled with your love and can bring that love to those who are starving."

When Pope John Paul II proclaimed, "Open the doors to the Redeemer," he used a word that means to open the door so hard that the hinges fall off. God wants to anoint us with his Holy Spirit, to empower us to do the works of Jesus in the midst of a world that is spiritually bankrupt and in poverty. Yet how easily we lose sight of our spiritual inheritance when we are being attacked by the enemy or being dragged down by our own low self-esteem. We need to keep reminding ourselves, "The Spirit of the Lord is upon me. He has anointed me."

WHO IS CALLED TO SERVE THE POOR?

Every Christian is called to serve the poor. Matthew 10:6–8 sums up our mission: "Go…to the lost sheep of the house of Israel. And preach as you go, saying, 'The kingdom of heaven is at hand.' Heal the sick, raise the dead, cleanse lepers, cast out demons. You received without pay, give without pay."

Jesus told us to "Go…and make disciples of all nations" (Matthew 28:19). Most Catholics seem to think he said, "Sit back and relax and let the Holy Father do it, let the bishops do it, let the priests do it." But Jesus said, "Go!" When we say yes, the Holy Spirit empowers us with divine energy and supernatural ability to get up and go. This is a great commission—to go into the whole world and make disciples of all nations. Yet it is the least obeyed command of Jesus Christ.

When I was about ten years old, I had the idea that when we stood before the throne of God in the Last Judgment, Jesus would ask us, "Do you remember on that certain day when you had bad thoughts and you committed this sin and that sin?" And then a movie of our sins would be shown to the whole world. This idea frightened me so much that I started getting headaches!

After I surrendered my life to the Lord and experienced his forgiveness and new life in the Holy Spirit, I realized that my understanding of the Last Judgment was wrong. So I said, "Well, Lord, what *are* you going to ask me when I come before your judgment seat?"

I believe the answer came to me. I believe he is going to ask, "Whom did you bring with you?" As followers and disciples of Jesus bound for heaven, we have got to be taking someone along! And the Lord is going to ask each one of us, "Whom did you bring with you?"

Many of us struggle with doubts and reject our ability to be used by God. *I'm not called… I'm not smart enough… I'm not a good talker… I'm not attractive enough… I'm not the one God wants to use.*

Yes, you are! You are just the one he wants to use. You are smart enough. You are not too fat. You are not too thin.

You may be too busy. If you are, then you can repent today and begin to be used by the Lord Jesus.

God wants to put you to work in his kingdom. If I asked you if you think you are qualified to be an ambassador for Christ, a representative, a witness, you would most likely say, "No, I'm not. And I feel so bad about it." Fortunately, God does not call the qualified, or none of us would be called. Rather, God qualifies the ones he calls. When you answer the call to make Jesus known to the world, he qualifies you with the gifts of the Holy Spirit. He backs you up all the way. You may be the only Bible that someone will read.

Many people argue, "I'm not healed enough to serve the poor. I'm not healed enough to be a witness for Jesus." I like to say, "He mends me to send me." When we begin to do the Lord's work, he will bring about the healing we need.

There are many gospels in the world today other than the Good News of salvation in Jesus Christ, even in parishes, even in church circles. Only one name sets people free. If we are going to serve the poor, then we must become experts at hearing his word and doing it. We must be able to say with Paul, "I am not ashamed of the gospel: it is the power of God for salvation to every one who has faith" (Romans 1:16).

What the world desperately needs today is a witness—even more than it needs a cure for cancer or hunger. Why? Because men and women are dying spiritually and have never heard the only name that saves, the name of Jesus Christ.

I have met young people, old people, people of every race and nation, who have said, "Why didn't someone tell me sooner? Why didn't someone tell me about Jesus Christ and his love?" If we do not bring Jesus to people, we have failed miserably. I like what one person said: "Unless we're willing to do the ridiculous, God will not do the miraculous."

A Hopeless Case?

One time when I was praying with a group of people, we felt that God wanted us to bring the gospel to people who had never heard it. So we went out into the hills of Juarez, Mexico, where the people are looked upon as downcast, outcast, with no hope. We set up a tent in the 110-degree heat and began to preach the gospel. Many who listened began weeping and giving their lives to Christ.

As we began praying with people, one of my friends went around to the back of the crowd. She handed a young man a picture of Jesus and said, "Jesus loves you." That is all she said. It is easy to say; it is the message of the gospel. That is all some people need to hear.

This young man started shaking and went home. He shook and wept the whole night. He said he felt as if a surge of electricity had hit him in the stomach. He told his mother, "Jesus loves me, and he wants me." His mother and his brothers laughed at him.

No one on our evangelism team was aware of the fact that this young man was a hopeless alcoholic, drug addict and thief, with every other vice that went along with these. Also, he had seen his sister burn to death when he was ten years old, and from that time on he stuttered.

This young man returned the next day as we were preaching the word of God and praying for the sick and those who were oppressed. As we prayed with him, he invited the Holy Spirit to take control of his life. In that moment God healed him. He was set free of the sickness and the heartbreak that had driven him into this life of vice.

Over the next several months God healed this man of stuttering and gave him the gift of preaching the gospel. He could not read well, he had never studied, but as he heard the word of God, he took it into his heart. That gift began to blossom, and today this former alcoholic and drug addict is preaching the gospel in the jails of Mexico. God will back up our small efforts to make his name known.

WHO ARE THE POOR?

Who are the poor? Jesus calls us to pray for the physically sick and mentally ill, to encourage those who are weak and fainthearted, to teach the lonely that Jesus loves them and is with them, to reassure the fearful that God's power can overcome any difficulty, to tell those who feel guilty and condemned that God holds out forgiveness, to comfort the brokenhearted with the Good News of Jesus Christ, to give sight to the blind, to proclaim release to prisoners, to clothe those who are in need, to share our bread with the hungry, to provide shelter for the oppressed and the homeless.

I became aware of this call several years ago. I was attending a conference, and we were praying to know the will of God. As I was sitting there, a thought came through my mind: I have something against you. When this gentle nudging would not go away, I began to think it could be the Lord—perhaps a message for some of the conference leaders I did not especially appreciate. I said, "Lord, if it's you, tell me what you want."

A line from Scripture immediately came into my mind: "He who closes his ear to the cry of the poor / will himself cry out and not be heard" (Proverbs 21:13). I felt as if I had been struck by lightning. I started weeping and pouring out my soul to God. "It's true. I don't even know who the poor are. I'm more concerned about my own comfort, my own reputation, my own security, than I am about your poor. Who are they anyway, Lord? Who are the poor?"

I felt so sad because I knew that my heart had grown cold, even though I was in full-time Christian work. I had entered the convent in 1960. I had given my life to evangelize, and yet I was far from what the Lord wanted. But I remembered that Ezekiel tells us that if we have a hard heart, a heart of stone, God can do heart surgery. He can take out our heart of stone and give us a heart of flesh, one that can feel the love of God, a heart that is interested and concerned about the plans of God.

So I said, "God, I need heart surgery. I just don't have a heart for the poor. I'm willing to change, but I can't change myself. Do something, Lord."

The very next day I was invited to go into the hills of Juarez, Mexico, for an evangelization outreach. I taught geography, but I did not even know where Juarez was. But I said yes because they had invited Sister Briege McKenna, a famous nun from Ireland with a healing ministry.

So in the middle of August I found myself sitting in the desert hills with pigs running around, garbage smelling and some of our workers falling over from heat exhaustion. I whispered to the Lord, "I'm getting out of here as fast as I can." Just then a lady leaned over and said, "I think the Lord wants you to come here and work with us."

"No way," I said. "My plane ticket is safe in my purse, and I'm using it tomorrow." I told the Lord that if he really wanted me there, he would have to give me a big sign, thinking of course that he could not do that. As I tried to relax and recover from heat exhaustion, I heard another man talking about how Jesus was still in the healing business. He said, "God heals today, and we're going to pray for the sick."

Oh, no, I groaned to myself. *That's going to take about three hours because everybody here is sick.* A lady ran forward and grabbed the microphone. She began to talk in Spanish, and everyone clapped, and they were laughing, and they got excited, and she kept pointing over in my direction. I thought she was pointing at Sister Briege, but my friend said, "No, she isn't! She's saying 'La gordita, the fat one, the fat one right there.' She's pointing at you!"

When I asked my friend to interpret, she answered, "Well, she says she lives in a shack by the dump and that last February she was dying. She was desperate because she had no money to go to the doctor, and she cried out, 'Jesus!' And when she looked up, Jesus walked through the door of the shack. And she said, 'That fat one, that one right there! I know that lady! I saw her, she was right behind him.'"

I knew it must be a sign. This woman had seen me with Jesus six months before I was even there! And God began to give me other signs that he wanted me to invest my life in his mission to make his name known among the poor.

WHEN THE POOR CRY OUT, JESUS SENDS HELP

A team of us recently finished building four houses for people who had been living in shacks or had no home at all. Each house has only one twelve-by-fifteen-foot room, but those people were so grateful. One widow told me, "I spent my nights on my knees asking God for help. I never dreamed there would be help. Now I'm on my knees thanking God that there are people who love him and who will come and help those who have no one to help."

James 1:27 tells us about looking after widows and orphans in their distress and about keeping ourselves unstained from the world for pure worship. I began to see that genuine compassion for the poor, the helpless and the oppressed was more important than correct doctrine about worship. James 2:5 goes on to tell us that God chose those who are poor in the eyes of the world to be rich in faith and heirs of the kingdom. The poor gladly come and gladly receive because they know their need.

We can reach the poorest of the poor, as I discovered when I returned to Juarez some months after my first visit. We began bringing people together for lunches, having prayer meetings, proclaiming the word of God, praying with the sick and expecting Jesus to act. Five hundred people walked for miles to attend our first prayer meeting.

One woman who came said she had spent nights in prayer begging God for help because her situation was so desperate. Having been seriously ill for a number of years, this woman had no money and nowhere else to turn. In fact, she had been living in a tent. When she came forward to give her life to Jesus, she was healed and renewed in the Holy Spirit. This woman became a radiant evangelist for the Lord and began to pray for her children, all of whom were involved in prostitution, drug addiction or other kinds of vice. By the end of the year, all of them had given their lives to Christ.

First Corinthians 2:4–5 tells us that people's lives are changed not by nice ideas, rational arguments in favor of Christ and lots of talk but by a demonstration of the power of the Spirit. Where the Holy Spirit is, good things happen, and people know God is in our midst. What convinced multitudes to follow Christ is seeing men and women being healed by Jesus' mighty power and evil spirits being driven out in his name.

My first initiation into this truth came at two o'clock one morning. Another nun asked me if I would go pray with a woman who was threatening to commit suicide. I felt Jesus urging me to get up and go. He can call on us twenty-four hours a day, and our job is to be available to him. I arrived at the woman's house to find her sitting there with a loaded gun. I was terrified. She said, "I'm going to kill myself. Nobody loves me."

This woman was an immigrant with no family. She was the poorest of the poor and had become a mean-spirited person in the midst of her poverty. I heard the Holy Spirit whisper to me, "Pray for her." So I knelt down and said the only prayer I knew up to then, but one that God answers every time: "JESUS, HELP!"

The woman fell over. I thought she'd passed out from liquor. But the Holy Spirit, God's love, had enveloped her, and she had fallen into a deep and peaceful sleep. She woke up the next morning totally sober—the first miracle.

During her sleep Jesus came to her in a dream and touched her. I found out later that she had a ninety-year-old grandmother in Denmark, and when she used to walk by her grandmother's room, she would see the old woman kneeling down and saying, "Jesus, what about little Krista? Jesus, take little Krista into your arms."

Upon awakening she said, "I know God loves me." Jesus had taken little Krista into his arms during the night. This woman was baptized, made her First Communion and yielded her life to the Holy Spirit. Those who knew her were amazed at the huge changes in the personality and character of a person one friend had described as "the meanest woman I ever knew." They thought it would not last, but she bore witness to Christ until she died.

WHERE DO YOU START?

Once you believe you are called to bring Good News to the poor, where do you start? Jesus said the poor you have always with you (see Matthew 26:11). I used to think that meant we could sit back and relax: "They're always going to be around, and there's nothing we can do about it." Now I know that Jesus meant that we will always have an opportunity to serve him in the poor. The Holy Spirit will lead us to the people he wants to touch.

The poor include the materially impoverished but also the spiritually impoverished, those who do not know Jesus Christ. Because we can't reach everyone, we often use that as an excuse to reach no one. But the world is won one by one. And God is going to bring people into your path—one by one, day by day, month by month—men and women he wants *you* to love and to pray with, that God would meet their needs.

At one point I was working with refugees from Vietnam, Laos and Cambodia. I was recuperating from hepatitis, but I learned that being weak or sick does not excuse us from being used by God. He always has us in a place and in a condition where he can use us perfectly.

It was during that time that I met refugees who had been abandoned by their sponsors. So we began to do the obvious things that needed to be done. We helped them find houses, brought them blankets to ward off the cold and taught them how to get their children into school.

While the three people on our ministry team were praying together one day, we received a prophetic word from the Lord: "It is not enough to feed them, I want to show them my power." And so we began to have a prayer meeting, a faith gathering, and developed a way to teach the gospel to these refugees, some of whom had never heard the name Jesus Christ.

We also had to overcome a language barrier. To our surprise, the Lord sent a young man from a church in Montana who spoke Vietnamese, Chinese and English. I would give the lesson, and he would translate it into two languages.

One day, as I was explaining the gift of the Holy Spirit and the new life in Christ—which I had planned would take about three months—a Chinese man said, "I want Holy Spirit! I want Holy Spirit now!" And the Holy Spirit came upon him. I saw that Jesus is the same yesterday, today and forever, as these refugees began to come alive in the Holy Spirit.

We are called not only to do the works of mercy but also to make disciples. One distraught young refugee told us that he had not been able to sleep for months, and no one could find a psychiatrist who spoke his language. His oppression was so great that the person taking care of him was going to have him hospitalized that week.

I said to him, "We're going to pray for you. Are you willing to accept Jesus Christ into your life?"

I did not know that this man had been a Buddhist monk for five years. We laid hands on him and prayed out loud, "In the name of

Jesus Christ, receive healing," just as Peter had prayed. Then I had him repeat a prayer asking Jesus to touch him and fill his life, to forgive him his sin.

The next week he returned, smiling and radiant. He said, "I have-been sleeping." That was the first good news, and everybody clapped. Then he said, "Buddha filled my mind, but Jesus filled my heart."

The Spirit anoints ordinary people like you and me to do extraordinary work in his power in order to demonstrate that Jesus is alive. I believe God wants all of us to be heroes in his kingdom. A hero is someone who has a lot of flaws but whose God is bigger than those flaws. You don't have to keep praying for the grace to evangelize. You have the grace, you have the anointing, you have the calling. Just do it!

You don't have to be perfect to share your relationship with God. You don't have to have it all figured out. You don't have to be eloquent. You need only to be in love with Jesus Christ and to be willing to share this tremendous Lover with others. The Spirit of the Lord is upon you to bring Good News to the poor—if you are willing to be his instrument.

Sister Linda Koontz is the director of Spirit of the Lord International Mission, an evangelistic outreach among the poor. For more information contact:

Spirit of the Lord International Mission
PMB 260
8900 Viscount
El Paso, TX 79925-5897
915-598-9015
fax: 915-590-5559
E-mail: solkoon@aol.com

CHAPTER 15

Evangelizing Married Couples

Frank and Gerry Padilla

The moral and spiritual condition of families will determine to a large degree the well-being of individuals and of nations. As Pope John Paul II asserted in his apostolic exhortation *Familiaris Consortio*, "The future of humanity passes by way of the family" (*FC*, 86).

At the core of renewing marriage and family life lies the evangelization of married couples. This is not an easy task. It is hard enough to evangelize in our modern secular milieu. It is doubly hard to evangelize married couples. Why? Because we need to evangelize *two* persons and not just one. Not only that, we need to evangelize not just any two people but a particular pair.

Rather than be discouraged, we need to see the reality of what

God is doing in the world today. Jesus issued the great commission to the eleven apostles: to proclaim the Good News to all creation (see Mark 16:15) and make disciples of all the nations (Matthew 28:19). This commission is still operative today and is the task of the church and of every Christian. In this task we should know that Jesus is still with us, until the end of the world (Matthew 28:20)!

Thus we should have faith about God's intent and God's provision. Despite the sorry condition of marriage and family life today, despite the tremendous difficulty of evangelizing married couples, God's plan is still operative: "to unite all things in him, things in heaven and things on earth" (Ephesians 1:10).

Jesus, who came into the world in order to bring us salvation, "is the same yesterday and today and for ever" (Hebrews 13:8). His mission, entrusted by the Father, also remains the same today. We can call upon the same power of the Holy Spirit, that power conferred on Pentecost, to be witnesses unto the ends of the earth. God has done his share; we need to do ours. We need to persevere in the task. We need to give of ourselves and be willing to make sacrifices. And if we do not lose heart, then we will reap the harvest (see Galatians 6:9).

Rather than evangelizing in a haphazard way, we need to develop a vision for the task—a deliberate, concerted, focused and corporate approach. There are basically three stages in evangelizing married couples: (1) attracting them; (2) converting them; and (3) keeping and growing them.

ATTRACTING THEM

Our efforts to evangelize married couples usually come up against three problems: sin, apathy and ignorance. There are those couples who are living apart from God, strongly influenced by the world and the devil. Then there are those who simply are not interested; they are busy living their lives and do not care about spiritual matters.

Finally, there are those who may be fairly good people but do not realize their need for Jesus as personal Lord and Savior.

Most married couples will not seek out the Lord on their own. We need to go after them. We do this in the normal day-to-day circumstances of our lives—in our family circles, in our neighborhoods, at our jobs, with our social contacts. Notice that we do not have to be missionaries or clergy or especially mature Christians in order to evangelize. We simply reach out to people with whom we have an opportunity to interact on a regular basis. (See diagram on page 191.)

We start evangelizing by building personal relationships, by becoming friends with people. The natural context of spending chunks of time with others affords us a unique opportunity. We can bide our time. We can choose the "when" and the "how" of speaking to them about the Good News.

We do not have to throw the gospel at someone. In fact, what we want to do is to build up a wordless witness. As people interact with us, they begin to notice how things are different with us: a healthier marriage relationship, better behaved kids, a more peaceful home. They begin to notice the difference in our speech, in our attitude, in our values.

In this context we will eventually find an opportunity to share about our life in the Lord. At that point we stress whatever we feel would be of particular interest to them. It could be in the area of family life, or music, or Christian formation, or service to the poor or fellowship. We should know a couple well enough to choose wisely which aspects of our renewed life would prove most attractive to them.

	WHAT	BY WHOM	HOW	WHY
Stage 1	Attracting them	Personal (person-to-person)	Develop a personal relationship Share Christ	Need tangible witness of life Show positive effects on daily life
Stage 2	Converting them	Communal	Programmatic	Work of body of Christ Utilize different gifts in body Introduce to Christian community
Stage 3	Keeping and growing them		Follow-up Formation courses Support groups Community life and mission	Ongoing work of renewal Goal: holiness, maturity Bring not just to Christ but to body Learn how to serve

Converting Them

Our goal in the first stage is simply to prepare people's hearts more fully to receive the Good News. Now comes the second stage: converting them. The term *conversion* is appropriate. We may be evangelizing among Catholics, but many are simply nominal or cultural Christians—in other words, "baptized pagans."

This second stage often makes use of "programmatic" evangelization. Here our Christian group or community steps into the picture. We invite those whom we have evangelized (attracted) to join a program for Christian renewal. It may be a Cursillo, or a Life in the Spirit Seminar, or a Christian Life Program or some other group evangelistic effort. Whatever program is utilized, it should basically contain two important elements: (1) an effective means of proclaiming the gospel and (2) an environment that can attract them.

Proclaiming the Good News

Proclaiming the gospel is done through a combination of teachings, discussions and personal witnessing. All three are important and reinforce one another. We must use authentic, clear and orthodox teaching to impart the meaning of the Good News of Jesus Christ. Small group discussions allow a greater retention of what is heard in these teachings. Personal witnessing gives life and particular relevance to what is taught and discussed.

These tools become even more effective when done by married lay people. Program participants can relate better to the program resource persons and identify more easily with the practical life implications of what is taught. It is not theology but a practical living out of the Good News.

It is also preferable, perhaps even crucial, that the program not be a one-shot affair—for example, a one-day Life in the Spirit Seminar or a one-evening evangelization rally. Solid conversion and growth need continuing proclamation and care. One of the more effective programs currently being utilized is the Christian Life Program of Couples for Christ, which extends over thirteen weeks.

Finally, a successful program should include not only a presentation of the basic truths of the Christian faith but also a clear call to repentance, a positive response to the lordship of Jesus and a prayer for empowerment (baptism in the Holy Spirit).

AN EFFECTIVE ENVIRONMENT

Many people can be attracted through person-to-person evangelization, attracted enough to agree to go to the formal program. At that point the challenge is to move from mere attraction to actual conversion.

During the program the evil one will be working more intently to deter married couples from pursuing a new life in Christ through this particular program. One of our jobs is to help them in deciding to come back week after week. Thus our program should have a number of appealing features. And since each couple differs in personality, needs, desires and expectations, our program should be multifaceted.

The first feature of attraction should be having an equal number of men and women comprise the team, a feature so simple yet so effective. A disproportionate number of women in groups and activities often deters men who may be searching for answers in the church. A significant obstacle in men's spiritual lives can be thinking that spiritual activities are mainly for women.

The second feature of attraction involves having men assume the primary role of leadership. It is hard enough to get men involved in spiritual activities, but often when they are attracted and then join a group led by women, their interest wanes. When they see other men taking leadership in the group, they tend to stay. And so God can continue to work in their lives through the church.

Male leadership in a group of married couples can present challenges. In the usual situation where the woman is the more spiritual
of the two, her husband often holds back and finds it difficult to
become more involved. But if the man is given an opportunity to
move on, without being spiritually overshadowed by his wife,
chances are he will "overtake" his wife and ultimately assume spiritual leadership in their married life—an outcome all wives would
welcome.

A third feature of attraction is encouraging warm fellowship. The
most effective atmosphere for evangelization is not somber or
formal or "churchy" but more like a social gathering. The team
members strive to be warm, friendly, caring, always reaching out.
Newcomers experience a powerful magnet when they see total
strangers welcoming them like friends, when they receive service
with a warm smile. Lively music and less formal prayer offer other
aids to warm fellowship.

Our goal in this second stage of evangelizing married couples is
to bring the program participants to repentance and conversion, to
the point of accepting Jesus as their personal Lord and Savior, to
receiving the empowerment of the Holy Spirit and to being inte-
grated into the Christian group or community.

KEEPING AND GROWING THEM

Now we come to the third stage. Our aim in evangelization is
renewal. Our goal is for the Good News of Jesus Christ to be lived
out in the lives of people. Our desire is for people to experience salvation now, leading to salvation in the hereafter. Thus we cannot
stop at the initial conversion of couples during the organized program. Otherwise many of them will fall back into their old lifestyle.
This lack of follow-up or follow-through is a major shortcoming of
many otherwise good programs in the church today.

Evangelization is an ongoing work. We do not stop at initial conversion but move on to implantation: planting people in the church in general and in a Christian group or parish in particular. Then we do not stop at implantation but move on to helping people in being formed and growing to Christian maturity. This growth process extends for the rest of a person's life. Furthermore, those evangelized have to move on and become evangelizers themselves, which is how the cycle of renewal continues in ever widening circles.

Thus we recognize a need for the evangelized couple to join a committed community of Christians. This could be the parish community, if it is structured to support Christians in their everyday lives, or it could be a lay group operating within the parish.

For such a community to continue effectively the task of evangelizing married couples, several elements should be present. First, commitments need to be clearly spelled out. Real community is not a matter of being included in the membership rolls but of faithfully living out the life of the community. Important areas of commitment would include regular personal prayer, Bible reading and attendance at meetings. We are called on in faithfulness in such areas by making a clear commitment to the Lord and to one another.

Second, there should be "cell groups." These are small support groups comprised of five to seven couples who meet regularly. These cell groups provide opportunities to grow in real friendships and to care for one another more intimately, thus addressing the common problem of anonymity in a large group.

Third, there should be weekly meetings. People involved in church groups may be used to meeting only monthly or fortnightly. But this sort of schedule leaves a couple too long in the world between meetings. For couples to realize the importance of the spiritual dimension of their lives, they need to come together with their brothers and sisters in Christ on a more regular basis.

Other elements that need to be offered by the Christian community are ongoing formation, a corporate life and identity, opportunities for service, a sense of mission and a clear vision for the group regarding its place in God's plan.

The task of evangelizing married couples is crucial for God's plan for the family to come to pass, for societies to have and live out Christian values, for the church to be strengthened, for disciples to be made of all the nations. We all need to apply ourselves to this task. We need to develop a vision for this work. Then we need to give of our time, our talent and our treasure. In all of this we must have the confidence that God is with us and will empower us with his Holy Spirit.

Frank and Gerry Padilla are leaders in Couples for Christ, a movement that focuses on renewing family life with specific ministries to couples, children, young adults, single men and women and widows. For more information contact:

Couples for Christ Global Mission Foundation, Inc.
349 Ortigas Avenue, Greenhills East
Mandaluyong City 1554
Philippines
+63(2)727-0682 to 87
+63(2)727-0707 to 12
+63(2)727-5777 (fax)
E-mail: cfcglobal@cfcglobalmission.org

In the United States contact:
Couples for Christ
P.O. Box 1833
Cranford, NJ 07016

CHAPTER 16

Evangelizing Teenagers

Frank Mercadante

How can we effectively reach adolescents with the Good News of Jesus Christ? Perhaps no other age group presents so many tough challenges.

Misconceptions about God and apprehensions about his desire can prevent teenagers from embracing the faith of their parents and enjoying the adventure of following Christ. Some of these misconceptions originate from the church herself, perhaps in sermons that depict Jesus as heavy-hearted, serious and sad. Adolescents may conclude that such a person offers no excitement and has no relevance to their lives. Young people naturally want to experience life as an adventure, not a funeral wake. They decide to set aside church until they grow older and more accustomed to the "mundane things in life."

My own faith adventure began in my senior year of high school when some friends invited me to a parish retreat. I heard other students describe a Jesus unknown to me. They sounded as if they knew him personally, almost as if they had had lunch with him that day! By the end of the first night, I too had met Jesus in a personal way and experienced his love.

That weekend altered the course of my life. After preparing in college, I began work as a full-time youth minister in a parish in the Chicago area. Our ministry grew from a meager beginning with fourteen students to a multifaceted outreach that involved over five hundred young people. Over fifty student evangelizers would meet before school on Tuesday mornings at six o'clock to pray and organize themselves to share the gospel with peers.

Jesus wants to send out many workers to gather young people into his kingdom. With this mandate, let's consider some fundamental principles of youth evangelization.

WHY SHOULD WE EVANGELIZE TEENAGERS?

Our young people are restless, searching among an overwhelming number of options for something to believe in. We are obligated by love to share Jesus with them, the only option that has the ability to truly satisfy the longing ache of one's soul.

Some of us might feel insecure because we do not want to be rejected. Approaching adolescents certainly can be intimidating. But this mission is too important to be stymied by any barriers, real or imagined. Christ can take us beyond our fears and deficiencies and help us to know that the Holy Spirit will guide us and supply whatever we need. Unusual and exciting encounters will follow. Let me suggest three reasons we should evangelize teenagers.

First, young people face a crisis of identity. One question looms large: *Who am I?* Developmentally, adolescence is a pivotal period in a person's journey. Many critical decisions will have lifelong consequences.

If the church is not there to offer answers, then peers or modern culture will. Most often the answer they will hear is "You're nobody unless you have...." Our consumer society tells us that we need things to be satisfied. Attaining the American dream is all that matters. If you have a three-car garage and a summer home, you are somebody.

The gospel tells us that we are "somebody" because God created us for a purpose and even died for us. We do not have to do anything or have anything to earn this love. God loves us for who we are.

Second, young people are dealing with questions of purpose. *Why do I exist? What is the purpose of my life? What direction will my life take? What is my life all about?* Again, contemporary culture stands ready with answers: Life is all about accumulating things, being popular, being attractive. Scripture teaches us much more profound values: Life is about loving, giving and serving.

Third, we need to evangelize adolescents so that we can benefit from their enthusiasm and idealism. Their emotions are not all straightened out and under control yet, but their zeal can be contagious and inspiring. Once young people have caught fire for the Lord, they can live out the Scriptures in an idealistic way that reminds us of the raw power of love.

EFFECTIVE YOUTH MINISTRY

Jesus' style of interpersonal evangelization illustrates some solid principles about evangelization. Instead of having a standard or "canned" approach, we need to identify an individual's need and then share the Good News in a way that speaks to that need. Implementing this approach requires knowledge of the Scriptures. We also need to be in touch with the Holy Spirit. Evangelization is not merely a human interaction. Conversion never happens apart from God.

Enter the world of the adolescent. Adolescents need to see us as approachable, credible, caring and worthy of trust. Relational youth ministry involves a willingness to be personally present to youth, to go where teens spend time, to venture forth into their world and walk alongside them. We should not embrace their culture without restraint but seek to understand it and be able to converse with them about it. Youth will take us seriously only when we take them and their experiences and perspectives seriously. A good rule of thumb is to *listen and learn first* and earn the right to be heard.

Move from being program-centered to being person-centered. A program-centered model attempts to reach youth with only content. A person-centered model reaches them with the "content" of our love and through our relationship with them. Interesting presentations will bring young people to a program a few times, but if these young people do not develop any significant relationships, they will not continue to come. We do not want to become so absorbed in *doing* the "right things" at meetings that we miss *being* present and expressing love.

Share your life and faith. After making contact and developing a relationship with a young person, we have a natural context in which to share God's action in our lives. They usually become interested and begin asking questions about our faith. It is also important to invite them to respond to the Good News. If they are open, pray with them and for their needs. Let them know that a "new life" is possible for them as well through a personal relationship with Christ.

Follow through. After bringing teenagers to a relationship with Christ, we need to help them grow in their relationship with Christ, teach them how to pray and explain the relevance of Scripture. Do your best to connect them with others who can help them grow as well. Try to incorporate them into the life of the youth and parish community. Introduce them to other students who can support them spiritually. Our ultimate destination is to make "disciples" of young people, so that they can embrace the mission of the church and be sent out to proclaim the gospel to others.

Relational outreach never conforms itself to a "neat and tidy" plan. Getting involved in other people's lives and letting them become part of ours entails vulnerability, opening ourselves up to feeling rejected. We need to push through our initial feelings of reluctance. By establishing relationships with young people, we will become a credible and significant influence in their lives. When the going gets tough, God will give us strength and grace to persevere.

LARGE-GROUP EVANGELIZATION

Much of the focus up to this point has centered on relational and interpersonal evangelization of youth. You may be in a position to develop a group program that could expand your opportunities for reaching young people with the gospel. What goes into large-group evangelization?

A large gathering does not provide a lot of intimacy or deep sharing but does offer more excitement with lots of other teens. Young people typically attend events because of who will be there. They want to meet new people and build friendships with each other and with caring adults.

First, we need to schedule a regular event for a particular day, time and location, and often enough to maintain some momentum. Consistency helps young people establish some element of routine in their busy lives and also cuts down on our need to publicize an event. If at all possible, we should give names to our programs that actually publicize for us. For instance, a group of young people meet in downtown Chicago for an event called "Second Saturday."

Second, we need to design quality events that carry an attractive and appealing image. Many young people assume a church-sponsored event will be boring. We need to develop innovative, fast-paced and high-energy programming that can successfully compete for a young person's time and energy. Youth meetings need to use a variety of methods to convey the gospel and move quickly from one activity to another before boredom sets in: perhaps a ten-minute skit, a ten-minute youth witness, a short talk by an adult, ending with a video that carries the same theme.

Large-group events need to breed a sense of enthusiasm and excitement. Young people typically have lots of energy and need physical activity. One of their highest priorities is to have fun. A successful large-group meeting is one people consider "the place to be." They are looking for opportunities to gather. What better place than the church?

Young people will attend a large-group evangelistic meeting because it meets their perceived needs. Once we convey our love and concern in this way, we can more readily address their deeper need for spiritual conversion. Teens may sense something missing in their lives or experience a longing for more, yet few will be able to express their need for God. A roomful of teens who are experiencing a good time is not enough. If we fail to invite them to Jesus and a deeper conversion of heart, we have fallen short of our goal. Each meeting should highlight the person and teachings of Christ in light of relevant teen issues.

Receiving a warm and enthusiastic welcome is often more meaningful to a young person than the content or activities. Adult and teen leaders can be planted at the door to greet teens as they arrive. Be careful to watch for any young person who might be standing alone. After a brief official welcome, the meeting can begin with a short and simple prayer that avoids theological language or sober imagery. After using humor or a fun activity to put people at ease, we should proclaim the gospel in a relevant and creative manner, with content rooted in the Scriptures and church teaching.

After closing the meeting, we do not want to give students the impression they have to rush away because the program is over and we "old people" are tired. Providing refreshments encourages them to hang around so that we can talk and interact with them. This is where real ministry occurs, especially in one-to-one interactions that elicit their response to the meeting.

Reaching Out

Large-group evangelization will attract the largest cross section of young people, but it will not touch everyone. We need to go beyond attracting just the interested and focus on unreached adolescents in our community. This may include jocks, troubled teens or unchurched kids.

This kind of outreach requires innovative thinking. First we must identify those students who are not being reached by our present efforts. Second, we need to find a common ground for meeting these groups. What might interest or attract them?

Once we find a point of contact, we need to develop a program, event, activity or relationship. We need to think carefully and consider all the details. If we wanted to reach the athletes in our community, we might sponsor a city-wide slam-dunk contest and specifically invite varsity basketball players. We could publicize the event throughout the city, inviting everyone else to come as spectators.

No matter what the program, we need to keep in mind our ultimate purpose, the sharing of the gospel. Our planning process should include some way to help break down barriers to faith and pave the way to a closer relationship with Christ. Sometimes building and creating a positive awareness and experience will suffice, the kind of experiences we can build on later. Or we may pursue more direct evangelization.

The youth of our nation will be evangelized. The question is: by whom or what? Will it be the church? Or will it be the contemporary

American culture, which packages its message with slick sophistication and catchy media?

I believe it is a myth that today's teens are not interested in spiritual things. We would not have such a problem with drugs, alcohol, sex and the occult if they were not spiritually hungry. Unfortunately, they are trying to fill deep spiritual needs with artificial substitutes. The church has the answer: Jesus Christ. Let's commit ourselves to applying excellence to our task by living and proclaiming the gospel in a relevant and creative way.

Frank Mercadante is the executive director of Cultivation Ministries, which helps parishes develop their own youth ministries to evangelize teenagers. For more information contact:

Cultivation Ministries
P.O. Box 662
St. Charles, IL 60174
630-513-8222
www.cultivationministries.com

CHAPTER 17

Evangelizing in Business and Government

Michael Timmis

Twenty-two years ago I had everything that the world tells us brings happiness: a wife, two handsome children, a successful career, wealth and stature in the community. Yet I was lonely, miserable, self-righteous and critical.

As my material wealth increased, I became spiritually impoverished. I felt empty inside. I expressed my mounting frustrations by being critical and demanding of those around me. My son viewed me as an adversary and was gradually retreating from me, and the only woman I have ever loved was becoming quieter and quieter in our marriage.

I would go to church each Sunday, receive Communion and pray that somehow I could bridge the gap between God and myself. While I totally believed in Jesus Christ and knew without doubt that he was my Lord and Savior, I did not have or feel any personal relationship with him. Feeling distant from God allowed me to adopt an indifferent approach to my faith. I convinced myself that I really didn't sin because I didn't commit adultery, I didn't cheat in business, I went to church faithfully and kept up the requirements of being a so-called "good Christian."

Then my wife asked me to attend a dinner with her at a local country club. When I asked her what the dinner was about, she told me that there would be a discussion on religion. Well, I had absolutely no desire to hear about religion! Having studied more philosophy and theology than most people, I thought I had heard it all, and I did not want to be preached to. But somehow my wife prevailed, and we went to the dinner.

That evening changed my life. I did not hear anything about religion, but I heard a lot about a person I really didn't know very well, the person of Jesus Christ. I listened to a professional athlete and his wife, who lived in Dallas, Texas, share their faith. They described how their marriage had been falling apart but how Christ intervened. They developed a personal relationship with him that saved their marriage and finally brought them true happiness.

I also heard a local businessman talk about his personal relationship with God. I could identify with him because he seemed to have the same kind of problems I had, yet his love for Christ was totally transparent.

At the end of the dinner, I said a simple prayer and committed my life to Jesus Christ and accepted him as my personal Savior. It is difficult for me to describe the incredible inner joy of what Jesus did in my heart that night. Some of my friends call it "being born again," others call it "being renewed," and still others say "committed to

Jesus Christ." Whatever you call it, I began to understand that the whole purpose of my life is to love Jesus Christ with all of my heart, soul, mind and strength and to learn how to love others for the love of him.

Becoming an Effective Advocate for Christ

My experience was so transforming that my children and many of my friends thought I had gone through some sort of mental change, and it frightened them. I remember going to a priest friend and explaining to him what had happened. I received no encouragement, no understanding and, quite frankly, no interest. I mention this detail because many of us think evangelizing in the marketplace includes reaching out to a social-economic group that is predominantly Catholic. When our efforts are met with suspicion or objection, it makes it doubly hard, and often the spirit of evangelism is snuffed out.

God was gracious to me and made it clear that he did not want me to join another denomination but rather follow the scriptural instruction to stay exactly where I was, continuing as I was when he called me (see 1 Corinthians 7:17). As I began to be renewed in all aspects of my spiritual life, I also began to be renewed in my Catholicism. I read the Vatican II documents, where it states that ignorance of the Scriptures is ignorance of Christ and that all Scripture is God-breathed or divinely inspired for our instruction.

As a lawyer and businessman, I had executed literally hundreds of contracts, all of which I had read personally because they affected me. Yet I had never read the most basic of all contracts, the New Testament, the new covenant between God and the human race. I realized how ignorant I was of the "contract" that God had made with me through my religious experience in the church and through the Scriptures, that it was something on which I could rely on a daily basis. I began to understand the absolute necessity of knowing God's word, as best described by an anonymous, fourteenth-century monk who authored a book called *The Cloud of Unknowing:*

> God's word, whether written or spoken, is like a mirror. The spiritual eye of your soul is your reason. Your spiritual face is your conscious-ness. And just as your bodily eyes cannot see where the dirty mark is on your bodily face, without a mirror, or without someone else telling you where it is, so with your spiritual faculties. Without reading or listening to God's word, it is not possible for the understanding, when the soul is blinded by habitual sin, to see the dirty mark on his consciousness.[1]

Reading Scripture convicted me of my responsibility to share with others what God was giving to me, first with my wife and children and then with my friends. I made the common mistake of becoming overzealous, preachy and all-knowing and very easily fell back into many of the traits that I had acquired before my rebirth in Christ. I discovered through painful experience that without someone to check you, advise you, lead you and make you accountable in evan-gelism, most likely you will end up being totally self-righteous, narrow and ineffective.

As a lawyer, I am a trained advocate, but in reality most business-men and women are also advocates. A good advocate can be very effec-tive in so-called evangelism, in presenting facts about Jesus Christ, but that is not the same as presenting the person of Jesus Christ.

When I think of evangelism, I think of *changed lives,* not people saying "I do" or "I will," raising their hands or coming forward at a crusade or altar call. Evangelism for me changed substantially when I began to *live* the life of Christ rather than *talk about* the life of Christ. A good friend of mine said to me early on, "You have been successful as a lawyer; you have been successful as a businessman; I am sure you will be successful in religion." And I would suspect that was a common feeling among the people who knew me.

One of the most profound experiences came approximately one year after this transformation. I met a man who ultimately became my spiritual mentor (and who still is today). He told me that if I wanted to be involved in evangelism, *I should first go home and learn how to love my wife and children and wait upon the Lord.* This is one of the best pieces of advice I have ever received; I encourage you to take it to heart for yourself.

I began to realize that evangelism means *being available* to the Lord as opposed to deciding "this is what God should do" and then dragging him into my project. True evangelism is like being an usher at a theater. An *usher* brings people in, sits them down and facilitates their watching the play. The central figure in the play is Jesus Christ. If I think of myself as the *major actor* in that play, I will not let the Christ in me evangelize those I am trying to serve.

To me evangelism has become basically representing Jesus Christ where I am. Many years ago my spiritual mentor told me that if I would be a light *where I am*, other people would be attracted to the light and thus to the word of God. I found that to be true. We usually think of evangelism as "going." I believe evangelism in the main is "staying" and being consistent.

Where Was God Calling Me to Proclaim the Good News?

As I started to change, I began to receive numerous invitations to speak about that change (early on those invitations came mostly from Protestant Evangelical organizations). I began to speak publicly about my relationship with Jesus Christ. When a businessman does that, he begins to set himself apart to some degree. As a friend told me many years ago, people are watching you to see if this is for real. And if you fall, you take many others with you. That helped instill discipline in me, because the one person I did not want to let down was Jesus Christ.

God called my wife, Nancy, and me to evangelize in several different arenas. These may suggest some ways in which you can share the Good News with others in the business world. As I mentioned earlier, I met the person of Jesus Christ at an outreach dinner. A group of us have put on a number of dinners in our community, where average people—homemakers, business leaders, professionals and political leaders—talk about Jesus Christ coming into their lives and making them the kind of people he wants them to be. We make these dinners a pleasant social experience and hold them primarily in homes. We ask people to bring their friends and sponsor a table by bringing their own china and silverware and so forth, so they can feel like an integral part of the event.

The Lord led Nancy and me to look around our community of Grosse Pointe, Michigan, and ask certain couples (covering the spectrum of local denominations) to come together and pray monthly to lift up Christ in our area. After twenty years, this group of seven couples is still together. Notwithstanding the fact that the group includes Protestant Evangelicals who have been following Christ for decades, they look to me as their leader—which proves that God does not call the qualified; he qualifies the called.

With this small prayer group as a starting point, we started Bible studies and prayer groups as well as other activities. Each of us decided that we would support the work undertaken by the others. Out of the prayers of our community group has come a fellowship program in Christ that reaches over 150 high school and middle school students each week, again including all the denominations of our area. We also put on an annual seminar, which brings together approximately 135 people for a weekend of fellowship in Jesus Christ to hear speakers from around the country—Catholic and Protestant—lift up Jesus Christ.

Two of us from the group volunteered to put on a mayor's prayer breakfast in our community, which became a regular event.

Approximately five hundred people attended the most recent one. When you are willing to do the necessary footwork, you can select speakers who make a breakfast a meaningful event rather than a "feel good" event, an event that really lifts up the person of Jesus Christ as opposed to an event that accomplishes virtually nothing.

When I am in Detroit, I regularly meet with two groups of men. One group is comprised of men my age who have met together for twenty years. We started out with just three of us, and now there are approximately twenty. When they first came, none of these men had a personal relationship with Jesus Christ, but all were hungry. Through the years all of them have been personally transformed and have transformed their marriages and families. Most of their wives have joined some form of prayer group or Bible study as well. The second group has met for over twelve years and has approximately twenty-five members who are between thirty-five and forty-five years of age.

Nancy and I feel that Christ has called us to lift him up to the poor. We do this in the city of Detroit through a number of projects. For example, we work with Cornerstone Schools, which are four Christ-centered inner-city schools formed in 1991.

In addition, God has called us to work in Third World countries. We work with other believers in Latin America and Africa, where our son lived for seven years. The whole thrust of these activities is to lift up the person of Jesus Christ and to offer his love through self-help projects.

REACHING OUT TO GOVERNMENT LEADERS

Another aspect of my life in Christ involves evangelizing government leaders. After traveling to over 110 countries in the last eighteen years, I have observed several basic consistencies among these world leaders. Whatever their religion, color or degree of power, most are lonely, depressed, distrustful, concerned. They face difficulties in their personal lives and have no close friends. In short, they are all hungry for the Good News of Jesus Christ.

In literally hundreds of meetings with political leaders (representing Christians, Jews, Hindus, Moslems, Buddhists and others), I have never once had an unpleasant experience. When we have talked about Jesus Christ and his message of reconciliation, I have never had a disagreement; I have never had anyone tell me that he was offended; and I have never had anyone say, "I do not believe you." The most common response was that we had told them about a Jesus Christ they had never heard of before.

I want to underscore a principle that I think is critical to evangelism: when I lift up Jesus Christ to someone, I do not lift up anything else. I do not lift up Christianity or any "isms" or any methodologies. I prayerfully concentrate on sharing the love Jesus Christ has given to me. I believe that this is the only biblical and effective form of evangelism that leads to changed lives, that opens the door so that Jesus can come into the lives of our listeners.

My first evangelistic trip was to Poland in 1988—before the fall of communism—where I had been asked to talk to Polish communist leaders about Jesus Christ. This struck me as quite preposterous, but the Spirit led me forward even though I knew very little about Poland and have no ethnic connection. I frankly did not believe that an ordinary person who is basically an unknown outside of his own community could be an effective witness to world government leaders.

To make a long story short, over the course of that trip I met with the vice president of Poland, most of the cabinet members and the head of the Polish K.G.B. All I did was share my experiences about Jesus Christ and his love. The reception I received was overwhelming. The day I left, my picture appeared on the front page of the Warsaw daily newspaper, showing me shaking hands with the vice president with the headline "American Businessman Comes to Discuss Jesus Christ with the Vice President."

This experience proved to me that when Jesus Christ is lifted up, he is irresistible to all men and women, whoever they may be. While I continue to be called to evangelize government leaders around the world, I have found that these same principles hold true on the local scene—with judges, with mayors, with members of the legislature, with the governor.

WORKING TOGETHER

One of the major developments in my life has been my work in Prison Fellowship. In 1990 Chuck Colson, founder of Prison Fellowship, approached me and asked the question, "Mike, who are the poorest of the poor?"

I had met many poor people, but I had never specified any group among them. He told me that the poorest of the poor were the imprisoned, because in addition to having nothing they did not even have their freedom. But then he told me something else that would become the signature issue of my life: unless Catholics and Evangelicals unite together in the person of Jesus across our historic divisions and differences and recognize each other as brothers and sisters in Christ, it is impossible to prevail in the issues of the day, such as abortion, same-sex marriage, poverty, drugs and so on.

And so I joined the board of Prison Fellowship in 1991. In 1997 Chuck asked me to take his place as chairman of Prison Fellowship International, which then covered approximately seventy-five nations. Today we have 108 chartered nations, with ongoing work in at least ten other countries. Over a hundred thousand volunteers go into the prisons of the world to proclaim the Good News of the salvation of Jesus and to serve prisoners, their families and their victims in many material ways, such as medicines, clothes, jobs and so forth.

Because of Chuck Colson's vision, I was the first Roman Catholic to chair an organization that started as a Protestant Evangelical movement. It is a great privilege to partner in the sharing of the love of Jesus with Catholics, Protestants and Orthodox believers as we reach out to the least, the last and the lost.

In the 1990s I joined the board of Promise Keepers as its only Roman Catholic member. Promise Keepers enabled me to see a work of the Holy Spirit that was penetrating American men throughout the country. In 1997 I was a member of the team that addressed over one million men in Washington, D.C., at a daylong event called "Stand in the Gap." God then led me to get specifically involved with the Catholic Men's Movement.

Promise Keepers has awakened many men to fellowship and the need for Scripture in their daily lives. But Catholic men needed something more. They needed to understand the importance of church teaching and the intimate connection between God and man that is found in the Eucharist. Today I am a member of the board of the National Fellowship of Catholic Men. It is a movement that is spreading all over the country, with daylong events leading to Bible study and fellowship groups in individual parishes.

EVANGELISM AS A WAY OF LIFE

What I have described to you is not a methodology, not a recorded series of projects, but rather a description of evangelism as a way of life. This way of life begins with taking Jesus Christ to the four corners of my mind before I take him to the four corners of the world. The four corners of my mind are: (1) my personal relationship with Jesus Christ; (2) my relationship with my wife, family and friends; (3) my relationship as it pertains to my human sexuality—my manhood; and (4) my career, which includes my wealth and my ego.

I have found that the area of career, wealth and ego is the most difficult for every business, professional or political person to face. Taking Jesus into this corner means realizing that I can only evangelize others if I first evangelize *myself*. Of course, that is an ongoing process, one that allows me to look back and evaluate how well I am doing only this morning or this afternoon.

I believe evangelism is not possible without daily prayer, and by that I mean praying for myself and others and meditative prayer. The older and busier I become, the more I realize how absolutely critical it is to spend a portion of each day in prayer *without fail*. On those few days when I let my day get away from me because of meetings from morning to night, I never go to bed until I finish a quality time of prayer. That takes personal commitment.

Second, Scripture reading is an integral part of every day. It is a time when I believe God conveys to me his thoughts, his encouragement, his advice and his admonition.

Third, I try to go to Mass on a daily basis. When I was wrestling with what God wanted me to do with my life, he made it clear to me that he wanted me to devote a portion of my life to evangelization in the Catholic church. I thought the best way I could do that was by becoming an exemplary Catholic, and so I started going to Mass every day—with the view that people then would not doubt my Catholic credentials when I talked to them about Christ.

That reason quickly became totally irrelevant. Through the beauty of worshipping at Mass, I discovered an even deeper intimacy with Jesus Christ through the sacrifice of the Mass and by receiving the Eucharist. On the days I find it impossible to get to Mass, I feel a deep sense of incompleteness. Now I plan my day around Mass. If I miss it in the morning, I try to get there at noon.

Fourth, as I said earlier, accountability is critical. I need to be accountable to someone—a person who is a good friend and a brother in Christ—who will tell me exactly what he sees in me: the good, the bad and the ugly.

WHAT IS OUR CALL?
In closing I would like to share three quotes from the Vatican II documents that provide a framework for evangelism in the marketplace.

So intimately are the parts linked and interrelated in this body (cf. Eph. 4:16) that the member who fails to make his proper contribution to the development of the Church must be said to be useful neither to the Church nor to himself. (*AA*, 2)

An apostolate…does not consist only in the witness of one's way of life; a true apostle looks for opportunities to announce Christ by words addressed either to non-believers with a view to leading them to faith, or to believers with a view to instructing and strengthening them, and motivating them toward a more fervent life. (*AA*, 6)

The apostolate of the social milieu, that is, the effort to infuse a Christian spirit into the mentality, customs, laws, and structures of the community in which a person lives, is so much the duty and responsibility of the laity that it can never be properly performed by others. In this area the laity can exercise the apostolate of like toward like. It is here that laymen add to the testimony of life the testimony of their speech. (*AA*, 13)

I can tell you that in all my years of attending Mass, I have heard only one homily on these principles, and that was given by Father Bodhan Kosicki of St. Lucy's Church in St. Clair Shores, Michigan, when he was pastor there. I suggest that less than 1 percent of Catholics know these principles, yet they are critical to our call to share the Good News with others. Before the laity can meet its responsibility in evangelism, we must understand the critical importance of evangelism to the average Catholic.

In the final analysis, each of us has to figure out the best way to proceed in evangelizing both ourselves and others. While we are all called to the same question, we are called to different answers. I hope my experience has at least stimulated your own thinking about how you can bring the Good News to those around you.

Michael Timmis serves on the boards of Promise Keepers and the National Fellowship of Catholic Men.

Promise Keepers National Headquarters
P.O. Box 11798
Denver, CO 80211-0798
303-964-7600
800-888-7595
www.promisekeepers.com

National Fellowship of Catholic Men
P.O. Box 86381
Gaithersburg, MD 20886
301-519-0646
301-519-0694 (fax)
www.nrccm.org

CHAPTER 18

Evangelizing Hispanic Americans

José (Pepe) Alonso

North American society is comprised of many ethnic groups with different cultures, languages and lifestyles. The Christian ideal is to achieve unity within this diversity, but we must not confuse integration with assimilation.

In the *National Pastoral Plan for the Hispanic Ministry*, issued in November 1987, the American bishops explain the difference between assimilation and integration:

> Through the policy of assimilation, new immigrants are forced to give up their language, culture, values, and traditions and adopt a

form of life and worship foreign to them in order to be accepted as parish members. This attitude alienates new Catholic immigrants from the church and makes them vulnerable to sects and other denominations.

By integration, we mean that our Hispanic people are to be welcomed to our church institutions at all levels. They are to be served in their language when possible, and their cultural values and religious traditions are to be respected. (*NPPHM*, 4)

Taking the oath for United States citizenship in no way requires a person to renounce his cultural identity. In just the same way, our efforts to bring people into the church must not infringe on their ethnic heritage. Unless we take into consideration the multicultural dimension of our society, our efforts to bring others to Christ will fail. We cannot evangelize with the mentality of stirring everyone into one big melting pot.

Saint Paul offers one of the clearest examples of effective multicultural evangelization:

> For though I am free from all men, I have made myself a slave to all, that I might win the more. To the Jews I became as a Jew, in order to win Jews; to those under the law I became as one under the law—though not being myself under the law—that I might win those under the law. To those outside the law I became as one outside the law—not being without law toward God but under the law of Christ—that I might win those outside the law. To the weak I became weak, that I might win the weak. I have become all things to all men, that I might by all means save some. (1 Corinthians 9:19–22)

In *Evangelii Nuntiandi* Pope Paul VI emphasized this same principle: "Evangelization loses much of its force and effectiveness if it does not take into consideration the actual people to whom it is addressed, if it does not use their language, their signs and symbols, if it does not answer the questions they ask, and if it does not have an impact on their concrete life" (*EN*, 63).

A Difficult Balancing Act

Hispanics are fast becoming the largest minority in the United States. Their continued resistance to giving up their language and culture offers clear evidence of the pride they take in their cultural heritage. The primary goal of Hispanics has been to participate in American society without being assimilated by it—an extremely difficult balancing act.

Certain historical factors help us understand why Hispanics have not followed the same pattern of assimilation as other large immigrant groups. For one thing, people of Spanish ancestry already occupied much of the United States well before other Europeans came to take possession of these lands. Mexicans were the first to colonize Arizona, Nevada, New Mexico, California and Texas.

Puerto Ricans possess American citizenship by birth, but the majority do not consider themselves *gringos*. Cubans, who came for political not economic reasons, arrived in large numbers and established concentrated Cuban communities. They live their own lives and maintain their own culture so well that they have never made irreversible changes.

The majority of Hispanics have not become separated from their homelands by vast oceans. Their countries are so close that they constantly travel back and forth, nourishing their roots in a way that allows their traditions not only to survive but even to thrive.

The term *Hispanic* is not applied exclusively to those born in one country but is a generic term applied to people from Argentina, Chile, Paraguay, Uruguay, Peru, Bolivia, Ecuador, Colombia, Venezuela, Panama, Costa Rica, Nicaragua, Honduras, El Salvador, Guatemala, Mexico, Cuba, Puerto Rico, Dominican Republic, Spain and the United States. In fact, according to the 2000 census, Hispanics from the United States make up the *fifth largest* Hispanic population in the world. America's 35.3 million is topped only by Mexico (104.9), Colombia (42.3), Spain (40.2) and Argentina (39.1).

Even though each one of those countries boasts a separate and well-established culture, not only a common language but also a similar value system is shared. According to the American bishops, values common to Hispanics include "a profound respect for the dignity of the person, a profound and respectful love for the family life, a marvelous sense of community, a fond thankfulness for life itself—a gift from God, and an authentic and solid devotion to Mary." The bishops go on to say that for Hispanic Catholics, "the culture has become a way to live the faith and transmit it" (*NPPHM*, 10).

SIGNS OF THE TIMES

In terms of the Hispanic presence in the United States and in the Catholic church, certain statistics can help us read the signs of the time in which we live. To disregard these signs when planning our evangelistic efforts would be a tragic error.

The 2000 census reports 35.3 million Hispanics living in the United States, which I believe to be a very conservative figure. They represent almost 12.5 percent of the United States population. The projection for the year 2050 is 102.6 million or 24 percent of the total population. In 1950 there were fewer than 4 million Hispanics; in 1980 there were 15 million, 9 million of whom were Mexican. From 1950 to 1980 the population of the United States grew by 50 percent, while the Hispanic segment increased by a whopping 270 percent!

The three largest Hispanic groups in the United States, according to the 2000 census, are Mexican Americans (almost 20.9 million), Puerto Ricans (over 3.4 million) and Cubans (over 1.25 million). Others totaled over 9.75 million more.

The three metropolitan areas with the most Hispanics are Los Angeles (over 4.7 million), New York (over 2.8 million) and Miami (over one million). Other cities with a large Hispanic population include San Francisco, Chicago, Houston, San Antonio, Dallas,

El Paso and Fresno, California. Five metropolitan areas in Texas have a large percentage of Hispanics: Laredo (93.9 percent), McAllen (85.2 percent), Brownsville (81.9 percent), El Paso (69.6 percent) and San Antonio (47.4 percent). In Miami, Los Angeles and Fresno about one-third of the total population is Hispanic.

It is estimated that there are some sixty-five million Catholics in the United States, of which twenty-five million (39 percent) are Hispanic and this percentage is rising much faster than that of non-Hispanic groups. Yet we see a huge disproportion in the pastoral leadership of the American church. Consider the following current statistics: out of fourteen cardinals, only one is Hispanic (Cardinal Aponte from Puerto Rico); out of 281 active bishops, 25 are Hispanic (five of whom are in Puerto Rico); and out of 46,000 priests, only 2,900 are Hispanic (6.3 percent).

How can we analyze these statistics? Perhaps the projections based on the 2000 census come up short due to the large number of illegal aliens, approximately 10 percent more than government records indicate. Although this group is not reflected by any official statistics, it cannot be ignored. These are real people who place significant demands on the Catholic church.

The rate of growth among Hispanics in the United States is enormous and appears to be increasing. We do not believe the pastoral resources of the church are capable of caring for this rapidly growing segment of the population, which may explain why certain sects, such as Jehovah's Witnesses, are winning thousands of Hispanics every month.

Because of the shortage of pastoral leadership, I believe it is the hour of the laity. Together with Hispanics and in communion with the hierarchy of the church, I pray that we lay people will wake up to the real needs before us. Only then can we carry out the mission of the church: evangelization.

REEVANGELIZING THE BAPTIZED: *KERYGMA* VS. CATECHESIS

In their analysis of the pastoral situation of Hispanics in the United States, the American bishops recognized the following: "It is more important than ever that Hispanics recover their identity and their Catholicism, be reevangelized with the Word of the Lord, and join together in a necessary union with all of the other Hispanics who have come from all over the world where Spanish is spoken" (*NPPHM,* 12).

Later in the same pastoral plan they state: "The great majority of Hispanics feel left out of the Catholic Church. Evangelization has been limited to the Sunday Liturgy and a sacramental preparation which has not focused on the kind of profound conversion which brings together all the dimensions of the faith, spiritual growth, and justice to transform society" (*NPPHM,* 37).

What the bishops are saying is that the church has taught Hispanics the catechism and made them Catholic but has not given them the basic fundamentals. We have not presented them with the Good News; we have not led them to a personal relationship with Jesus. We have catechized them but left out the first step: the *kerygma*, which is the proclamation of the gospel.

Many Catholics do not make any distinction between *kerygma* and catechesis. Consequently they carry out an enormous number of activities labeled "evangelization" that in fact are something else. If our evangelization of Hispanics is to be effective, we need to examine the fundamental differences between *kerygma* and catechesis—even though the dividing line is thin and difficult to discern.

It is possible to say that *every action of the church is evangelization,* that there are different stages and levels of evangelization and that this activity never terminates. Nonetheless, for clarity of understanding, I would like to define *evangelization* more narrowly within this particular context as the first stage, or the *kerygmatic* evangelization, or the first proclamation of the gospel.

Etymology: The Greek word *kerygma* comes from the verb *keryssein,* which means "to proclaim or shout." The word *catechesis* stems from the Greek word *katechein,* which means "to teach or retain."

Objectives: The general objective of *kerygma* is to be born again, to have life. The objective of catechesis is to grow in Christ, to have an abundant life.

Content: The content of the *kerygma* is one person, Jesus, who died, rose from the dead and was glorified. Christ is Savior, Lord, Messiah. The content of catechesis is the doctrine of the faith: morality, dogma, biblical study and so on.

Methodology: The methodology of *kerygma* consists of proclaiming Jesus as the Good News. *Kerygma* addresses the will and is typically accompanied by personal testimony. The methodology of catechesis consists of teaching in an orderly and progressive manner. Catechesis addresses the understanding and is accompanied by the faith of the whole church.

Agent: The agent in *kerygma* is the evangelist, a witness full of the Holy Spirit. The agent of catechesis is the person doing the catechizing, a teacher filled with the Holy Spirit.

Goals: The specific goals of *kerygma* concerning a person being evangelized are an experience of the love of God and of one's own state of sin; a personal encounter with Jesus through faith and conversion; the acceptance of Jesus as personal Savior and Lord; the reception of the gift of the Holy Spirit; and integration into the church community. The goals of catechesis are more limited: an encounter with the body of Christ, which is the church, and growth in the holiness of the people of God.

Response: The response to *kerygma* is personal: *my* Savior, *my* Lord, *my* Messiah. The response to catechesis is communitarian and social: *our* Savior, *our* Lord, *our* Messiah.

Time frame: The time frame for *kerygma* is *now*. The time frame for catechesis is sometime soon. Catechesis must be *preceded* by *kerygma.*

Hispanics Must Be Integrated into Parish Life

The *kerygma* consists of six basic topics: God loves us unconditionally; sin has ruptured this relationship; Jesus is the only hope of salvation from the consequence of sin, which is death; we need to have a personal experience of Jesus the Savior through faith and conversion; Jesus promises to send the Holy Spirit to enable us to live this new life in Christ; we can maintain this new life only by joining together with our brothers and sisters in Christ.

These six points of proclamation set the stage for effective catechesis and integration into the life of the church, where Christians can best grow in their personal faith. Every instance of evangelization should focus on fleshing out these central ideas in a personal way, adapting the presentation to the situation. However, in no circumstances should the basic message of the *kerygma* be altered.

Many Hispanics live in poverty, especially in Central and South American countries and in the Caribbean islands. While the church needs to be concerned with the material needs of mankind, we cannot neglect the primary importance of spiritual poverty. The "theology of liberation," as taught and practiced over the last generation, has focused attention on how best to meet these needs. Clearly the church must oppose unjust and oppressive social structures as part of her service to the poor, but our methods must be in accordance with the teachings of Jesus.

In evangelizing Hispanics it is of singular importance that the process not stop with the acceptance of the gospel in the heart of the convert. The person's spiritual growth must be watched over and guided within the church and particularly drawn into the life of the local parish.

However, there is a big difference between Latin American parishes and the typical American parish. The American bishops make this observation: "The Hispanic community recognizes that the parish is, historically and ecclesiastically, the basic organizational unit of the church in the United States and will continue being so" (*NPPHM*, 37). Recognizing the importance of the parish to the Hispanic, the bishops propose that it is necessary "to create an inviting atmosphere which among other things will recognize the culture of those on the fringe" (*NPPHM*, 45).

This proposal gives rise to obvious challenges.

- First, a parish that does not welcome Hispanics paves the way for competing gospels. Of particular danger are the various "sects" that cater to the Hispanic and lure away thousands of our brothers and sisters to sometimes misguided heresies.

- Second, a parish that does not have a pastoral plan to include Hispanics will fail in its evangelization efforts. The Hispanic will not be content to be a mere spectator of the show: he wants to be an integral part of it.

- Third, the parish that evangelizes Hispanics must make a special effort to know and understand these diverse cultures, since each one contains valuable elements and traditions that can enrich parish life.

If a parish truly wishes to evangelize and welcome Hispanics, it must change from being simply an administrative unit to being a highly pastoral parish. Hispanics cannot be just another number on our weekly envelopes and in our computers. Because of their deeply rooted cultural values, they must experience being welcomed and accepted as valued human beings and being given pastoral opportunities to grow in holiness and to share their talents in the life of the parish.

In order to achieve this goal, the American bishops propose a vehicle that fits well with the Hispanic cultural tendency: *communities*. "At the same time it is recognized that their conversion and the sense of being church is experienced best in small communities, within the parish, which are more personal and make the members feel more like participants" (*NPPHM*, 37).

They further recommend that our efforts of evangelization to Hispanics make a priority of these goals:

> Recognize, develop, accompany, and support the small ecclesiastical communities and other groups within the church (Cursillos de Cristiandad, Emmaus, Family Christian Movement, RENEW, Charismatic Movement, prayer groups, etc.) which together with the bishop are effective instruments of evangelization for the Hispanic. These small ecclesiastical communities and other groups within the parish framework promote faith experiences and conversion, the missionary movement, interpersonal relations, fraternal love, prophetic questioning and pro-justice movements. These communities are a prophetic challenge to the renewal of the church and to the humanization of our society. (*NPPHM*, 40)

The *National Pastoral Plan for the Hispanic Ministry* proposes as a next step the formation of Hispanics as agents of evangelization: "To prepare visitation teams to be of the Word and of the Love of God and to form communities with the families visited and thus create a 'bridge' between the fringe members and the church" (*NPPHM*, 48).

I see three primary implications from the bishops' proposal:

1. The Hispanic should not only visit other Hispanics on the fringe of the church but should also evangelize them.

     In order for this to take place, it is necessary to prepare or train Hispanics. The evangelist is not born but made.

2. Evangelization schools are necessary in our Catholic world, since the majority of us have been trained to catechize but rarely trained to evangelize.

3. The Hispanic is the best agent to be the bridge to other Hispanics.

The American bishops call on the great Hispanic people of the United States to commit themselves to this missionary vision. We can accomplish the evangelization of the Hispanic world only with God's help and through the instrumentality of the church.

José (Pepe) Alonso is the mission director of Kerigma Asociación Misionera Hispana, which promotes the evangelization of Hispanics in the United States, especially through evangelization schools and rallies. For more information contact:

Kerigma Asociación Misionera Hispana
P.O. Box 557206
Miami, FL 33255
305-661-0590

PART 5

EVANGELIZING AS A PARISH

CHAPTER 19

The Story of an Evangelizing Parish

Father Marc Montminy

Only a decade ago Ste. Marie parish in Manchester, New Hampshire, was a struggling inner-city parish with a huge debt; funerals far out-numbering baptisms and marriages combined; and a church with a 250-foot brick spire towering above a rectory, schools, convents, a gymnasium, all looking tired and worn.

Today Ste. Marie shines as a humble beacon of renewal: a staff committed to evangelization and praying for a deeper release of the Holy Spirit; a Sunday renewal liturgy grown ten times over; more than five hundred attending ongoing Scripture study groups, Cursillo groups, contemplative and charismatic prayer groups and youth groups, with involvement at every age level; and a shrinking debt of just over one hundred thousand dollars, with renovations happening in every corner.

How did all this come about?

GOD KNOWS HOW TO PUT ALL THE PIECES IN PLACE

When first appointed as priest liaison to the Catholic charismatic renewal and the Cursillo Movement in 1982, I would visit twenty to thirty prayer groups each year, hold leaders' conferences and direct diocesan-wide events. Through these events I became convinced that the Holy Spirit was doing something new in the church. Having experienced the "baptism in the Holy Spirit" and a Cursillo weekend as a seminarian, I had seen the power of God manifested in a variety of ways. It became evident to me that those methods had to be brought into parish life.

We began by offering retreats for men and women, couples' retreats, young adult weekends, family weekends, men's and women's breakfasts, high school retreats, days of renewal and healing services. People started coming out of the woodwork. One hundred thirty men at a retreat, thirty couples at another, 240 people at a family weekend.

Within five years two young men were added to my diocesan staff as full-time associates. The name of our ministry was changed to Spiritual Renewal Services (S.R.S.) to reflect a broader vision: to bring a deeper release of the Holy Spirit to as many people as possible in a variety of ways. The vision for renewal burned in my heart and in the hearts of those with whom I collaborated.

Eleven years later the renewal office was financially sound, with ample funds being contributed by monthly donors and through scheduled events. Sixty healing services were being conducted a year, as well as eight parish missions, over twenty weekend retreats, monthly days of renewal and eight parish missions a year. With this model we were able to reach clergy and laity in fifty-two parishes, well over a third of the total number in our area.

A center for spiritual direction was established during this period. A staff of ten religious and priests began doing part-time spiritual direction for over 130 people. A young adult ministry was established in the diocese to help people familiarize themselves with the teachings and traditions of the church and give them a greater sense of self-worth as members of the body of Christ.

In the meantime, on June 15, 1988, much to my surprise, the bishop appointed me pastor of this large and struggling inner-city parish. Although I had been living in the rectory and doing part-time ministry at Ste. Marie's on a limited basis, I had never been able to implement the vision that I felt could change the face of this flock. My new assignment meant that I could bring that vision to the people of God to whom I had been sent as shepherd. It was during this time that I began to realize that God was about to do something great.

I began by introducing my parishioners to the Cursillo movement, and through the weekend experience it became evident that they were being transformed by this short course in Christianity. An Ultreya (an ongoing support group for people who have attended a Cursillo) was soon formed in the parish, and it flourished. Also a group of laity gathered together in the parish and devoted themselves to the Holy Spirit and renewal.

As time went on, however, I noticed that young adults and men were missing from the picture. Prayer moved me to seek new directions for renewal. I felt the need to expand renewal so that it could become all things to all people. Limiting ourselves to charismatic prayer groups or even the Cursillo movement had become an obstacle for many. New models were needed.

Having given an overview of the scenario, I would like to now share some important aspects that have helped this parish in renewal, that in fact have been instrumental in bringing about a revived interest in evangelization and catechesis.

PRAYER

Jesus tells us to pray always. Becoming even more convinced of this as I began shepherding the large debt-ridden parish, my associate and I began praying at least three mornings a week for one hour, petitioning the Lord to confirm and strengthen the vision.

We were not alone. In 1987 I had opened an old convent on the property as a house of contemplative prayer. A sister who was hired to direct this ministry began to pray daily for the renewal of the parish. I then asked the existing staff to pray and pleaded with parish organizations, prayer groups and individuals to join me in this most important task.

Within a matter of months we could see the power of God moving within and beyond the parish. I remember one morning pleading with the Lord for an evangelist. The parish had no means of supporting such a person, but I knew in my heart that this was a missing link in our efforts at renewal. The following day the parish received a check for twenty thousand dollars from an anonymous donor, who asked that this money be used for whatever purpose we deemed necessary.

On Christmas Eve of that same year, the parish staff met at ten o'clock at night to pray before the crib that had been set up in the church. We came together to plead for a greater outpouring of the Holy Spirit on the entire parish community. Twelve hundred people attended midnight Mass that night, one being an elderly woman who donated seventeen thousand dollars to be applied to the parish debt. I began to see lives changing, people returning to the sacraments and an empty church once again being filled with living stones.

I had started a young adult prayer group in 1983, and I also begged these young people to pray with me for the renewal of the entire parish community. At times over one hundred of them would show up on Wednesday evenings to worship God and to intercede for a fresh outpouring of the Holy Spirit.

George Curran, who served as codirector of S.R.S., had envisioned households for single young adults. Four of these households existed in the parish when I became pastor. These twenty-five young people met with me and my associate pastor five days a week for daily prayer. The time: six o'clock in the morning. A widowed woman who felt called to a new lifestyle moved into the house of prayer and began to intercede throughout the night for a new Pentecost. The main priority of the staff and of parish members became prayer.

Today this need and desire to have prayer as the center of our parish life has grown in the following ways:

- ✤ The parish opened a eucharistic adoration chapel in preparation for the Great Jubilee. The Mother Riviera chapel is open seven days a week, twenty-four hours a day, and has well over four hundred people adoring the Lord every week. Every hour of the day and night is dedicated to a group in the parish.

- ✤ Our entire staff meets to pray every other week in one of the parish chapels. We pray the Divine Office and then take time to intercede for every group and organization in the parish.

- ✤ Our pastoral council meeting always begins and ends with prayer, which will last a minimum of thirty minutes.

- ✤ Each first Friday of the month, between sixty and a hundred men join with the parish priests to pray before the exposed Blessed Sacrament. These men pray for their families, jobs, friends and parish.

✢ For more than twenty years the parish has prayed the Novena to the Holy Spirit, in which over a hundred people participate.

✢ In recent years our religious education coordinators have initiated eucharistic adoration for all the children who are involved in the program. Imagine seeing over a hundred children in the sanctuary of the church learning how to pray before the consecrated host.

VISION AND MISSION

Without a vision, a people perish. Prayer should always lead us to a vision. When I became pastor of Ste. Marie, I realized that the model for the pastor and pastoral council was to do what most councils do: they decided on the purchase of new boilers, concerned themselves with the debt, decided which roof to fix next and were often burdened with issues that really belonged to the realm of other competent staff.

During my first month as pastor, I met with the pastoral council. I started by asking them to pray and to dream with me. For the next five months our meetings consisted of an hour of prayer and an hour of sharing our dreams of what we would like the parish to look like in the next five to ten years. Our deacon, who works for a large government firm, gave a workshop on vision and shared with the members of the council the importance of visionary people in the history of civilization.

With a solid foundation of prayer and vision, the pastoral council wrote a mission statement, in collaboration with every existing committee, society and organization in the parish. A town meeting was held to ask parishioners to share their own hopes and dreams for this parish. One man became so excited about the prospects for growth that he donated three huge spotlights to illuminate our church building, which happens to stand on one of the highest points in the city. The lighted church can now be seen from the highway and from every bridge in the city.

Appropriately enough, our vision statement is based on Matthew 5:14, 16: "You are the light of the world. A city set on a hill cannot be hid.... Let your light so shine before men, that they may see your good works and give glory to your Father who is in heaven." Our mission statement reads as follows:

> As we look back on the rich heritage of the community of Sainte Marie, we see a community that sought to bring dignity and hope to an immigrant people by being a beacon of light shining in the darkness.
>
> Over one hundred years ago, Monsignor Hevey raised up a vision that gathered and empowered a community of French Canadian Catholic immigrants to establish a church, hospital, orphanage, schools, convents, cemetery, and credit union. These signs of their commitment stand tall among us today as a monument to them and a challenge to us.
>
> We remember with joy and are grateful for all that God has done in and through the community of Ste. Marie. We are proud of our heritage and are rooted in it; and we are convinced that God continues to work among us today. He makes present his kingdom among us as we evangelize, celebrate the sacraments, and provide pastoral care and religious education. Through these means, God is forming us into one body, a community of disciples, gifted by his Spirit and sensitive to the needs of all who are near.
>
> God's call to our community today remains the same: to proclaim Jesus Christ in word and deed! This is a call to renew our baptismal commitment where we pledge to live for God and to be his light in the world.
>
> We feel a particular urgency to live this call today in the midst of a disintegrating society marked by such manifestations of darkness as alienation, loneliness, and despair. Only the light of Christ can overcome this darkness; only his love can bring life out of death.

As we continue our journey with God, we will keep our eyes on the cross of Christ, our ears attentive to his word, and our hearts docile to his Spirit. In that same Spirit we offer what follows as means through which we will fulfill God's plan for our community today:

- By providing a eucharistic liturgy marked by living faith, prophetic preaching, and inspiring music, in the midst of a welcoming environment.

- By emphasizing the power of prayer—both in community and in the silence of our hearts—as a source of strength and nourishment for our spiritual journey.

- By developing and nurturing small faith communities where individuals can experience spiritual and personal growth and form supportive relationships of brotherhood and sisterhood with others in the group.

- By offering diverse catechetical programs for community members of all ages, which will lead them to a deepened understanding of our faith.

- By promoting social justice as a community through financial means and personal sacrifice and through community programs.

- By being an evangelizing community, who reaches out with the gospel to families, friends, and co-workers, and welcomes into our midst all those who seek Jesus: the Way, the Truth and the Life.

As an extension of our mission statement, every staff group, organization and society was asked to write a statement with clear goals and objectives that would complement the greater parish mission. The results were quite helpful. Since the mission statement was written in 1988, the six objectives mentioned at the end of the statement have come to fruition.

WORSHIP AND COMMUNITY

The parish has four Sunday Masses, each appealing to different congregations while maintaining sound liturgical principles.

- ❖ As people enter the church, they are warmly welcomed by teams of greeters, who make them feel at home and loved by God.

- ❖ Competent musicians who have been touched by God's presence lead the assembly in song.

- ❖ Lectors, extraordinary ministers of the Eucharist and servers abound. At present we have up to forty servers at our 11:30 A.M. Mass and twenty to thirty at the 9:30 A.M. Mass.

- ❖ Many baptisms take place in the context of the Sunday liturgy, where family and friends witness the power of the praying community welcoming new life in its midst.

- ❖ Communion under both species has become a traditional part of both Sunday and weekday celebrations.

- ❖ Prayer teams are available after Sunday Masses to pray with people who may have a variety of needs.

- ❖ Over fifty men and women bring Communion to the homebound and to the sick at the local hospital as an extension of our celebration.

- ❖ Twelve men visit the state prison on a weekly basis, sharing the power of the Holy Spirit and imparting a greater hope in God.

- ❖ At two of the Masses, the parish provides childcare for children who are under four years old. For children who are four to first Communion age, a children's lectionary is also offered.

- ❖ Often at the end of the Eucharist parishioners give witness talks, which may pertain to healing, reconciliation or new life received by participating in a particular group.

Realizing that the Eucharist is "the source and summit" from which everything flows (*LG*, 11), new parishioners are encouraged, at an introductory evening with the pastor, to make Sunday Mass a priority. From this source and summit we have seen a great growth in the celebration of the sacrament of reconciliation and a tremendous thirst to participate in the sacred Triduum.

Imagine being able to welcome over a thousand persons at the Holy Thursday Mass and then having over six hundred people march through the streets of the city as the Blessed Sacrament is carried to a neighboring church for adoration. On Good Friday over nine hundred attend the stations of the cross in the morning, at which time young people from the youth ministry dress like the characters of Jerusalem and lead us through the streets of our cemetery in prayer and song. Some seven hundred return in the evening for the celebration of the veneration of the cross. The Easter Vigil draws a full church, as every year many adults, young adults and children are welcomed into the life of the church through the RCIA process.

Members of the parish visit the homebound as well as nursing home residents on a weekly basis. Not only do they bring them the Sacrament but also keep them informed on the life of the parish, so that they will feel more connected to the community.

BUILDING PARISH LIFE THROUGH SMALL FAITH COMMUNITIES

Through the work of full-time evangelists, small faith communities have been established. At present over 180 parishioners meet weekly in homes to share and pray the Scriptures. Over a hundred adults meet weekly at a charismatic prayer meeting, and a number of Cursillo group reunions are held throughout the month. Vintage Couples (fifteen years married and more) and Cana Couples (less than fifteen years) meet on the third Saturday of every month to share a meal and their faith. Groups for the bereaved, for the divorced and separated, as well as for cancer survivors find a place at the heart of the parish.

Young families, young adults, men, women and young mothers have formed support groups to meet the needs of a growing population who want to connect more deeply with the church. An annual Family Day in June is attended by over seven hundred people of all ages, featuring teachings, games, athletics, historical walks, dinner, dance and card games for the elderly.

The parish has organized a variety of ministries that allow for diversity while at the same time creating a greater sense of unity. Experiencing Life in the Spirit Seminars are held for young people preparing for the sacrament of confirmation as well as for adults who desire to experience the power of the Holy Spirit in their lives. For those who may be at a different place in their spiritual lives, the parish has also offered seminars on the Ignatian exercises and Carmelite spirituality. One of the former convents (Joseph House) serves as a house of prayer, where a variety of contemplative retreats are offered on a monthly basis.

EVANGELIZATION AND CATECHESIS

As a result of our mission statement, the pastoral staff and pastoral council have felt a great urgency to introduce parishioners to solid Catholic teaching. We have opened a parish bookstore, offered catechetical programs on basic church teachings and held parish seminars in apologetics, featuring speakers such as Peter Kreeft, Scott and Kimberly Hahn, Father Francis Martin, Dr. Thomas Howard, Sister Ann Shields and Father Michael Scanlan. Every summer the parish has a "tent rally," at which time noted area priests and laity lead people to a renewed faith through music, Scripture and liturgical prayer and teaching.

The mission of our religious education programs has been to assist parents in their role as primary catechists. The process takes the four "pillars" of the *Catechism*—the Creed, the sacraments, morality and prayer—and over a four-year period introduces the parents, and they in turn their children, to basic Catholic teaching. The program is designed to integrate catechesis, evangelization, community life, ritual and sacraments. *The General Directory for Catechesis* tells us that "family catechesis precedes…accompanies and enriches all forms of catechesis."[1]

Catechesis involves all ages. Through the efforts of Mary Mosher, a mother and catechist, the parish has developed a Family-Based Religious Education Program, which has worked with hundreds of families, integrating the *Catechism of the Catholic Church* into the heart of family life.

For parents who are not as motivated or who cannot find the time to make such an extensive commitment, a religious education program is offered for all children, which once again attempts to integrate the needs of the modern family. This program also works to integrate catechesis, evangelization, community life, ritual and sacraments into the catechetical experience. For example, morning retreats are offered for the parents and their children who are preparing for the sacraments on a yearly basis, a Mardi Gras party and a Thanksgiving meal are held for the entire family, and prayer times are celebrated during Advent, Lent and May, when the family has an opportunity to gather for prayer and enrichment.

Every year the parish conducts workshops for adults on marriage enrichment, church teachings, sacred Scripture, prayer, spirituality and liturgy, theology and apologetics, the lives of saints and interpersonal relationships. Parish missions have been extremely successful in capturing the hearts of our people; days of prayer and renewal are held on a monthly basis.

An organization to foster the involvement of young dads as shepherds of their families has been extremely successful. Over a hundred men now make up the "Men of Joseph," a group that fosters weekly family prayer time, Sunday Eucharist as a family, the sacra-ment of confession at least twice a year, attendance at a weekday Mass every three weeks and a monthly reunion of prayer before the Blessed Sacrament every first Friday from 9:00 to 10:00 P.M. The Men of Joseph now sponsor the "Sons of Joseph," through which dads spend quality time with their sons camping, praying and socializing in the context of small Christian community.

Women's groups in the parish have flourished. We have a monthly breakfast, named "Women of Mary," where guest speakers challenge women to greater holiness as disciples, wives, mothers and daughters. A support group for young mothers, called "Mom's Connection," meets monthly. Teachings, socials, Scripture and sup-port are seen there as important components for growth in the Christian life.

Every year over 150 women who are part of the Women's Biblical Ministry attend a weekend conference on leadership skills and in turn help hundreds of women who are in need of physical, emo-tional and spiritual support.

In 1989 the parish hired a full-time youth minister, whose office presently coordinates all junior high, high school and confirmation activities. With the help of other adults, our total youth ministry program has evolved into a vibrant community where our young people are evangelized and catechized through weekly community meetings. This focus on the evangelization of our youth forms them in prayer and discipleship through prayer services, Life in the Spirit Seminars, pilgrimages to shrines, conferences at Steubenville East, attendance at diocesan and parish retreats, attendance at confirma-tion class, participation in work camps and working with the poor. Recently, through New Hampshire Catholic Charities, the youth office has initiated Rainbows for All God's Children, a support group for children and teenagers who have experienced the pain of separa-tion, divorce or death within their families.

THE EVANGELIZING PARISH AND WORKS OF MERCY

The parish also tries to reach out to the poor. An active St. Vincent de Paul community visits the sick and the poor, bringing them not only the Good News but also the basic needs of human existence: food, clothes, furnishings and a renewed sense of respect. Every Thanksgiving and Christmas the Vincentians distribute food and gifts to hundreds of families. The parish also owns and operates a St. Vincent de Paul store, which is open six days a week, to help those who are in need. The parish has also "adopted" parishes in South America and in Kentucky, where parishioners have become actively involved.

As well as the ministers of Communion, who bring the Sacrament to the sick and homebound, there are other ministries that reach out to those in need. An example would be the ministry to the grieving and to the deceased, which was developed and implemented through the parish's cemetery. A trained staff member at Mount Calvary cares for the grieving family and assists them in their funeral planning needs. Members of the Catholic War Veterans serve at all the funeral Masses.

SERVANT LEADERSHIP

Leadership is a crucial component not only in establishing the vision but also in carrying it out. A pastor is called above all to be a servant, to wash the feet of his people. Rather than an exercise in futility, leadership is based on the belief that there is a greater power at work within us. A priest has received extraordinary strength to capture the vision and to live the vision that is the kingdom of God. Paul sums up these vast resources in his prayer for the budding community at Ephesus:

> I do not cease to give thanks for you, remembering you in my prayers, that the God of our Lord Jesus Christ, the Father of glory, may give you a spirit of wisdom and of revelation in the knowledge of him,

having the eyes of your hearts enlightened, that you may know what is the hope to which he has called you, what are the riches of his glorious inheritance in the saints, and what is the immeasurable greatness of his power in us who believe, according to the working of his great might which he accomplished in Christ when he raised him from the dead and made him sit at his right hand in the heavenly places, far above all rule and authority and power and dominion, and above every name that is named, not only in this age but also in that which is to come. (Ephesians 1:16–21)

The world in which we live is alien to that call. It often mocks, degrades and confuses the role of a priest. Because of this, many priests have become confused in their role, many times living like bachelors rather than celibate priests. If a priest is confused about his role, imagine how the rest of the community feels!

A priest will not be renewed or empowered simply by taking more time off, delving more deeply into self or attending continuing education classes or convocations. A priest who strives for servant leadership will discover his true identity only by entering into the heart of Christ, the Christ who prays to the Father, who admits his vulnerability and who is empowered by the Spirit to bring forth the kingdom of God. If a priest is to be a servant leader, he must embark on that same journey and teach others by example that the kingdom of God is in our midst.

Regardless of the number of talented people who may be available, if a pastor is not present to his people as one who washes feet, a parish cannot grow. It has been my experience over many years of diocesan work that priestly leadership is vital for the spiritual and physical renewal of any parish community.

A pastor in servant leadership must believe in his staff, affirm them and be willing to trust in their gifts. He must work closely with his pastoral council, challenging them to help him in carrying out the vision that God has given the parish. He must shepherd his extended staff: the maintenance staff, the secretaries, the teachers in the school, the housekeeping staff and the volunteers. He must challenge them to spiritual growth and be with them in their pain and in their joy. A pastor, then, is called to *ignite* the hearts and souls of the people placed in his care.

Parish Spirituality

Spirituality is a particular style or method of following Christ. It has elements and a pattern to help people develop a deeper life in the Spirit.

For centuries many thought the only way to holiness lay in monastic life or in religious orders, which often adapted monastic spirituality. The word is out: Jesus wants *everyone* to be holy! Spiritual growth is for everyone, which means that the ordinariness of everyday life is meant to be caught up in the vision of Jesus and the power of the Holy Spirit. For that to happen, each one of us must hear the Good News and respond.

But growing into the magnificent people God created us to be is filled with obstacles and dangers. The parable of the farmer and the seed in Luke 8:5–8 tells us that sometimes the word reaches us when we are like rock or at the side of the road. Most of the time we fail to recognize the weeds and thorns in ourselves that can choke the life within us.

From time to time God brings forth men and women who are outstanding in holiness, who not only yield a hundredfold but often help others avoid dangers and cultivate their own hearts to yield the fruit of the Spirit. Holiness is all around us. One of the joys of shepherding a parish is discovering the many saints around us and learning how to tap into the richness of their spirituality.

Twice a year we have an evening for young married couples. Usually thirty to forty couples will come to hear a husband and wife who have been together a lot longer witness to the pains and the joys of married life. On one occasion a couple who had been married sixty-five years shared how they had never missed their evening prayer, with the exception of a few times when the husband had to be out of town on business. The young couples were moved and began asking them more about prayer.

On another occasion a couple who had been married for twenty-five years shared their regret at having used birth control as a means of avoiding pregnancy. To my great amazement, the younger couples began asking questions and relating their own discomfort at often taking on the values of the world rather than the values of the kingdom.

Parish spirituality means being open and alive to the present moment. The adult converts who assemble around the font at the Easter vigil are immersed in the baptismal waters of new life. The community gathers at the cemetery to pray with a young couple who recently lost their three-month-old baby. A group of women bake for the families who mourn their loved ones and then serve them after every funeral liturgy. This is all an integral part of parish spirituality.

The renewed parish seeks to help people discover God in all the ordinary events of daily life. We come together to celebrate our life in Christ at Sunday Eucharist, with all the messiness that such a communal gathering entails: families walking in late, babies crying during the homily, altar servers fighting in the sanctuary and the lector arriving one minute before Mass. Spirituality means learning how to follow Christ in the midst of the very ordinary turbulence of human life.

A DEEPER RELEASE OF THE HOLY SPIRIT

Another important element of parish renewal has been the development of the Catholic understanding of the baptism in the Holy Spirit. At times charismatics have unnecessarily alienated themselves from the mainstream of parish life by defining this experience too narrowly. For example, many deeply spiritual priests, bishops and laity have not been considered "Spirit-filled" if they have not completed a Life in the Spirit Seminar and spoken in tongues.

Unfortunately, this narrow view can quickly divide noncharismatics from those charismatics who believe they alone possess the fullness of the Holy Spirit. Power struggles often follow, with charismatics being pushed to the fringe.

I have come to believe that baptism in the Holy Spirit is a process of being totally immersed in the life of Christ. Our parish currently has two charismatic prayer groups: one adult group made up of about 130 people and a young adult prayer group consisting of about fifty to sixty young adults. The overall number of charismatics is small when compared to the twenty-three hundred registered families, who total between seven and eight hundred people.

Charismatic prayer groups cannot be clubs for the spiritually mature. They must be a part of God's great plan for his church. Their role is not to safeguard the spiritual gifts or to make the parish charismatic but to bring as many people as possible to a deeper love of Christ through the baptism of the Holy Spirit. Theirs is only a training ground.

It is my belief that there are many other ways within the parish community by which people can experience a deeper release of the Holy Spirit. Ste. Marie's offers Experiencing New Life Seminars three times a year. They usually take place on a weekend and are conducted by the office of evangelization. Hundreds have gone through these seminars and have been deeply blessed and touched by the power of God.

Another model we have used for many years is a novena to the Holy Spirit. For nine evenings we invite parishioners to attend a prayer service, during which lay persons witness to their lives in the Holy Spirit. The novena concludes with a Pentecost Vigil celebration, attended by well over one thousand people. We have seen noticeable fruit from these novenas.

Praying for the release of the Holy Spirit has become commonplace in our liturgical assembly. Often parishioners are invited to be prayed with after the Sunday liturgy. The Prayer of the Faithful often includes petitions for a greater release of the Spirit.

At Sunday liturgies the priest reminds the parishioners who are coming forward to receive the Body and Blood of Christ of their call to ongoing conversion: to accept Jesus Christ as Lord and Savior of their whole lives and to seek greater wisdom, power, healing and strength through the power of the Holy Spirit.

CONCLUSION

The vision and ministry of the parish community is to bring the light of Christ to all people. It is not a matter of having everyone at the same level of spiritual maturity or even of having everyone be faithful. It is simply a matter of revealing Jesus Christ to all and of meeting them wherever they are along the way. It is important for a community to remember, with understanding and compassion, the many tortuous routes that human beings take and to always respond, worship and teach through faith and love.

Developing a sense of community is at the center of our parish vision. Always remembering that we are not simply seekers after the truth, we are called to share a life together, a life with one another in Christ. Jesus Christ did not die on the cross and send his Spirit just so that we could be nice to each other, organize a lot of parish activities or commission groups who could take care of the needs of the poor. He died, rose and sent the Holy Spirit primarily so that we would know him and through him love the Father with all our hearts and souls and minds—and love each other with the overflow of his life in us.

The best of parishes will never be without its problems: its addicted and rebellious youth, its broken marriages, its forgotten lonely and people losing their first fervor of conversion. Part of the vision is that in the midst of the many people who are hurting, parish members can be found who are alive in the Spirit, mature, settled and convinced of the deep love that God has for all of us.

The priest or deacon must use every opportunity to evangelize and catechize, whether it be at the time of baptism, a small group meeting, marriage preparation or homily. Parish renewal comes about only through hard work, committed prayer and belief in a power greater than one's own. I hope our experience at Ste. Marie's proves helpful in your own efforts toward renewal. These observations are simply a feeble attempt to put on paper what I have come to believe so deeply in my heart: that parish life is not only necessary but more than ever vital for the people of our generation.

God has called us to a life of holiness. The word is out: Jesus wants *everyone* to be holy! Spiritual growth is for everyone, which means that the ordinariness of everyday life is meant to be caught up in the vision of Jesus and the power of the Holy Spirit. For that to happen, each one of us must hear the Good News and respond to it.

Father Marc Montminy
Ste. Marie Church
378 Notre Dame Ave.
Manchester, NH 03102
603-622-4615

CHAPTER 20

Evangelizing as a Parish

David Thorp

When Catholic theology thinks of the "local church," it turns its discussion primarily to the diocese. Where Catholics meet the "local church," however, is in the parish where they attend Mass, celebrate sacraments, grow in understanding the faith through religious education and spiritual development programs and reach out in service to others in a great variety of ways. The Catholic parish, present in almost every town or neighborhood, is also where most people who are not Catholic or who are not active in their Catholicism will meet the Catholic church—for the first time or once again.

In every town or neighborhood Catholic parishioners have the opportunity to present the gospel of Jesus Christ to others and to draw people into communion with God in a local parish. Having parishes become evangelistic, having parishes living fully the gospel and intentionally reaching out with the gospel, is essential for Catholic evangelization.

Becoming an evangelistic parish does not equate with doing evangelistic activities. In fact, it is possible to have a committed core of parishioners who are busily engaged in a variety of evangelistic efforts—home visitation, leading Bible studies, welcoming newcomers—and yet not have an evangelistic parish.

Herein lies the great temptation and, in the long run, the death of evangelization: to segregate evangelistic activities and those involved in them. Other members of the parish praise their efforts by exclaiming, "We are grateful for all that you're doing! We are so fortunate that you are such good evangelizers." Translation: "Boy, are we glad that *you* are doing the evangelizing, because that means we're off the hook!"

If evangelization is just another "what," just another activity that we do and not the "how" and "why" in every dimension of our corporate life, then a parish can easily remain essentially unchanged. Having parishioners involved as evangelizers is vital, but even more important is the need to articulate and implement a vision for the evangelizing parish.

WHY EVANGELIZE?

Vision is the starting point for action. I may not be able to articulate the vision all the time, but unless I am grasped by it—if only in a "I-can-feel-it-in-my-guts" way—then I probably will not be involved in action. But once I have been grasped, there is no stopping me.

Before getting a wide-angle picture of what evangelization is, there are some challenging questions to face: *Why do I evangelize? Why do I see evangelization as important to my life and to the life of my parish?*

If I have trouble answering these questions, I will certainly have great difficulty in evangelizing. Each person's answers will bear some similarity to those of others but also will be stamped with that person's unique relationship with the Lord Jesus Christ and with his or her own set of human relationships. Here are a few general reasons why we evangelize.

We do so first of all because Jesus commanded us to. He gave the church, on the day of the Ascension, "the unending task of evangelizing as a restless power, to stir and to stimulate all its actions until all nations have heard his Good News and until every person has become his disciple" (*GMD*, 28; see Matthew 28:18–20).

Second, we evangelize because we have become convinced that what we have to share is *Good* News—indeed, the *best*. We echo the words of Peter when many disciples of Jesus no longer followed him: "Lord, to whom shall we go? You have the words of eternal life; and we have believed and have come to know, that you are the Holy One of God" (John 6:68–69). We share the gospel with others because salvation is offered to every person in Jesus Christ, because in him people can be brought enlightenment and be lifted from error, because he bears a unique message (see *GMD*, 32).

Third, we evangelize because we are surrounded by people who are hungering, thirsting and literally dying for the Good News. While they may not express their need in such direct fashion, many are undoubtedly wondering to themselves: *Is anyone there? Does anyone care? Is there hope? Is there any sense and meaning to life? Is life possible?* When we have the answer for their questions, to withhold the Way, the Truth and the Life is to violate the rights of others and to place ourselves in peril, as Pope Paul VI pointed out so well in *Evangelii Nuntiandi* (80).

Fourth, we evangelize because of love for others. "Because we have experienced the love of Christ, we want to share it. The gifts God has given to us are not gifts for ourselves.... Faith makes our hearts abound with a love-filled desire to bring all people to Jesus' Gospel and to the table of the Eucharist" (*GMD*, 33).

VIEWING EVANGELIZATION WITH A WIDE-ANGLE LENS

Evangelization is growth up and out: *up* because it attempts to help those who are already Christians to make progress in the spiritual life; *out* because the church must reach beyond her existing membership and seek to add members to the body of Christ.

Those who have begun with the Lord need to renew their life in him in an ongoing way lest they grow stale. In the Christian life there is always *more*. Having experienced conversion once, we must be converted continually lest we become just "tired old believers."[1]

However, evangelization is not just for the sake of renewing the church or adding muscle to her own life. We seek renewal so that the church can grow out. A congregation of one hundred should be praying about and planning ways of adding twenty-five new members; a parish with five hundred families should be looking for ways of having six hundred. While we are not the lords of the harvest and cannot control the results, we can set our sights on steady growth. We do so not merely to add to our numbers and so become *bigger*; we do so in obedience to God and so that he may be honored more fully by the people for whom Jesus Christ died and rose.

When we think in terms of those whom the church is trying to reach, evangelization means *inspiration, invitation and perspiration*. The parish is trying to *inspire* its active Catholics to live fully the life into which they have been grafted through the confession of faith and their baptism. Many may be "simmering" in the Christian life, not allowing themselves to be grasped fully by the power of the word and Spirit, settling for less than the Lord offers. There needs to be a "fanning into flame" of the Holy Spirit in their lives.

The parish is also trying to reach out to inactive members, who for many different reasons no longer participate in the congregation's life of worship, teaching and service. Many adults send their children for religious instruction even though neither they nor their children worship with any regularity. We need to find ways of establishing contact with these people so that we can *invite* them into full life with the community of faith. In reaching out we need to listen to their stories: how they neglected their life of faith, how they were neglected by the community, how they walked away and how some believe they were driven away.

Then too the parish is trying to reach the increasing number of men and women who have no church community to call their own, who have no religious tradition or who profess non-Christian religions. Such outreach will cause us to *perspire*. If we are not willing to dedicate ourselves to the "hard work" of being faithful over a long period of time, even when we see little fruit, we will have a short life span as individual evangelizers or as an evangelizing community. One lay evangelizer sums it up this way: "If you want to evangelize, throw away your watch and stop counting heads."

HELPING OTHERS TO SEE WITH AN EVANGELISTIC LENS

To quote a pastoral worker who attended a meeting about evangelization, "I hate that word." Many in our pews are put off or confused about evangelization. While we should not give up the word, we can talk about evangelizing activity without ever using it. With this in mind, how can we point out ways in which evangelization is occurring and clearly name an activity as evangelistic?

One way to draw attention to this essential ministry is through the weekly parish bulletin. A number of brief pamphlets that describe evangelization can be used as inserts. Another way is to plant seeds in people's minds through a brief column in the weekly bulletin, something like "Sharing Your Faith" or "Reaching Out to Those Around You." One parish has developed twenty-six brief statements about evangelization. Along with a notice about specific outreach activities, a different statement appears in each week's bulletin.[2]

Evangelization can become part of the weekly public prayer of the congregation. Have people begin to pray specifically for individuals with whom they are in regular contact, that the Lord will bring them to a conversion of mind and heart.

Such methods raise people's consciousness about evangelization, reminding them that the life they have received is meant to be shared freely and generously with others. Challenge the worshipping congregation to look for opportunities to invite others to hear the gospel and be touched by the grace of God. Most people will not say on their own initiative, "This is a great parish. I think I'll tell others about it and look for ways to help them meet the Lord here as I have." They need to keep hearing this call and receive hints on how to talk to others about the Lord and his church.

A Catalyst for Parish Action

In my family it is everyone's responsibility to make sure that the house stays clean. But we all know what happens when something is everyone's job: no one does it because we are all waiting for the "other guy" to do it. However, with the right catalyst (almost always my wife or I), everyone gets to work.

Evangelization is the privilege and the duty of every Christian. But without a catalyst to help move a parish to action—specifically to pray and think about evangelization, to plan for evangelization, to recruit evangelizers, to help carry out special projects, to develop an evangelistic attitude in every ministry—very little evangelization will be sustained in the life of the whole parish.

A parish evangelization committee can be the kind of catalyst that helps move vision into specific actions. Recruit basically friendly people with these characteristics: an interest in parish renewal and growth; a personal conviction about the gospel message (you cannot share what you do not have); a conviction that they have something of great value to share with others; a desire to share faith; a conviction that life in Christ as a parish member will enrich and bless others; a concern about inactive or alienated Catholics and the unchurched.

Print notices in the weekly bulletin about the formation of an evangelization committee and extend a broad invitation to become part of the committee. Also be sure to issue a personal invitation (a phone call, a handwritten letter, a face-to-face conversation) to those who have the interest and the gifts from God in this area. Such contacts themselves provide wonderful opportunities for evangelism: to affirm people in their gifts, to call forth these gifts, to establish and deepen a relationship with an individual.

THINKING SMART: DEVELOPING A PLAN THAT WORKS

A plan is a guide that includes the goals and objectives of a parish, an assessment of current and future conditions and specific strategies and tactics for reaching those goals. A plan is a blueprint of how we can get from where we are today to where God wants us to be in the future. Some people think that planning and walking in the Spirit are diametrically opposed. They argue, "We want to be open to the movement of the Spirit in all that we do. We don't want to rely on merely human wisdom to dictate our actions."

People filled with the power of the Holy Spirit sometimes want to explode with that power. Explosions certainly create a sensation, but after the big bang the power may be all spent. What if we allowed the power to be channeled through a plan that allows for a sustained—yet no less powerful—burn?

Having a plan is akin to taking fire and placing it in a fireplace. The fire's glow and warmth, contained in the right place, are not diminished but are actually increased. We don't have to forget "explosions" entirely in our evangelizing activities (just think of the initial flare-up when a fire is lit in the fireplace); we just want to make sure there is a way to sustain that lighting of faith's fire with follow-up.

A plan identifies and clarifies the problems that can prevent the parish from growing and the methods that can be used to produce growth. Until we clearly understand our situation, we cannot respond to problems in an intelligent and creative way or take advantage of available opportunities. A plan transforms the dream into reality; a plan gives "legs" to the vision. You can inspire people to great things, but unless you give them the tools to implement that vision, nothing tends to be done.

A plan helps to prioritize the ministry objectives. Formulating a plan means that we are willing to say: Here are the strengths, the gifts we have received from the Lord; here are our weaknesses, the areas in which God has much work to do with us; these are the opportunities the Lord has given us to witness to and share the gospel; these are our present resources that we place at the Lord's disposal; these are the resources we need in order to accomplish God's plan for us; here is what we can do and cannot do at this time; here is what we must and must not do at this time so that we can be faithful to God's call.

Of course, if we had unlimited resources and unlimited time, planning would be unnecessary. Most of us, however, have obvious limits. We need to maximize the resources we do have, harnessing them for the service of the Lord and his kingdom. Planning helps us to reduce any waste of precious gifts: the grace God offers us; the talents he has placed in our care; the opportunities he has given to us; the goodwill and the assets of others who want to join us in reaching out to others.

Planning establishes responsibility and accountability. We take time to identify people who will help accomplish the plan, and we call them to move ahead in dynamic and creative ways. Giving them specific responsibilities also means that they can be made accountable.

How Can We Develop an Effective Evangelistic Strategy?

Developing an evangelistic strategy involves responding to the question, *What does God want us to do now?* There's importance to each of the four main elements of this question: *God, us, to do* and *now.*

God

Since the call to evangelize comes from God, we need continually to seek his plan for outreach in a particular parish. The question is not so much "What do *we* want to do?" as it is "What does *God* want us to do?" In responding to God's call to us, we need to discern *carefully* what God already is doing to call individuals to himself. Like Jesus, we want to see and hear what the Father is doing and then join in that work (see John 5:19–30). We need to move *confidently*, out of an awareness that God anoints with his grace all whom he appoints to a task.

Since God desires that others know the Good News through our efforts, he will grace us abundantly to share it with others. We need to avoid becoming so task-oriented that we neglect praying together and sharing with one another the good things God has done for us.

Us

Since God is calling *us*, we need to know who we are, how we have been gifted, what God has established in the parish at this time. Each person and parish is different. Congregations vary in size, age, history, finances, resources, leadership. Because of these differences, no two parishes have exactly the same experience of church life. And no two parishes have exactly the same opportunities to reach out to others with the gospel. There is no cookie-cutter approach to evangelization as a parish. Yet each parish, unique in its gifts and present opportunities, can be used by God to evangelize.

In order to come to a clearer understanding of our current parish situation, we need to focus on the positive elements in our shared life. These strengths form the foundation from which we reach out; these are the resources that God will use to bring others into a deeper relationship with himself and his people. God is not looking for *perfect* parishes and parishioners; none are to be found. He is looking for *willing* parishes and parishioners. If we waited until we were perfect, we would never even begin to evangelize. God simply asks us to place who we are and what we have been given at his disposal.

This aspect of the planning process need not be overwhelming. Much of this information is readily available or can be obtained with a minimum of research or a few "interviews" with staff members. You will be amazed to discover how many parishioners—even those who are serving on an evangelization commission or otherwise committed to sharing the Good News—remain unaware of the nature of the parish and what resources are available.

Understanding *us* can mean many things: taking a look at existing programs or resources; taking a look at parish priorities, examining how we make use of our time and money or how we employ our key people and our energies; taking a look at the parish's overall schedule in terms of busy times, times with less activity and annual events.

Specific questions can also be directed toward resources and possible avenues for evangelization. For example, what spiritual gifts are found within our parish, and how can they be used for evangelization? What existing structures within the parish can be utilized as entry points into the life of the parish? What vehicles do we have for reaching out to inactive and alienated Catholics and those who are without any church family to call their own? What natural contacts exist by virtue of kinship, occupation and ethnic background that might provide bridges for sharing the gospel and the life of the community with those outside of our parish?

The New Testament describes a common way of bringing people into the kingdom, one that could be called *oikos evangelization*. *Oikos* is the Greek word for "household." When one member of the family hears and responds to the Good News, often the whole family is brought into the faith community. If we view this concept in a more expanded way, we could consider others with whom we share our lives: those who live on my street or in my neighborhood; those with whom I work; those in my extended family; those who enjoy the same things I enjoy. How can these already existing relationships be opportunities to share the gospel with others and invite them to a relationship with God in our parish?

We could also take a closer look at the area the parish serves. How large is it geographically? Does it encompass neighborhoods, defined areas or subsections? Are there higher or lower concentrations of housing? Do we have a way to touch all parts of the parish? Realistically, what areas are possible to reach or more easily reached than others?

What is the total number of people living within the geographical boundaries of our parish? Has there been any notable change in the population: rapid influx, steady growth or decline? Has there been any significant new construction of single-family homes, apartments or condominiums?

What are the characteristics of the population in terms of ethnic groups, race, religious heritage, national origin, age? How has this changed over the past five, ten, fifteen or more years? How does the registered Catholic population compare to the general population: is it the same or very different? What points of commonality can be identified? How do those who actively participate in the parish compare with those who are simply registered members?

What are the socioeconomic characteristics of the population: How are people employed, what is the employment level, what is the extent of formal education? What churches and synagogues exist within the area? Who have they reached? How? Why? What other evangelizing efforts are being made?

To Do

When trying to discern where we would begin, there are a number of questions to consider. Our answers should be based on experience, either past or present. We cannot plan adequately if we remain within cloistered walls, behind rectory doors, within the church's meeting rooms. We will fail to help people see the importance of the gospel for their lives unless our planning is based on reality.

Of all the groups in our parish, which ones can we reach at this time? No one church can reach every group within a city or town. Certain churches are better equipped to touch some people than others. Keep this simple principle in mind: when launching a new outreach venture, target your efforts to those whose backgrounds are most similar to your own. Match up the parish profile and the community profile. It is easiest to reach those with whom you have the most points of contact.

Perhaps a parish could begin with a concentrated outreach to Catholics who are baptized but not actively participating in the life of the faith community. Perhaps an ethnic or racial link between parish members and the unchurched who live in the area may make this kind of outreach possible. Try to understand the level of resistance or receptivity of these groups to the gospel message. Why are Catholics separated from the parish community? How could they be invited to reconsider the message and life of the church?

Since the Good News is not just abstract doctrine but a real response to real people, it would be good to know more about their felt needs, concerns and aspirations. What are the pressure points in this group, and how does Christianity address them? Their needs may be *physical* (food, clothing, housing), *psychological* (to be loved, accepted, supported, welcomed), *spiritual* (hope, mercy, forgiveness, understanding Christianity or the church) or *social* (a place to belong or gather). What hopes and desires motivate this group, and how does Christianity fulfill or bring about the realization of that dream? How can we capture their attention?

In thinking about how we can communicate effectively with our target group, we may want to examine the dominant social dynamics and structures. In what sorts of groups do people tend to gather? Is the group we are trying to contact best reached by large meetings (parish missions, feast day celebrations, healing services, celebrations of popular piety), through small groups (prayer groups, discussion or adult education studies, neighborhood Bible studies) or one-to-one conversation?

What methods of communication would be the most effective? Is this group apt to be reached by print (mail, posters, newspaper, bulletins, brochures), by electronic media (radio, TV) or by personal contact (telephone or face-to-face)? Do people react more favorably to casual invitations or to more formal contacts? What has worked in the past as we sought to make our message and our programs known to others?

Now

The best goals, objectives and action steps are those that are SMART: *specific, measurable, achievable, reviewable and time-defined.*

- ✧ *Specific* means that we know who is going to be doing what and when they are going to do it.
- ✧ *Measurable* means that we have an idea of what we are trying to accomplish in some way that can be quantified; for example, we are going to visit fifty homes in the Green Street area.
- ✧ *Achievable* means that we do not seek to reach beyond our resources—leaving room, of course, for God to do wondrous things with those resources and our willingness to reach out to others. "Our parish will reach the world for Christ" is not an achievable goal.

↬ *Reviewable* means that we are able to analyze and learn from our outreach so that we can better plan and expand our efforts.

↬ *Time-defined* means that our plan has a beginning and an end. If not, we may never get started at all. Having an end does not mean we will be finished with evangelization at some point but that we are able to finish one particular project and then move on to the next activity as God directs.

Every parish is called to be an evangelistic parish. However, this does not happen overnight or even over a few months. Your evangelistic parish will not be a carbon copy of the one in the next town. God wants to use every parish to reach its entire people—and beyond. If we are *willing* to be messengers of the Good News, God will send us to those who hunger and thirst for the Word of Life. If we are purposeful and deliberate without being in a rush, if we are zealous without being frantic, our parish can be transformed into an evangelistic parish.

David Thorp
Spiritual Life Center
P.O. Box 639
Medway, MA 02053-2121
E-mail: dmthorp@comcast.net

CHAPTER 21

Transforming the Sacramental Parish Into an Evangelizing Community

Father Ernesto I. Elizondo

The parish is the fundamental structure for the pastoral ministry of the church and one of the primary places where people can learn and embrace the Christian faith. We urgently need to rediscover the importance of evangelizing at the parish level, to transform the parish into an evangelizing community. Why this? The church is mystery and sacrament of communion (see *LG,* 1), and "the task of evangelizing all people constitutes the essential mission of the Church" (*EN,* 14). Therefore, the parish needs to be an evangelizing community.

The pope's call to a new evangelization urges each congregation to seek for new ways to *be* church and to fulfill the mission of the church in its entirety. When we meditate on the church's mission, we are focusing on the mission of the people of God, *our* mission. The church is not only the bishops and priests, nor is it the building in which we meet to worship. The church is the people of God, the body of Christ. The church is communion in the Holy Spirit.

We know that there is but one mission, *the mission of Jesus Christ* to bring the Good News to all people. We are ambassadors of the mission that Jesus himself left us. Ambassadors do not go to other countries to fulfill their own personal agenda. Every ambassador represents a particular government. As ambassadors of Christ, we are called to continue his mission and to fulfill it in its entirety.

Jesus is our example. He did not weigh all the options and personally choose what to say or do. His attitude was clearly one of submission to his heavenly Father: "My food is to do the will of him who sent me" (John 4:34); "I always do what is pleasing to him" (John 8:29). Jesus in turn says to his disciples, "As the Father has sent me, even so I send you" (John 20:21).

Jesus Christ has left us a specific mission to fulfill. It is not up to the pastor of the parish to choose the mission; he has the duty to fulfill the mission that has been entrusted to him—and to all the church—by our Lord. While we can distinguish within this single mission a diversity of ministries, we do not have the right to choose our own mission or adjust it to suit ourselves.

We as the people of God also need to view our call in an *integral* manner. We cannot fragmentize or mutilate the mission and pick and choose the part that we like the best. We are called to fulfill the *whole* mission of Christ. The Holy Spirit has been given to empower us to continue that mission.

We need to foster the vision of transforming each parish into an *evangelizing community* and all of our parishes into a community of communities or, as Pope John Paul II described it, a family of families.

WHAT IS EVANGELIZATION?

Many Catholics lack a clear and precise understanding of what *evangelization* means. We need this clarity in order to respond fully to Pope John Paul II's exhortation. We can distinguish four aspects of evangelization that are meant to follow one after another:

1. *Kerygma*: The first missionary announcement proclaims the Good News of salvation. It is realized through "the primary proclamation," directed to nonbelievers, to those who have chosen unbelief, to Christians who live on the margins of Christian life and to those who follow other religions (see *EN*, 51–53). This *kerygma* experience is the greatest lacuna, or gap, in the Catholic church; it is a void that needs to be filled in every parish.

2. **Ministry of the Word**: This is a dynamic process in stages:
   a. It includes *kerygma*, the primary proclamation, the rousing of faith.
   b. Continuous education in the faith, also known as "permanent catechesis." This should be systematic, well organized and gradual, complete and for all (children and adults).
   c. The liturgical function of the ministry of the word, when realized within the context of a sacred action, is an integral part of that action. It takes different forms, but the most important among them is the homily.
   d. The theological function: Theology needs to confront philosophical forms of thought, various forms of humanism and the human sciences and dialogue with them.

3. **The Entire Mission of the Church:** The mission of the church manifests itself in four dimensions of ministry: ministry of the word, ministry of communion (that is, building up community, *koinonia*), liturgical ministry and social action (*diakonia*).

4. **Social Transformation:** Building and establishing the kingdom of God by transforming the unfair structures of society by the power of the Holy Spirit.

When evangelizing, we need to provide each of these elements and in this order. They are not alternative choices. The church's mission of evangelization needs to be accomplished in its entirety! It is not enough to provide only sacraments, not enough to only catechize children, not enough to build small communities, not enough to engage in social transformation. All of these are important and necessary, but all are based on the foundation of the *kerygma*.

The primary goal of evangelization is to bring the Good News to others at every opportunity. It is not a matter of waiting for people to come to the parish but of reaching out in search of those who have left the church or those who have no church.

Sacred Scripture challenges each and every one of us: "But how are men to call upon him in whom they have not believed? And how are they to believe in him of whom they have never heard? And how are they to hear without a preacher? And how can men preach unless they are sent? As it is written, 'How beautiful are the feet of those who preach good news!'" (Romans 10:14–15).

It is important that all parishioners actively go out and share their faith, motivated and empowered by the Holy Spirit. Catholics need to be more active in using our feet and going out to preach the gospel to all the parish territory. An evangelizing parish is in a permanent state of mission.

To whom are we going to bring the Good News? Jesus said, "Go into all the world and preach the gospel to the whole creation"

(Mark 16:15). Within the scope of each individual parish, the "whole world" especially includes every person within the geographical boundaries of that parish. An evangelizing community should view these people as the primary recipients of the gospel message.

GO TO ALL!

The concept of "integral evangelization" means, first of all, that we need to bring the Good News to *all* people. We must begin by going out to all Catholics within the parish boundaries and inviting them to join the parish family. Statistics tell us that out of the approximately sixty million Catholics within the United States, more than half miss Sunday Mass. That means we need to bring back to the church those thirty million or more Catholics who do not regularly participate in the parish community.

Jesus tells us in the parable of the Good Shepherd that when one sheep was lost, the Good Shepherd left the ninety-nine and went in search of that one. When he found that sheep, he loved and healed it and brought it back to the flock. Within our parishes it is often the other way around. Time is spent with one sheep, caring for it and pampering it, while the ninety-nine are lost! Each one of us is called to go out in search of each and every lost sheep.

In the majority of our parishes, people come to church when they choose to and when they can. Many come with the idea of receiving a "service" and experience the parish as a "religious service station" at which they can quickly refill their spiritual gas tanks. They want to attend a parish where they can receive the best and fastest service: where the homily is shortest; where requirements for marriage and baptism are minimal; where the best choir sings and so on. In a word, many parishioners lack any sense of commitment and belonging. Many people attend the parish with the same mentality that can be found at a country club, where people pay a fee to receive certain benefits of membership. In our efforts to promote evangelization, we must bring Catholics to an awareness of the necessity for personal commitment to the parish.

GIVE THEM ALL!

People will ask, "What does the parish offer me if I return to the Catholic church?" We need to give them all, every dimension of the mission of the church. When we were baptized as children, we became members of Christ in his roles as prophet, priest and king. This fact tells us that the three main dimensions of the church's mission are the *prophetic* ministry, the *priestly* ministry and the *kingly* ministry. Every Catholic needs to be spiritually nourished through all of these ministries.

The prophetic ministry: Jesus the Prophet spoke in the name of his Father. The prophetic ministry of Jesus includes *kerygma* (announcing the Good News of salvation), a systematic and gradual catechesis, homiletics and theology.

The priestly ministry: Jesus the Priest practices his priestly ministry primarily through the liturgy and the sacraments. Jesus offered sacrifices to the Father, the ultimate sacrifice being his life. The sacraments and every other aspect of our worship celebrations define this dimension of the church's mission.

Unfortunately, the majority of our parishes are primarily liturgical and sacramental parishes. Their strength lies in providing this liturgical dimension of the total mission of the Catholic church, but to a certain extent they neglect the other three dimensions. Clearly the sacraments are vital and a necessary treasure for us as Catholics. *The Eucharist alone is the summit and source of the Christian's life* (see *SC*, 10; *LG*, 1). However, we also need to emphasize the importance of the other three dimensions of the mission of the church.

The kingly ministry: Jesus the Good Shepherd also exercises part of his kingly ministry, when we gather as a parish community, by uniting and congregating his sheep. Community, or *koinonia* in

Greek, does not automatically and immediately come into existence. Of paramount importance in our mission as followers of Christ is our duty to *build* community, day by day, day in and day out.

The fact that we attend Mass at the same parish and hold hands to pray the Our Father does not mean that we are already community. There needs to be a sharing of our lives on a deep level with our brothers and sisters in Christ. The experience of the first Christian communities, as recorded in the Acts of the Apostles, offers a clear example.

Jesus also exercises his kingly ministry through social action, *diakonia* in Greek. As Christians, we build a kingdom of justice and peace through serving the needs of others. This is clearly a desire within the heart of Jesus, as exemplified in his washing the apostles' feet at the Last Supper. Jesus came to serve, not to be served.

Through social action, a genuine liberation can come into being, with communities living new models of life, where a new world is built in fraternal solidarity. We as Catholics need to state and demonstrate a clear preferential option for the poor. We need to work toward the elimination of need, oppression and exploitation. This can be accomplished only by fostering gospel values within our society.

Involving All

For centuries we have believed that priests and religious were the only ones responsible for fulfilling the mission of the church. However, Pope John Paul II's call to a new evangelization has reminded us that sharing the Good News is the mission of the whole church. We need to be guided and led by the church's pastoral leadership, but every member of the church needs to participate actively.

Our mission as the people of God and the body of Christ is to evangelize: "They [the laity] exercise a genuine apostolate by their activity on behalf of bringing the gospel and holiness to men, and on behalf of penetrating and perfecting the temporal sphere of things through the spirit of the gospel.... On all Christians...is laid the splendid burden of working to make the divine message of salvation known and accepted by all men throughout the world" (*AA*, 2, 3).

Each parishioner has gifts and charisms for the building of the kingdom of God. Some are called to be evangelizers, some prophets, some pastors, some teachers (see Ephesians 4:11). What is important is that each of us discern and actively use these gifts. It is important that we give not only our talents but also a tithe of our money and time toward our primary mission of evangelization. If you spend forty hours at your job, a tithe or one-tenth of that time would mean committing a minimum of four hours a week to extend the kingdom of God, or perhaps one week per year to participate in an evangelizing missionary outreach.

We also need to help other members of the parish become more aware of the importance of our mission. We are called to be apostles of Christ not because of a shortage of priests and religious. Even if we enjoyed an abundance of priests and religious, the laity would need to participate actively in the mission of the church. Evangelization is both a duty and a privilege for every Christian. Pope Paul VI said, "Finally, the person who has been evangelized goes on to evangelize others. Here lies the test of truth, the touchstone of evangelization: it is unthinkable that a person should accept the Word and give himself to the kingdom without becoming a person who bears witness to it and proclaims it in his turn" (*EN*, 24).

TRANSFORMING THE PARISH

In order to fulfill the mission of the church in its entirety, parishes need a well-organized and systematic plan. The Systematic Integral New Evangelization Pastoral Process, which was initiated by Father Alfonso Navarro, M.SP.S.C., is now being implemented in many countries around the world. This plan is not designed for a particular type of parish—rural or urban, rich or poor—or for a particular country or culture or language. Since it presents the essential mission of the church, this plan can be implemented by any parish in any continent or country.

This pastoral plan begins with the experience of a Kerygmatic Retreat for people who are ready to listen and respond to Jesus' invitation to salvation and new life in him. At the end of the retreat, all are called to continue in their spiritual growth both as *disciples* and as *apostles*. This Kerygmatic Retreat is an experience of "the permanent priority" of the mission of the Church, for "in the complex reality of mission, initial proclamation has a central and irreplaceable role" (*RM*, 44).

After this experience—which in many cases is a life-changing experience—parishioners choose to live as *disciples* of Christ by participating in small Christian communities and by receiving a systematic and well programmed catechesis that they apply to their lives. The fruit they experience from encountering Christ in these ways is a renewed and revitalized sacramental life.

The call to be *apostles* is also emphasized. Those who continue in their small communities are invited to discover their gifts and to use them within the evangelizing parish. They are invited to be apostles both by giving a witness of word and deed and by committing themselves to mission in the parish. They will not only belong to the parish but will participate more actively in their parish in the extension of the kingdom of God.

Some may feel called to host meetings in their homes. For a month before Kerygmatic Retreats or parish missionary outreaches, home meetings take place to prepare new people to encounter the Lord. Others serve on home-visitation teams, which visit inactive Catholics in their geographical area and invite them to the home meetings or other evangelistic activities.

Once a year all who have accepted the call to the apostolate participate in a missionary outreach to visit as many people within the geographical bounds of the parish as possible. To facilitate this, the parish territory is divided into smaller sectors. The "apostles" invite those they speak with to come to a mission at the parish during the evenings that week.

If this pastoral plan has the full support of the pastor and is implemented in the name of the parish, it can succeed.

Father Ernesto I. Elizondo
St. Joseph Parish
Hwy 290 E, Loop 212
Manor, TX 78653
512-353-8969

PART 6

EVANGELIZATION AND CHRISTIAN UNITY

CHAPTER 22

Ecumenical Issues in Evangelization

Father Peter Hocken

We might wonder if evangelization is a promising field for ecumenical collaboration, given the fact that the Christian world seems to be polarized between two camps: mainline denominations, for which evangelization has not been a high priority, and the "nonsacramental" streams, for which evangelism has been a high priority and church has not. These latter streams include Evangelicals, Holiness Christians, Pentecostals and independent charismatics.

Positive relationships have been hindered by mutual disdain. Members of mainline denominations easily regard the evangelistic streams as bastions of "conservative fundamentalism," while the latter typically perceive mainliners as lost in "lifeless liberalism." Ecumenical relationships are further complicated by widespread anti-Catholic sentiments inherited by the "nonsacramental" streams, for whom the Church of Rome symbolizes the triumph of outward religion and thus "the false church."

It is not hard to see why evangelization is a difficult ecumenical issue. The Catholic church has dialogued with most mainline denominations that are not currently strong on evangelization, while the evangelistic streams have been suspicious of the ecumenical movement. The latter also tend to group Catholics along with non-Christians as targets for evangelism. Meanwhile, Catholics often see the "nonsacramentals" as sects to be fought rather than as potential allies of any kind.

How can we cooperate in evangelization across this major divide? Is there an ecumenical alternative to squaring off for a war of polemics between the Catholic church and "the sects"? I want to suggest that significant collaboration is possible; indeed it is already happening in a few places.[1]

WHY DOES CATHOLIC EVANGELIZATION HAVE AN ECUMENICAL COMPONENT?

First, Vatican II's acceptance of the ecumenical movement as a work of the Holy Spirit has affected all areas of church life. Evangelization necessarily has an ecumenical dimension, because ecumenism is a dimension of everything Christian and ecclesial.

Second, the rise of the charismatic renewal has made possible new forms of collaboration across the church-stream divide. The charismatic renewal has an inherently evangelistic thrust. Through it God has given vast numbers of ordinary Catholics an inner power and motivation to proclaim their faith in Christ to others. This inner equipping was not the result of any training program but flowed from the baptism in the Spirit. Evangelistic zeal was not so much the grace sought as the natural concomitant of a transformed relationship to God and to Jesus.

This current of renewal has affected virtually all church traditions, with the same grace being poured out on all. Charismatics quickly discovered that the new life they had in common could be exercised together. Not only could they pray together and share their witness together; they could speak together about Jesus to others. Thus the rise of shared evangelism was at the beginning as spontaneous as the desire to evangelize itself.

This ecumenical cooperation in evangelization has been taking three main forms. The first is the ordinary evangelistic outreach of ecumenical communities that have grown up within the charismatic renewal. The second is the formation of ecumenical teams for evangelistic work. These may be one-time events, perhaps organized by councils of churches or by an offshoot of an ecumenical mission, or the work of more permanent teams, such as La Tente de l'Unité in France. Catholics have sometimes participated in Billy Graham's campaigns, though this is generally limited to having Catholic counselors who can refer Catholic "converts" to Catholic parishes. The latter is really evangelical evangelism with an ecumenical follow-up.

A third pattern is of Evangelical-Catholic collaboration resulting from Evangelical Christians' rethinking negative attitudes toward the Catholic church. Into this category fall the initiatives of Evangelicals desiring to help renew the faith of Catholics and to train them as effective evangelists. The most striking example is in the work of Youth with a Mission (YWAM), which in several countries now has Catholics on staff and which has formed a specific branch for outreach to Catholics called "Kerygma Teams."[2] Another striking example is the ministry of Evangelical David Bjork, not a charismatic, who has worked for twenty years among Catholics in France, seeking always to explain his ministry to Catholic authorities.[3]

THEOLOGICAL ISSUES

I believe that the ecumenical sharing that has been developing in recent years is not an aberration to be corrected but a response to the Spirit of God. However, theological reflection on these developments is needed. I will try to identify the major theological issues involved.

The Distinctiveness of the *Kerygma*

Theologians and catechists today commonly acknowledge that Christian formation involves distinct phases, which can be described as (1) the initial proclamation to the unconvinced; (2) the preparation of the convinced for baptism and reception into the community of faith; and (3) post-baptismal formation. The greatest potential for ecumenical sharing is found at the first stage.

The New Testament indicates a basic initial proclamation of salvation in Christ (*kerygma*), often called the gospel or the Good News. The basic preaching of the apostles and disciples included these essential elements: the advent of the kingdom of God; the mighty saving deeds of God in history, reaching their climax in the passion, death, resurrection and ascension of Jesus; the return of Christ for judgment at the end of the age. This proclamation seeks to bring hearers to repentance and faith. Those who accept the Good News of salvation in Christ are baptized. They receive the forgiveness of sins and the gift of the Holy Spirit.

The twentieth-century renewal of the Catholic church, centered on Vatican II, involved a recovery of the distinct phases in Christian formation and thus a recovery also, though more gradual, of the *kerygma*. The stages in the RCIA are the most obvious example. The distinction of the basic *kerygma* from subsequent catechetical teaching is clearer in John Paul II's *Catechesi Tradendae* (25) than it had been in Paul VI's *Evangelii Nuntiandi* (22). More recently, it has been set out in the *General Directory for Catechesis* of 1997 (*GDC*, 47–49, 61, 88).[4]

All these documents reflect the Catholic concern to bring the gospel to bear on all aspects of life, and so they mean by "evangelization" something much wider than what most Protestants mean by "evangelism." However, they all recognize that there is an initial proclamation that is necessary and distinctive. *Catechesi Tradendae* indicates that this initial proclamation is ordered to conversion and precedes catechesis (see *CT*, 19, 25).

The recovery of the *kerygma* is not simply a work of theological research but an action of the Holy Spirit in the church. The Spirit is particularly using the new ecclesial movements to recover the *kerygma*, not simply in theory but in action.

First, the Holy Spirit teaches the Christian inwardly of the truths expressed outwardly in the word of God and the teaching of the church. The gift of the Holy Spirit, consciously received, both clarifies the content of the message to be preached and internally equips the Christian for evangelism. It is the Holy Spirit within the Christian who gives the desire and the capacity to evangelize. Only as the gospel message is brought to life within the Christian can he or she proclaim that gospel with faith and power. This is why exhortations to evangelize to people who have no personal testimony to conversion will have no effect.

Second, the *kerygma* proclaimed with faith has the power to elicit interior conversion of heart in others. The differentiation of the *kerygma* from subsequent catechesis holds the key to effective evangelization. The Christian evangelist is a herald (*kerux*) who announces a death and resurrection that have the power to produce the hearer's conversion—itself a death and resurrection.

The Basis for Joint Proclamation of the *Kerygma*

The degree of faith agreement necessary for jointly proclaiming the gospel will vary according to the nature of the collaboration: less would be needed for unofficial efforts, like the spontaneous initiative of a neighborhood group; more would be needed for official, institutionalized and ongoing collaboration, like an interconfessional missionary society.

For a more official outreach, we could take as the necessary content of the *kerygma* what Pope Paul VI described as "the foundation, center and at the same time summit of its dynamism," that is "a clear proclamation that, in Jesus Christ, the Son of God made man, who died and rose from the dead, salvation is offered to all men, as a gift of God's grace and mercy" (*EN*, 27).

The 1994 statement *Evangelicals and Catholics Together* (*ECT*) at least implies that joint proclamation of the gospel is possible.[5] The authors affirm together the contents of the Apostles' Creed. At the same time, they include a statement of the conditional nature of this agreement, one which could be used by all participating bodies in formal patterns of joint evangelism: "These differing beliefs about the relationship between baptism, new birth and membership in the church should be honestly presented to the Christian who has undergone conversion."[6] The ECT group signed a second statement in 1997, which affirms that "we rejoice in the unity we have discovered and are confident of the fundamental truths about the gift of salvation."[7]

Such joint proclamation is not possible with all Protestants: for example, with those of very liberal tendencies who deny central elements in the *kerygma* or with those who hold doctrines that deviate from the basic gospel message. Catholics are more united with Evangelicals and Pentecostals on the *kerygma*, where our characteristic differences of emphasis are complementary rather than inherently opposed. An obvious example is the Evangelical emphasis on the "substitutionary atonement" (Christ died in our place) and the Catholic preference for the language of "representation" and "solidarity" (Christ represents all humanity before the Father). One without the other leads to imbalance.

An ecumenical approach can help us as Catholics to see the links between doctrinal emphasis and evangelistic impact. In particular, it can help us to view more positively the Evangelical accent on conversion as a critical rupture with the past. Catholics need to recognize the necessity for a radical turning to God, one that takes seriously the New Testament teaching that spiritual rebirth entails a death to the old life and a resurrection to a new life of the Spirit (see Romans 6:3–11; 8:13; Galatians 5:24; Colossians 2:11–12; 3:3).

In fact, this death to the old life is at the heart of the sacramental symbolism of baptism and is expressed in the threefold renunciation of Satan and sin. Only converts who have experienced this spiritual death and resurrection and a radically changed life in Jesus Christ will have a personal testimony with the power to evangelize others.

The Relationship Between Evangelization and Church

Here is where we meet the most difficult theological questions. The Catholic church is concerned with affirming the full ecclesial instrumentality and context for the work of evangelization as well as the unique relationship of the Catholic church to the one church of Jesus Christ. In the Catholic understanding, the gospel is proclaimed by the church so that new life may be generated within the church for the church. This view affirms the maternal role of the church, formed and moved by the Holy Spirit. The evangelized thus have a Spirit-formed mother as well as a life-giving Father.

Perhaps the most crucial theological issue concerns the Catholic sense of the total inner coherence of divine revelation. For the Catholic, the divinely revealed Good News of salvation in Christ necessarily bears an inner orientation to the whole mystery of the church. Thus deficiencies in faith concerning the full mystery of the church can have a distorting effect on the basic gospel message. Consider, for example, the distorting effects produced by an individualistic view of faith. This concern for the inner coherence of all revealed truth was evident in the Vatican *Instruction on the Church as Communion,* particularly the observations on the relationship of papal primacy to ecclesial communion.[8]

The basis for anything separated Christians do in common is what they share of the Spirit in Christ. Catholic documents on ecumenism have emphasized the basis for this sharing in our common baptism. In the Catholic understanding this sharing in divine things is to be understood not in an individualistic way but in an ecclesial framework. That is to say, Christians act as members of churches or ecclesial communities, and their acts of sharing are instances of "partial communion" between separated churches or ecclesial communities.

Catholic participation in joint evangelistic ventures need not be seen as positing an initial nonecclesial stage of joint evangelism followed by a stage of separate ecclesial initiation. It can be practiced as a "partial communion" between ecclesial communities, leading to converts being received into "partially separated" churches and ecclesial communities. However, joint proclamation at the official level requires some agreement on these two points: evangelization as an expression of the church and an absence of impediments to converts' choosing the full Catholic process of initiation.

The coherence of the whole Catholic faith has important ecumenical consequences. This works both ways, for evil and for good. On the one hand, objective error, defects in faith and prejudice would operate to weaken and subvert an individual's faith, whether Catholic or Protestant. On the other hand, the authentic presence of Christ and the Spirit of God always works to increase the truth and life by which one is possessed.

On this basis we could propose a complementary principle: Wherever the Holy Spirit is at work in other Christians, and the reality of salvation in the God-man is confessed, there exists an inner orientation to the fullness of Christ. Such a perspective underlines the gravity of all prejudice and the grace required to overcome it.

Allowing the Holy Spirit to accomplish this work of grace moves us further along the path from sectarianism to full catholicity.

Ecumenical collaboration in evangelization represents an abandonment of competition as well as of attitudes of hostility and prejudice between the churches. As stated in *Evangelicals and Catholics Together*, "We do know that existing patterns of distrustful polemic and conflict are not the way."

We must also recognize, however, that ecumenical cooperation founded on a theology of partial communion more obviously applies to mainline Protestant denominations than to the Evangelical and Pentecostal sectors. The potential for collaboration could be evaluated by asking potential Protestant partners a key question: Do they understand that evangelization essentially means bringing a person into a local church as an expression of the body of Christ?

Here we need to take note of some significant stirrings in parts of the Evangelical and Pentecostal world in relation to church. Spurred partly by an awareness of the debilitating spiritual effects of rampant individualism and partly by the growth of "church planting" strategies, many Evangelical Christians have been paying more attention to the church issue. One of the fastest-growing sectors is the independent charismatics, sometimes called "nondenominationals," among whom one often finds a real tension that is not so obvious among Pentecostals and traditional Evangelicals: a tension between the desire to be (and "do") church as a covenant relationship in the body of Christ and the voluntary and competitive character of such assemblies that easily results in further divisions. While this new attention to church has an ambiguous side and is still far from the Catholic sacramental-liturgical understanding, it nonetheless marks a significant trend that could favor increased ecumenical cooperation.

Joint evangelism expresses in a visible way the reconciling power of the gospel being proclaimed. This proclamation is weakened and contradicted by competitive and polemical evangelism. Like any other ecumenical activity, joint evangelism brings to fuller expression the "imperfect" unity between our churches and ecclesial communities. Each expression of "partial communion" inevitably deepens that partial communion and helps move us toward full reconciliation and full communion.

Ecumenical learning is a two-way street. Working with Catholics who have a strong sense of church can help other Christians to consider with greater seriousness the church and the corporate character of Christian life. However, the growing Evangelical-charismatic focus on building the body of Christ can invigorate Catholics, whose emphasis on church can often be more external—whether institutional or sacramental. We all need to be reminded of the importance of living together in love, of team leadership and of reaching a common mind in Christ.

TOWARD AN ECUMENICAL STRATEGY

An ecumenical strategy for world evangelization would have two thrusts: (1) a policy of developing positive relationships with the most evangelistic non-Catholic Christians, helping them to become not less evangelistic but more ecumenical; (2) the firm rooting of Catholic evangelization in church renewal, of which ecumenism is an intrinsic dimension. Such a strategy would help to encourage and develop ecumenical attitudes within the Evangelical, Pentecostal and charismatic streams.

Most lasting changes in attitude begin through personal contact. At Vatican II the daily interaction between the bishops and the non-Catholic observers changed many hearts. YWAM's changing attitudes toward the Catholic church began through meetings between its Protestant leaders and charismatic Catholics. Other impetus for closer contact has come from collaboration on pro-life and other moral issues.

We cannot control or organize such openness to the Catholic church on the part of Protestant or parachurch bodies, but we can help the process by our prayers, our friendship and our assistance when invited. We as Catholics also have much to learn in order to collaborate with the Evangelical and Pentecostal streams. We need to be as well informed about what is happening in this dynamic sector as our ecumenical specialists are in regard to the "mainline" denominations. This is not easy, because their world is more fluid and changes more rapidly.

Finally, only a renewed church can evangelize. Only a renewed church will have the desire to evangelize. The only way that the Catholic church can stem the hemorrhage of baptized Catholics to other churches is through our own renewal. Only when Catholics preach a message that is as life-giving as that of other preachers and evangelists will the major motive for leaving be removed.

Unfortunately, division has led us to oppose and reject elements that belong to the full Catholic and biblical heritage. A heart for renewal means a heart open to all the biblical truth and life found among other parts of the body of Christ.

What appears to be a problem at first glance turns out to be a grace and an opportunity. Vatican II intuitively grasped this essential link between renewal of the church and ecumenism: that each tradition, including the Roman Catholic, needs the witness of the Spirit in other traditions for its own full vitality and vigor.

An essential element in this renewal is repentance for our failings in the past and the present. As a church we score more highly in modern times for rethinking our theology and adapting our structures than we do for publicly admitting our failures. This has important spiritual repercussions. Because an authentic renewal requires a change of heart before God, becoming an effective evangelizing church may require a corporate humbling before the Lord, along with the confession of our weaknesses and failings in this area.[9]

This radical link between ecumenism and renewal, between authentic ecumenism and authentic renewal, suggests that the Holy Spirit is challenging the Catholic church to trust in the power of the truth given by the Lord. In a context of deep renewal, ecumenical collaboration will lead not to the frequently lamented evils of confusion and false irenicism but to a greater sharing in revealed truth. Together we can make major strides toward the realization of the prayer of Jesus that "they may all be one" (John 17:21).

CHAPTER 23

A Great Springtime for Christianity

Eduardo J. Echeverria, Ph.D.

"God is preparing a great springtime for Christianity," our beloved John Paul the Great proclaimed throughout his pontificate of almost twenty-seven years.[1] To prepare for that rich harvest, the people of God, the whole church—especially the lay faithful, the Holy Father stresses—must be committed to the new evangelization. "The new evangelization that can make the twenty-first century a springtime of the Gospel is a task for the entire People of God, but will depend in a decisive way on the lay faithful being fully aware of their baptismal vocation and their responsibility for bringing the good news of Jesus Christ to their culture and society."[2]

If the new evangelization is to meet the challenge of this hour, the first and most urgent imperative is that the church must remain true to her *evangelical* identity. As Paul VI wrote, "Evangelizing is in fact the grace and vocation proper to the Church, her deepest identity. She exists in order to evangelize, that is to say, in order to preach and teach, to be the channel of the gift of grace, to reconcile sinners with God, and to perpetuate Christ's sacrifice in the Mass, which is the memorial of His death and glorious resurrection" (*EN*, no. 14).

In other words, the church will fulfill the task in which her deepest identity is based when she proclaims throughout the world "the full truth of the Gospel...with renewed vigor, '*Jesus Christ, the one Savior of the world, yesterday, today and for ever.*'"[3]

Pope John Paul II called his Christ-centered approach to the transformation of culture "the new evangelization." Why does he call this evangelization new? He described in *Ecclesia in Europa* the reason that comes readily to mind in reference to Europe, but surely a similar point could be made about America: "*the loss of Europe's [and America's] Christian memory and heritage,* accompanied by a kind of practical agnosticism and religious indifference whereby many Europeans [and Americans] give the impression of living without spiritual roots and somewhat like heirs who have squandered a patrimony entrusted to them" (*EE*, no. 7).

Significantly, there is also the advance of secularism, which includes a relativistic attitude toward truth itself, in the flow of the culture and society; gradually changing cultural institutions, such as marriage and family; and broader societal structures like mainstream media, political, legal, educational and health care institutions. With the Christian faith under attack by this advancement, many Christians have *privatized* their faith, adopting a "citadel mentality," retreating behind the walls of the church and hoping that secularization will not reach them. Thus:

> Many people are no longer able to integrate the Gospel message into their daily experience; living one's faith in Jesus becomes increasingly difficult in a social and cultural setting in which that faith is constantly challenged and threatened. In many social settings it is easier to be identified as an agnostic than a believer. The impression is given that unbelief is self-explanatory, whereas belief needs a sort of social legitimization which is neither obvious nor taken for granted. (*EE*, no. 7)

Alternatively, "European culture gives the impression of 'silent apostasy' on the part of people who have all that they need and who live as if God does not exist" (*EE*, no. 9). In sum, John Paul adds, "We are witnessing the emergence of a *new culture*...whose content and character are often in conflict with the Gospel and the dignity of the human person" (*EE*, no. 9).

Western culture is failing because its Christian roots are eroding. This failing culture has reached its lowest point in the emerging *culture of death*, which is antithetical to what John Paul II called the culture of life in the 1995 encyclical *Evangelium Vitae*. There are four specific roots of the culture of death: individual autonomy, a debased notion of freedom as detached from objective truth, the eclipse of the sense of God and, in consequence, of the human person and the darkening of human conscience—indeed, moral blindness—resulting in a confusion between good and evil in the individual and in society (see *EV*, nos. 19–24).

In short, the church is engaged in a battle for the soul of Western culture. What is the consequence of this conclusion for the church? What ought we to do in engaging this failing culture?

In response, John Paul II has provided us with an all-embracive "plan of action" involving the whole church in the whole spectrum of life and in the whole culture.[4] We are called to be the people of God at the *service of life*. We need to bring the gospel of Jesus to the heart of every man and woman. There is a deep spiritual hunger in every human heart "for fullness of life and truth."[5] In no uncertain terms John Paul boldly proclaims the truth of the gospel: Jesus Christ is the answer to the question that is every human life. "No demand…is more urgent than the 'new evangelization' needed to satisfy the spiritual hunger of our times."[6]

Most important for her overall approach to culture, the church must have a vision of how Christ relates to culture as a whole. The *culture* that embodies the *Gospel of Life* is opposed to the *culture of death*—abortion, infanticide, physician-assisted suicide, euthanasia, cloning, along with issues regarding bioethics, sexual ethics, marriage and family life.[7] Christians are called not only to be *against* these practices but also to be agents of Christ-centered cultural *renewal*. The church must evangelize—indeed, transform not only individuals but also cultural institutions and broader societal structures to support and promote the *Gospel of Life*. God's people are called to be in service to life by *building a new culture of human life*.

At the core of the new evangelization is the good news that *human life is a good, a gift of God*: man is made in the image of God (see Genesis 1:26), who is the crown of creation given dominion over all of creation (Genesis 1:28), possessing human dignity and incomparable value. Man's image was marred by sin but is "restored, renewed and brought to perfection" in and through the redemptive incarnation of the eternal Son of God, Jesus Christ (*EV*, no. 36). Pope John Paul II said, "All who commit themselves to following Christ are given the fullness of life…. God's plan for human beings is this, that they should be 'conformed to the image of his Son' (Romans 8:29)" (*EV*, no. 36). Furthermore: "The dignity of [human] life is linked not only to its beginning, to the fact that it comes from God, but also to its final end, to its destiny of fellowship with God in knowledge and love of him" (*EV*, no. 38). Thus, "the Gospel of God's love for man, the Gospel of the dignity of the person and the Gospel of life are a single and indivisible Gospel" (*EV*, no. 2).

In order to be fully equipped as God's people to be at the service of life, this "single and indivisible Gospel" must be taught and lived from the outset in the life of the family. Indeed, the family has a decisive and irreplaceable role to play in building a culture of life. Children must be raised with the understanding that *procreation* is about receiving, not possessing, the divine *gift of human life*.

Human life is not only a *gift*, however; it is also a *task*. Children must learn that in receiving this gift they have a concomitant responsibility to affirm and protect human life as a good by making choices that show respect for others, not only their rights. Indeed, chiefly they need to learn to make the sincere *gift of self* in being hospitable, engaging in dialogue and generous service, bearing each others' burdens and expressing solidarity with others. At the root of this self-giving is the divine commandment *to love, respect and promote life*, especially but not only where life is weak and defenseless, challenged by hardship, sickness, rejection and suffering. "Human life is sacred and inviolable at every stage and in every situation; it is an indivisible good" (*EV*, no. 87; see also nos. 52, 92–93, 96).

But the truths of this single and indivisible Gospel of Life must be taught thereafter "in catechesis, in the various forms of preaching, in personal dialogue and in all educational activity" (*EV*, no. 82). Yet there is more: the Gospel of Life should be culturally embodied. As John Paul II constantly urged, "A faith that does not become culture [that is, inculturated] is a faith not fully accepted, not entirely thought out, not faithfully lived."[8]

To that end we must support and express solidarity with agencies and centers of service to life—such as hospitals, clinics and convalescent homes—by emphasizing the intrinsic and undeniable *moral dimension* of their responsibility. In particular, to be actively pro-life for the common good of society requires Christian health care professionals—doctors, nurses, pharmacists, administrators and chaplains—to bear witness to the Gospel of Life in their respective areas of responsibility. This is in keeping with the Vatican II teaching on the role of the laity:

> Their apostolate is exercised…when they endeavor to have the Gospel spirit permeate and improve the temporal order, going about it in a way that bears clear witness to Christ and helps forward the salvation of men. The characteristic of the lay state being a life led in the midst of the world and of secular affairs, laymen are called by God to make of their apostolate, through the vigor of their Christian spirit, a leaven in the world. (*AA*, no. 2)[9]

This apostolate is particularly important today, given the current temptation of health care professionals "to become manipulators of life, or even agents of death." This temptation may be resisted by recovering the meaning of the Hippocratic oath, "which requires every doctor to commit himself to absolute respect for human life and its sacredness" (*EV*, no. 89).

Furthermore, Christians involved in the political, social and civic arenas of cultural life are also responsible for implementing the Gospel of Life by "shaping society and developing cultural, economic, political and legislative projects which, with respect for all and in keeping with democratic principles, will contribute to the building of a society in which the dignity of each person is recognized and protected and the lives of all are defended and enhanced" (*EV*, no. 90). Moreover, Christian scholars—philosophers, theologians, indeed all those intellectuals engaged in the study of man, at work in institutions of higher education, centers, institutes and committees addressing bioethical questions—are also obligated by virtue of their calling in Christ to contribute to building a new culture of life.

Last but not least, the intrinsic goodness and moral inviolability of human life is a fundamental value for all human beings, indeed for the common good of the whole of human society, and hence moral knowledge of this good can be had by the light of human reason.

> The Gospel of life is not for believers alone: *it is for everyone*. The issue of life and its defence and promotion is not a concern of Christians alone. Although faith provides special light and strength, this question arises in every human conscience which seeks the truth and which cares about the future of humanity. Life certainly has a sacred and religious value, but in no way is that value a concern only of believers. *The value at stake is one which every human being can grasp by the light of reason; thus it necessarily concerns everyone.* (*EV*, no. 101, italics added to last sentence)

Christians should therefore form alliances with all men of good will and sound judgment who share a commitment to the sanctity of human life, unconditionally respecting "the right to life of every innocent person—from conception to natural death—[as] one of the pillars on which every civil society stands" (EV, no. 101).

What is more, they should communicate this commitment and other moral principles on the field of rational debate, in the public square, dispelling the misconception that pro-life principles are a matter of *pure faith* rather than rationally grounded beliefs about human nature. In the words of Princeton professor and author Robert P. George, "These principles are available for rational affirmation by people of good will and sound judgment, even apart from their revelation by God in the Scriptures and in the life, death, and resurrection of Christ."[10]

Of course, the Christian urges his cultural cobelligerents to notice not only that biblical revelation enriches our understanding of human dignity but also, chiefly, that the whole truth about human dignity is revealed in Jesus Christ, God truly become man. In other words, "When he presents the heart of his redemptive mission, Jesus says: 'I came that they may have life, and have it abundantly' (John 10:10). In truth, he is referring to that 'new' and 'eternal' life which consists in communion with the Father, to which every person is freely called in the Son by the power of the sanctifying Spirit. It is precisely in this 'life' that all the aspects and stages of human life achieve their full significance" (EV, no. 1). In a nutshell, this is the *leitmotif* of John Paul II's call for the *new evangelization*, echoing Vatican II: "In reality it is only in the mystery of the Word made flesh that the mystery of man truly becomes clear,"[11] which is to say that there is no true self-knowledge apart from Jesus Christ.

Pope John Paul II summed up the call:

> Indeed, the Church's mission of spreading the Gospel not only demands that the Good News be preached ever more widely and to ever greater numbers of men and women, but [also] that the very power of the Gospel should permeate thought patterns, standards of judgment, and the norms of behavior; in a word, it is necessary that the whole of human culture be steeped in the Gospel. The cultural atmosphere in which a human being lives has a great influence upon his or her way of thinking and, thus, of acting. Therefore, a division between faith and culture is more than a small impediment to evangelization, while a culture penetrated with the Christian spirit is an instrument that favors the spreading of the Good News.[12]

This last point makes clear the intrinsic connection between the new evangelization and the commitment to the renewal of culture, indeed, the whole spectrum of life. This renewal is ongoing because it is caught in the eschatological tension between the present ("the now") and future ("not yet") dimensions of the kingdom of God until its culminating fullness at the end of time.

Eduardo J. Echeverria, PH.D., is an associate professor of philosophy at Sacred Heart Major Seminary in Detroit, Michigan.

313-883–8793
E-mail: Echeverria.eduardo@shms.edu

Notes

Introduction

1. Pope John Paul II, "The Task of the Latin American Bishops," *Origins*, 12 (March 24, 1983), pp. 659–662.

Chapter 1: John Paul II and the New Evangelization: What Does it Mean?

1. The present paper is an adaptation and updating of my article "John Paul II and the New Evangelization," *America*, 166 (February 1, 1992), pp. 52–59, 69–72.

2. Dogmatic Constitution *Pastor Aeternus*, chap. 1, in Denzinger-Schonmetzer, *Enchiridion Symbolorum, definitionum et declarationum de rebus fidei et morum* (1965), 3053. The

reference here is to the written Gospels, not to the gospel message.

3. English translation *On Evangelization in the Modern World* (Washington, D.C.: USCCB, 1975), hereafter abbreviated *EN*.

4. Pope John Paul II, Arrival Speech in Mexico City, May 6, 1990, *L'Osservatore Romano* (English ed.), May 7, 1990, pp. 1, 12.

5. Pope John Paul II, Opening Address, Santo Domingo, October 12, 1992, no. 6; English translation in Alfred T. Hennelly, ed., *Santo Domingo and Beyond* (Maryknoll, N.Y.: Orbis, 1993), pp. 44–45.

6. John Paul II, "The Task of the Latin American Bishop," Address to CELAM, March 9, 1983, English translation in *Origins*, 12 (March 24, 1983), p. 661.

7. English title "The Mission of the Redeemer." For text see *Origins*, 20 (January 31, 1991), pp. 541–568.

8. Pope John Paul II, Address to Italian Bishops' Conference, May 18, 1989, *L'Osservatore Romano* (English ed.), June 5, 1989, p. 16.

9. Pope John Paul II, Message for World Mission Day, October 21, 1990, *L'Osservatore Romano* (English ed.), June 11, 1990, p. 9.

10. *Christifideles Laici*, December 30, 1988, hereafter cited as *CL*. Text in *Origins*, 18 (February 9, 1989), pp. 561–595.

11. Pope John Paul II, Opening Address at Santo Domingo, 1992, 22; see also *Redemptoris Missio*, hereafter cited as *RM*, nos. 52–54.

12. English translation in *Origins*, 21 (May 16, 1991), p. 19.

13. *Origins*, 17 (October 1, 1987), p. 263.

14. Pope John Paul II, *Ad Limina* Visit of Puerto Rican Bishops, October 27, 1988, *L'Osservatore Romano* (English ed.), December 5, 1988, p. 14.

15. See *First Things*, 43 (May 1994), pp. 15–22.

16. Quoted by Pope John Paul II in Opening Address at Santo Domingo, 1992, no. 6.

17. Pope Paul VI, "Opening of the Second Session of the Ecumenical Council," *The Pope Speaks*, 9 (1963), p. 130.

18. Pope John Paul II, *Ad Limina* Visit of Bishops of Southern Germany, December 4, 1992, *L'Osservatore Romano* (English ed.), December 23–30, 1992, p. 5.

19. Pope John Paul II, To Italian Bishops on Liturgical Course, February 12, 1988, *L'Osservatore Romano* (English ed.), March 14, 1988, p. 5.

20. Ad Limina Visit of Polish Episcopal Conference, January 12, 1993, *L'Osservatore Romano* (English ed.), February 3, 1993, p. 6.

Chapter 2: What Is Our Message?

1. Peter Kreeft, "Luther, Faith, and Good Works," *National Catholic Register*, November 10, 1991, p. 8.

2. Peter Kreeft, "Protestants Bring Personal Touch to the Life of Faith," *National Catholic Register*, April 24, 1994, pp. 1, 7.

3. Pope John Paul II, "New Catechism Will Promote National Recatechising Effort," *L'Osservatore Romano* (English ed.), March 24, 1993, p. 3.

Chapter 4: How Must Catholics Evangelize? Evangelization and the Power of the Holy Spirit

1. Pope John Paul II, Valladolid-Valencia, Spain, September 23, 1991.

2. Pope John Paul II, April 8, 1987.

3. Cardinal Hyacinthe Thiandoum, Archbishop of Dakar, Senegal, Address to the Special Assembly of the Synod of Bishops for Africa, spring 1994, par. 7, www.ewtn.com.

4. Pope John Paul II, Address for the Fifth Centenary of the Evangelization of America, October 28, 1991.

5. Pope John Paul II, January 1993.

Chapter 5: The Fundamental Mission of Every Believer

1. Pope Paul VI, Address to the College of Cardinals, June 22, 1973, quoted in *EN*, no. 3.

2. Pope John Paul II, speaking from the Vatican, November 27, 1988, www.vatican.va.

Chapter 6: Go and Make Disciples: The United States Bishops' National Plan for Catholic Evangelization

1. *National Pastoral Plan for Hispanic Ministry* (Washington, D.C.: USCCB, 1988).

2. *Here I Am, Send Me: A Conference Response to the Evangelization of African Americans and "The National Black Catholic Pastoral Plan"* (Washington, D.C.: USCCB, 1988).

3. Robert Wuthnow, *Christianity in the Twenty-first Century, Reflections on the Challenges Ahead* (New York: Oxford University Press, 1993).

4. Dean R. Hoge, William D. Dinges, Mary Johnson, S.N.D. de N., and Juan L. Gonzales, Jr., *Young Adult Catholics, Religion in the Culture of Choice* (Notre Dame, Ind.: University of Notre Dame Press, 2001).

5. Wade Clark Roof, *A Generation of Seekers: The Spiritual Journeys of the Baby Boom Generation* (San Francisco: Harper Collins, 1993), p. 176.

6. Roof, p. 233.

7. William V. D'Antonio, James D. Davidson, Dean R. Hoge, and Katherine Meyer, *American Catholics, Gender, Generation, and Commitment* (New York: Altamira, 2001), p. 43.

8. See *The Unchurched American* (Washington, D.C.: The Paulist National Catholic Evangelization Association, 1988), introductory summary.

9. Winseman, Albert, "How Many Americans are 'Unchurched'?" The Gallup Poll, (October 11, 2005), www.Gallup.com.

Chapter 7: Evangelization and the Experience of Initiation in the Early Church

1. Paul F. Bradshaw, *The Search for the Origins of Christian Worship* (New York: Oxford University, 1992), pp. 161–184.

2. *Dialogue with Trypho* 29:1.

3. *On Jeremiah* 2:3.

4. *On the Trinity* 2:12.

5. *Catechetical Lectures* 16:6, hereafter cited as *CL*.

6. More extensive biblical and the postbiblical evidence is presented in Kilian McDonnell and George Montague, *Christian Initiation and Baptism in the Holy Spirit: Evidence from the First Eight Centuries* (Collegeville, Minn.: Liturgical, 1991). I am not entering into the exegetical material but refer the

reader to the first section of the book, pp. 3–80, where the biblical witness is laid out. A popular presentation of the same material is found in Kilian McDonnell and George Montague, eds., *Fanning the Flame: What Does Baptism in the Holy Spirit Have to Do with Christian Initiation?* (Collegeville, Minn.: Liturgical, 1991).

7. *On Baptism* 1:1.

8. *The Prescription Against Heretics* 32:1; *Against Marcion* 4:5, 3; 4:29.

9. He protests against infant baptism. *On Baptism* 18.

10. *On Baptism* 20.

11. Tertullian writes as a Catholic; this treatise contains no hint of his later Montanism.

12. *On John* 6:33.

13. *On John* 6:33.

14. *On John* 6:33.

15. Basil, *On the Holy Spirit* 29:73. After his death Origen's speculations, which went unchallenged during his lifetime, were dogmatized, which brought down condemnations, now seen as largely unjustified. His doctrine of baptism was never challenged, either during his lifetime or after his death. He was one of the most influential theologians in the East during the first thousand years.

16. Hilary, *Tract on the Psalms* 64:14.

17. Hilary, *Tract on Psalm 118*, 12, 4.

18. *On the Trinity* 8:30.

19. *On the Trinity* 2:35.

20. *CL* 16:22.

21. *CL* 16:22.

22. Both occur in *CL* 16:12.

23. *CL* 16:22.

24. *CL* 16:26.

25. *CL* 17:14.

26. *CL* 17:15.

27. *CL* 17:18.

28. *CL* 17:19.

29. *CL* 17:35.

30. *CL* 16:6.

31. *CL* 17:37.

32. *CL* 18:32.

33. *On the Holy Spirit* 26:61.

34. *On the Holy Spirit* 26:61.

35. *On the Holy Spirit* 9:23.

36. *Fifth Theological Discourse* 28.

37. *Fifth Theological Discourse* 29.

38. *On 1 Corinthians* 29.

39. *On Romans* 14.

40. *On 1 Corinthians* 29.

41. *On Romans* 14.

42. *On 1 Corinthians* 32.

43. *On 1 Corinthians* 36.

44. *Discourses* 9:263.

45. *Discourses* 9:289.

46. *Discourses* 2:27. Letter of Sebastian Brock, Oriental Institute Oxford, May 27, 1990, to Kilian McDonnell. Brock also thinks that Joseph Hazzaya (Abdisho) implies the charisms.

47. *Dialogues and Treatises* 10:117.

48. *Dialogue on the Soul and the Passions* 9, 10.

49. *History of the Monks in Syria*, Prologue, 8, 10.

50. *On Prayer* 25.

51. See A. Mingana, *Early Christian Mystics* (Cambridge: Heffner, 1934), pp. 165–167.

52. *The Holy Spirit in the Syrian Baptismal Tradition*, Syrian Church Series 9 (Kottayam, Kerala, India, 1979), p. 134.

53. *The Holy Spirit in the Syrian Baptismal Tradition*, pp. 137–139.

54. S. Brock, *Spirituality in the Syriac Tradition* (Kerala, India: St. Ephrem Ecumenical Research Institute, 1989), p. 74.

Chapter 8: The New Evangelization in Africa

1. Ralph M. Wiltgen, *Gold Coast Mission History 1471–1880* (Techny, Ill.: Divine Word, 1956).

2. Allister MacMillan, *The Red Book of West Africa* (London: Frank Cass, 1968), p. 142.

3. Similar conversions of chiefs and their baptisms took place in the Congo (King Alfonso I in 1491), Zimbabwe (the king of the Mistapa kingdom in 1560), Nigeria (chief of Benin in 1491) and the king of Mombasa, who later became a Muslim sultan.

4. Wiltgen, pp. 12–13.

5. Wiltgen, p. 25.

6. In 1622 Pope Gregory XV founded the Congregation for the Propagation of the Faith (*Propaganda Fide*) to direct and to supervise mission work. It was to this congregation that all matters about missions were to be referred.

7. Wiltgen, p. 29. It is not clear whether the vicar's evaluation of the missionary labors of the Portuguese missionaries in El Mina can be applied to other situations and places of Portuguese evangelization, such as São Tomé, Congo, Benin, Gambia, Liberia, Tanzania and Zimbabwe. The case of Angola, however, is exceptional, for Angolans, taken to Lisbon and baptized there, returned later to serve as catechists. Accordingly, already in 1596, Angola had a diocese (see *Guida delle Missioni Cattoliche 2005* [Vatican: Congregation of the Propagation of the Faith, 2005]).

8. Wiltgen, pp. 52–53.

9. Wiltgen, p. 55. Several other places, for various reasons, also experienced breaks and interruptions in their missionary work. For example,

   ⮡ A Monophysite mission, which had been in the Sudan since the sixth century, would be interrupted in the thirteenth century (1275–1325) by Muslim Arabs. Mission work would resume under the Comboni missionaries in the nineteenth century.

   ⮡ Portuguese Augustinians, who had established convents in Tanzania in 1449, would be expelled by Arabs in 1698. The mission would be revived only in 1860 by the bishop of Réunion.

   ⮡ The Portuguese mission in Zimbabwe would be interrupted by the chief at the instigation of Muslim traders. Christianity would disappear between 1609 and 1759.

- ◈ The sixteenth-century Portuguese mission in Mombasa would be interrupted and persecuted when the baptized chief converted to Islam and became a sultan.

- ◈ Like El Mina, the Portuguese mission and church at Mossel Bay would be overrun by Protestantism, and South Africa would not be accessible to Catholicism until the nineteenth century, with the arrival in 1804 of three Dutch priests in the Cape.

10. See the case of South Africa cited in note above.

11. In 1856 a French bishop who had returned to France from India founded at Lyons a congregation of missionary priests and brothers for missionary work among the "most deprived" (*les plus abandonnés*). He was Bishop Marion de Bresillac, and his missionary congregation was the Society of the African Missions, known as S.M.A. for the order's name in Latin, *Societas Missionum ad Afros*. See Patrick Gantly, *Mission to West Africa 1: The Story of the Society of African Missions (S.M.A.), 1856–1907* (Brighton, U.K.: Pen, 1999); Jan van Brakel, *The First 25 Years of S.M.A. Missionary Presence in the Gold Coast (1880–1905)* (Nymegen: n.p., 1992).

12. Sir William Marshall was a Scottish Anglican minister who converted to Catholicism but remained in the lay state on account of an amputated arm. He served the British colonial government in the Gold Coast Colony as chief magistrate and a judicial assessor (see van Brakel, pp. 9–10).

13. Wiltgen, pp. 133–134.

14. Wiltgen, p. 138.

15. Wiltgen, p. 141.

16. *Fante* is a language spoken in and around El Mina and most of the coastal settlements of the Gold Coast (Ghana).

17. The arrival at almost the same time of Protestant Reformation groups and Catholic missionaries in the eighteenth through twentieth centuries meant that Catholic converts in Africa, by contrast with their European counterparts, made contact early with the Bible through their Protestant neighbors. This Catholic contact with the Bible was, however, not officially recognized and reckoned with. This exposed Catholics to Protestant interpretations of passages.

18. The report about a Capuchin school program on the west coast of the Gold Coast in the seventeenth century is instructive: "With surprising rapidity the children learned the Apostles' Creed, the Our Father, the Hail Mary and other prayers. Adults had classes too. As the catechetical instructions progressed, more and more were received into the Church by the saving waters of baptism. The priest's absolving hand again and again was raised over penitents who had made an intelligent and contrite confession, and Our Lord through the Sacrament of the Holy Eucharist came to dwell in their hearts" (Wiltgen, p. 43).

19. Otherwise, how was it possible for Rwanda, whose population is 47.3 percent Catholic, to sink so low into internecine carnage? At the outbreak of the "bush wars" of Liberia and Sierra Leone too, missionary sisters who were fleeing the war could identify some of the soldier rebels as former students of their Catholic schools.

    It is also the case that educated and articulate lay men and women cannot always easily bridge the gap between their faith and life; and in the houses of formation and studies, there are priests, seminarians and religious who need to ground their studies and vocation in conversion experiences and personal love for Christ.

20. Cardinal Joseph Ratzinger, "The New Evangelization: Building the Civilization of Love," Address to Catechists and Religion Teachers, Jubilee of Catechists, December 12, 2000, www.ratzingerfanclub.com.

21. See Ratzinger, section 1, no. 1.

22. Some churches are as big as 40 to 50 percent of the national population, such as Angola (49 percent), Uganda (43 percent), Rwanda (47 percent), Mozambique (53 percent), Gabon (44 percent), Democratic Republic of the Congo (49 percent), Congo Brazzaville (48 percent) and Equatorial Guinea (93 percent). Some have become self-reliant in their personnel needs, having a fully local clergy with little or no missionary help (Nigeria, Ghana, Uganda and Democratic Republic of the Congo). Others, however, have small Catholic populations and still depend heavily on missionaries (Botswana, Republic of South Africa and the Islamic countries of the northern and northeastern parts of the continent). See *Guida delle Missione Cattoliche, 2005* (Rome: Congregazione Pro Gentium Evangelizatione, 2005).

23. See Pope John Paul II, *Crossing the Threshold of Hope* (New York: Knopf, 1994), p. 102.

24. See *Guida delle Missioni Cattoliche, 2005.*

25. This represents a consistent increase from 55 million (12.4 percent) in 1978 to 144 million (17 percent) in 2003, and now 146 million (20.3 percent) in 2005. According to *New People* (No. 91, July–August 2004), a magazine of the Comboni missionaries, the total population of the continent stands at 862 million. Of this number only 16.6 percent are Catholic, 16.6 percent constitute the other Christians, 40 percent are Muslims, and 26.7 percent adhere to traditional religions.

26. See "Address of Pope John Paul II to the Sixth Meeting of the Council of the General Secretariat of the Synod of Bishops of the Special Assembly for Africa in Luanda," June 9, 1992, quoted by Bishop Anthony Gbuji in *New Evangelization in Nigeria: A Pastoral Contribution to the Synod for Africa* (Onitsha, Nigeria: EMMAUS, 1994), p. 1. See also *EN*, 13–15.

27. In Ghana the African Synod and its vision of new evangelization and renewal for the church have inspired almost every diocesan synod that has been held. In 1994 the diocese of Kumasi held a synod with the theme "The Evangelizing Mission of the Church in Kumasi Diocese." In 1996–1997 the archdiocese of Accra celebrated a synod with the theme "Renewal of Evangelization in the Archdiocese of Accra." In 1997 the Ghanaian Catholic Church held a pastoral congress to "implement with great fidelity the decisions and orientations" in the post-synodal exhortation *Ecclesia in Africa*. In October of the same year the new diocese of Keta-Akatsi held a pastoral congress on "The Church of Keta-Akatsi and Its Evangelizing Mission." From 1995 to 1998 the diocese of Wa deliberated in synod the theme "Let Evangelization Shine Forth in a Renewed Life of Faith." In August 2000 the diocese of Ho gathered in synod with the theme "Effective Evangelization for Living the Christian Calling in the Third Millennium." In the same year the diocese of Sunyani held a synod with the theme "Renewal for a New Millennium: Proclamation of the Faith to a New Generation," and in December 2000 the diocese of Navrongo-Bolgatanga also gathered in a synod to consider "Walking Together to Fulfill the Mission of Christ." In 2004 the diocese of Koforidua gathered in synod to explore "The Church as Family of God and Its Evangelizing Mission." Finally, the archdiocese of Cape Coast hosted a synod in July 2005 under the banner "'Lord, that I

may see!' Toward a New Vision of the Evangelizing Mission of the Church in the Archdiocese of Cape Coast."

Chapter 9: Which Churches Are Growing and Why?

1. C. Peter Wagner, *Your Church Can Grow: Seven Vital Signs of a Healthy Church* (Ventura, Calif.: Regal, 1976), pp. 124–125.

2. Wagner, pp. 69–155.

3. Dean Kelley, *Why Conservative Churches Are Growing: A Study in Sociology of Religion* (New York: Harper Collins, 1972).

4. Wagner, pp. 38–39.

5. Carl George, "Selecting Leaders," *How to Plant a Church*, Fuller Theological Seminary church growth lectures (1983), p. 637.

6. David B. Barrett, *World Christian Encyclopedia: A Comparative Survey of Churches and Religion in the Modern World, A.D. 1900–2000* (New York: Oxford University Press, 2001).

7. David Barrett, George T. Kurian and Todd Johnson, *World Christian Encyclopedia: A Comparative Survey of Churches and Religions in the Modern World, 2nd ed., 2 vols.* (New York: Oxford University Press, 2001).

8. Barrett (1982), p. 14.

9. These figures appear in an article by David Barrett, Todd Johnson and Peter F. Crossing in *The International Bulletin of Missionary Research*, Vol. 29, No. 1 (January 2005), pp. 27–30.

10. See Vinson Synan, *In the Latter Days: The Outpouring of the Holy Spirit in the Twentieth Century* (Ann Arbor, Mich.: Servant, 1984), pp. 12–19.

11. Barrett (1982), p. 6.

12. For the relationship between the church-growth movement and the Pentecostals, see Grant McClung, *Azusa Street and Beyond* (South Plainfield, N.J.: Bridge, 1986), pp. 109–132.

13. John Wimber, *Power Evangelism* (San Francisco, Calif.: Harper & Row, 1986), pp. 15–31.

14. For a discussion of reasons for Pentecostal growth, see Vinson Synan's "Pentecostalism: Varieties and Contributions," in *Pneuma: The Journal of the Society for Pentecostal Studies* 9, no. 1 (Spring 1987), pp. 31–39.

15. Barrett (1982), p. 6.

16. Wagner, p. 28.

Chapter 10: Six Steps to Effective Evangelization

1. *Religion in America*, The Gallup Report No. 222, March 1984.

2. M. Scott Peck, *The Road Less Traveled* (New York: Simon and Schuster, 2003), p. 81.

Chapter 11: Employing Charisms in Evangelization

1. Pope Paul VI, pontifical audience of October 16, 1974, quoted in Kilian McDonnell, ed., *Open the Windows: The Popes and the Charismatic Renewal* (South Bend, Ind.: Greenlawn, 1989), p. 8.

2. *L'Osservatore Romano*, March 16, 1994.

Chapter 13: Preaching Evangelistic Homilies

1. Billy Graham, quoted in *Newsweek*, April 11, 2005, p. 53.

Chapter 17: Evangelizing in Business and Government

1. *The Cloud of Unknowing* (New York: Paulist, 1981), pp. 188–189.

Chapter 19: The Story of an Evangelizing Parish

1. Congregation for the Clergy, *General Directory for Catechesis*, approved by Pope John Paul II August 11, 1997, 226. See *Matthew 5:48*; *LG*, 11, 40b, 42e.

Chapter 20: Evangelizing as a Parish

1. Benedict Groeschel, "On-going Conversion: The Challenge and the Chore," *New Catholic World* 229, no. 1370 (March/April 1986), pp. 57–60.

2. Three publications from St. Anthony Messenger Press are recommended: *Ten Top Reasons to Be Catholic* by Kathy Coffey; *The Mission of Christ the Redeemer: Key Passages of Pope John Paul II's Redemptoris Missio: On the Permanent Validity of the Church's Missionary Mandate*; and *How to Share Your Faith Today: A Short Course for Modern Evangelizers* by Jack Wintz, O.F.M. In addition, there is a fine article by Father Tom Forrest, C.SS.R., "Twenty Little Thoughts about Evangelization," that is available from Evangelization 2000, 3112 7th St., NE, Washington, DC 20017. For a revised version of the twenty-six bulletin inserts, contact David Thorp at Marian Community, P. O. Box 639, Medway, MA 02052.

Chapter 22: Ecumenical Issues in Evangelization

1. For the full text of the original paper, see *One in Christ*, 31 (January 1995).

2. For the origins of this development see Peter Hocken, "Youth with a Mission," *Pneuma*, 16 (1994), pp. 265–270.

3. See David E. Bjork, *Unfamiliar Paths: The Challenge of Recognizing the Work of Christ in Strange Clothing* (Pasadena, Calif.: William Carey Library, 1997).

4. On magisterial teaching on the stages in evangelization, see Peter Hocken, *Blazing the Trail* (Stoke-on-Trent: Alive, 2001), pp. 142–150.

5. "Evangelicals and Catholics Together: The Christian Mission in the Third Millennium," *First Things*, 43 (May 1994), pp. 15–23.

6. An Irish adaptation, *Evangelicals and Catholics Together in Ireland* added "We repent together" and "We pray together" to the five statements of common action.

7. "The Gift of Salvation," *First Things*, 79 (January 1998), pp. 20–23.

8. The Congregation for the Doctrine of the Faith, "Letter to the Bishops of the Catholic Church on Some Aspects of the Church Understood as Communion," June 15, 1992.

9. The necessity of a Catholic confession of sin, particularly for the sins against unity, was urged by John Paul II in his encyclical letter *Ut Unum Sint*, May 25, 1995, 34–35.

Chapter 23: A Great Springtime for Christianity

1. See Pope John Paul II, *Springtime of Evangelization: The Complete Texts of the Holy Father's 1998 Ad Limina Addresses to the Bishops of the United States*, Father Thomas D. Williams, ed. (San Francisco: Ignatius, 1999), p. 38.

2. *Springtime of Evangelization*, p. 89.

3. *Springtime of Evangelization*, pp. 40, 42.

4. *Springtime of Evangelization*, pp. 59, 76; see also *EV*, nos. 78–101.

5. *Springtime of Evangelization*, p. 56.

6. *Springtime of Evangelization*, p. 148; see also pp. 44, 58, 85.

7. *Springtime of Evangelization*, pp. 148–149.

8. John Paul II, Letter Instituting the Pontifical Council for Culture, May 20, 1982, AAS LXXIV (1982), 683–688, as cited in Pontifical Council for Culture, "Towards a Pastoral Approach to Culture," May 23, 1999, no. 1.

9. Austin P. Flannery, *Documents of Vatican II* (Grand Rapids, Mich.: Eerdmans, 1978), p. 768.

10. Robert P. George, *The Clash of Orthodoxies: Law, Religion, and Morality in Crisis* (Wilmington, Del.: ISI, 2001), p. 7.

11. Vatican Council II, *Gaudium et Spes*, Pastoral Constitution on the Church in the Modern World, December 7, 1965, no. 22, in Flannery, p. 922.

12. John Paul II, "A Deep Commitment to Authentic Christian Living," in James V. Schall, s.j., ed., *The Whole Truth about Man* (Boston: St. Paul, 1981), p. 89.

Index

abortion, 68, 291

Africa, 305n16

  charismatic renewal in, 109–111

  churches in, 106–107, 307n22, 307n25

  evangelization of, 94–111, 121, 303n3, 304n9, 304nn6–7, 305nn11–12, 306n17

  missionaries in, 3, 101–106, 305nn11–12, 306nn17–19, 307n22

  Portuguese missionaries in, 94–101, 303n3, 304n9, 304nn6–7

  Protestant evangelization in, 100

  religious growth in, 120, 121

  Synod of, 107–109, 308nn26–27

Alexander VI (Pope), 161

Americas, missionaries in, 3

apostles, 44–45, 270

  parishioners as, 272–273

apostolic age, baptism in, 88

apostolicity, 84

Asia, missionaries in, 3

assimilation, into church, 218–219

astrology, 8

baptism

  adult vs. infant, 89–91

  in apostolic age, 88

charisms and, 85, 86, 87, 88,
301*n*15
as Christian initiation, 80–86, 91,
92, 93
early church, 80–84
in Holy Spirit, 81, 83, 85–86, 88,
91, 92, 93, 231, 246, 277
Pentecost and, 87, 90
baptistery, 80–81, 82, 83
Baptists, 119
Catholics *vs.,* 17–18
church growth of, 119, 122
Barrett, David, 118, 119, 122
World Christian Encyclopedia of,
117
Basil of Caesarea, 87–88
Benedict XVI (Pope), 106
bishops. *See* United States Catholic
Bishops
Bishops' Committee on
Evangelization, 67
body of Christ, 161
business evangelization, 207, 208,
209, 216

Calvin, John, 3
Catechesi Tradendae (John Paul II),
279, 280
catechesis, 25, 105, 223, 225, 241
kerygma vs., 223–225, 279, 280
in parish renewal, 237, 240–243
permanent, 266
Catechism of the Catholic Church, 241
catechumens (neophytes), 83, 84,
86
Catholic(s)
on abortion, 68, 291
active, 125, 126–127, 253

attitudes toward gifts of Holy
Spirit, 141, 142
baby-boomer, 68
Baptists vs., 17–18
church growth of, 113, 117,
118–119, 120, 121, 122
early immigrant, 67–68
Evangelicals and, 11–12, 213, 278,
281, 282, 284
evangelization and, 9–10, 13–14,
24, 49, 65, 124, 151
evangelizing doubts of, 178–179
"good," 68
gospel message and, 18
inactive, 125, 126, 253–254, 268
mission of, 49–61, 64, 176, 265,
270–271
reevangelization of, 127, 253
relationship with Jesus of, 22
U.S. population of, 222
Catholic evangelization, 2. *See also*
specific topics
of active Catholics, 125, 126–127,
253
aspects of, 266–267
call to, 43, 45, 58, 61, 67, 125, 152,
164, 178–179, 189, 216, 255,
265, 288–289
challenges for, 68, 254
considerations for, 151–152,
158–159
ecumenical component of, 277
goals of, 54–55, 58, 60, 160, 267
growth of, 253
history of, 2, 4
Holy Spirit and, 15, 29, 39–48
of inactive Catholics, 125, 126,
253–254, 268

inspiration in, 253
invitation in, 253, 254
love and, 35, 37, 252
meaning of, 60, 151, 266–267
in modern world, 51–52
perspiration in, 253, 254
prayer and, 46, 215, 255
programmatic, 193
Protestant vs., 9, 10, 11, 49, 50, 109, 110, 125, 280, 306n17
qualifying for, 153–155
reasons for, 29–37, 251–252
targets of, 125–126
temptations for, 161–164
training for, 227–228
of the unchurched, 125, 126
urgency for, 32–33, 35–37, 40
Catholic evangelization, effective
befriending people, step of, 129–131
conversion invitation, step of, 134–135
discipleship, step of, 128–129
faith sharing, step of, 131–133
gospel proclaiming, step of, 133
new people integration, step of, 135–138
six steps to, 128–138
Catholic evangelization methods, 39, 45–48, 125, 151, 159, 212
of early missionaries, 98–99, 106
for inactive Catholics, 126
for laity, 160–161
of later missionaries, 104–106, 306nn18–19
for parishes, 254–256
street, 155–158, 159

Catholic evangelization strategy
customizing, 258–260
God in, 258
prioritizing actions in, 261–262
"SMART," 262–263
Catholic Evidence Guild, 151, 154, 158, 159, 160, 161, 163, 164
Catholic Men's Movement, 214
Catholicism
Evangelicalism and, 14, 15
secularization vs., 59, 67, 68–69
Centesimus Annus (John Paul II), 8
charismatic renewal, 83, 92
Catholic, 231, 232, 277–278
as new evangelization tool, 109–111
charismatics, 247, 276, 284, 285
church growth of, 117, 118, 119, 120, 121, 122
Holy Spirit baptism and, 246–247
charisms, 84, 87, 140, 142, 144. See also miracles; sign-gifts
attaining, 144–149
baptism and, 85, 86, 87, 88, 301n15
Christian initiation and, 87, 90, 91
disappearance of, 88–89
Christianity, 3
polarization in, 276
as religion of love, 34
of Roman Empire, 14
world survey of, 117
Christians
churched/unchurched, 127, 128
Gallup study of, 127–128
white vs. nonwhite, 118
Chrysostom, John, 88–89

church(es), 2
  African, 106–107, 307n22, 307n25
  integration vs. assimilation in,
    218–219
  local, 250
  of missionary evangelization,
    106–107, 307n22
  pathologies of dying, 114–115
Church (Catholic), 52, 59, 163, 264
  on abortion, 68, 291
  early architecture of, 80–81, 82
  evangelization and, 7, 52, 53,
    282–285
  mission of, 265, 267, 269–271
  true treasure of, 12–13
  work of, 52–53
church growth
  Baptist, 119, 122
  biological, 119–120
  Catholic, 113, 117, 118–119, 120,
    121, 122
  charismatic, 117, 118, 119, 120,
    121, 122
  conversion, 119–120
  Evangelical, 122
  evangelization and, 112–113
  movement, 113–117
  Orthodox Christian, 117
  pastoral leadership role in, 116
  pathologies of, 114–115
  Pentecostal, 113, 117, 118, 119,
    120, 121, 122
  Protestant, 117, 119, 121, 122
  studies on, 114–122
church planting, 116
churched Christians
  highly spiritual, 127, 128
  nominal, 127, 128

Communion, 238, 283
confession, 312n9
Congregation for the Propagation
  of the Faith, 100, 101, 102,
  106–107
Constitution on the Church, 23
conversion, 20, 47, 80, 91, 280
  as church growth factor, 119–120
  effective environment for,
    193–194
  gospel proclamation in, 192–193
  of married couples, 192
  superficial, 106
Council of Trent, 3
Creed, 241
culture of death, 290–291
culture of life, 291, 292
Cursillo movement, 232, 239
Cyril of Jerusalem, 86–87

D'Azambuja, Diego, 96, 98
diocese, 250
disciples
  charisms of, 140
  miracles of, 139–140, 141–142
  parishioners as, 272
  sign/gifts of, 139–140
"Dogmatic Constitution on the
  Church." See Lumen Gentium
Dominus Iesus, 23

earth worship, 8
Ecclesia in America (John Paul II),
  56
Ecclesia in Europa (John Paul II),
  289

ecumenical issues, in evangelization, 10–11, 276–278
theological issues and, 279–285
Edwards, Jonathan, 165, 166
ethnic diversity, 218–219
Eucharist, 26, 238, 239, 269
  and gospel, 25–27
eucharistic liturgy, 237
eucharistic room, 80–81, 82, 84
Europe, Christianity in, 3
Evangelicals, 2, 276, 285
  Catholics and, 11–12, 14, 213,
    278, 281, 282, 284, 286
  church growth of, 122
Evangelicals and Catholics Together,
  281, 284
Evangelii Nuntiandi (Paul VI), 5, 6,
  8, 9, 41, 50, 51, 52, 53, 54, 57, 65,
  66, 70, 219, 252, 264, 279
Evangelium Vitae (John Paul II),
  290
evangelization. See also Catholic
  evangelization; new evangelization; specific topics
  accountability and, 215
  as church growth factor, 112–113
  classic, 106
  of cultures, 8
  effective, 13
  institutional, 136
  integral, 268
  meaning of, 70–71, 72, 124–125
  multicultural, 219
  proselytization vs., 9, 10
  relational, 136
  source of, 79
  three levels of, 55
  through history, 3, 4

as way of life, 214–215
world, 285
"Evangelization in the Modern
  World." See Evangelii Nuntiandi
Evangelization 2000, 37–38

faith, 18, 20–22, 30
  kerygma with, 280
  salvation through, 17, 20–22
faith healers, 141
Familiaris Consortio (John Paul II),
  188
families
  catechism in, 241
  moral/spiritual condition of, 188

Gallup study of Christians,
  127–128
Gathered and Sent (Los Angeles
  archdiocese), 55
George, Carl, 116
Go and Make Disciples: A National
  Plan and Strategy for Catholic
  Evangelization in the United
  States (United States Catholic
  Bishops), 54, 64–65, 76–78
  genesis of, 66–67
  goals/strategies of, 72–76, 128,
    172, 173
  implementation resources for, 66,
    78
  vision section of, 70–71
God
  love of, 19
  words/deeds of, 143
God's kingdom, 143–144
Good News, 18, 19, 25–26, 35,
  252, 267

gospel, 8
  Catholicism and, 2, 3, 4
  Eucharist and, 25–27
  evangelization and, 4, 7, 13
  message of, 17, 18, 19
  proclamation of, 172, 192–193,
    223–225
Gospel of Life, 291, 292, 293, 294
government evangelization, 210,
  211–213, 216
grace, salvation through, 17, 18–19,
  20
Graham, Billy, 167
Grammar of Assent (Newman), 14
Gregory XV (Pope), 304n6

heaven, 30
  reality of, 25, 26
  salvation for, 24–25
hell, 23–24
*Here I Am, Send Me: A Conference
  Response to the Evangelization of
  African Americans,* 66
Hilary of Poitiers, 85–86
Hindus, 31
Hispanic Americans
  catechesis of, 223
  characteristics of, 221
  evangelization of, 218–219, 225,
    226, 227–228
  integration *vs.* assimilation of,
    218–220, 225–228
  numbers of, 220, 221–222
  reevangelization of, 223
holiness, call to, 43
Holy Spirit, 280
  apostles and, 44–45

baptism in, 81, 83, 85–86, 88, 90,
  92, 93, 231, 246, 277
charismatics and, 246–247
charisms and, 87
Christ and, 44
Christian initiation and, 91, 92
evangelization and, 15, 29, 39–48,
  59, 61, 66, 280
evangelizing community and, 59
in parish renewal, 246–248
Peter and, 43, 44–45
prayer and, 46, 233, 248
homilies, evangelistic, 165
hope, 32–34
Houck, William R. (Bishop), 67

immigrants, 218–220
initiation, Christian, 85
  architecture of, 80–81, 82
  baptism as, 80–86, 91, 92, 93
  charisms and, 87, 90
  as evangelization source, 79–80,
    93
  Holy Spirit and, 91, 92
  integration, into church, 218–219,
    225–228

Jehovah's Witnesses, 222
Jesus Christ
  Catholic church and, 52
  evangelization and, 5, 13, 40,
    41–42, 44
  gospel of, 3
  Holy Spirit and, 44
  life apart from, 23
  life of, 42
  miracles of, 141, 142, 143, 146
  mission of, 265

personal relationship with, 13–14,
    22, 223
poor and, 176–177, 178, 183–185
on prayer, 233
salvation through, 31
treasures of, 13
John Paul II (Pope)
    on African Synod, 108, 308n26
    Catechesi Tradendae of, 279, 280
    Centesimus Annus of, 8
    on charisms, 142
    Ecclesia in America of, 56
    Ecclesia in Europa of, 289
    on Eucharist, 26
    Evangelium Vitae of, 290
    Familiaris Consortio of, 188
    on Holy Spirit, 15
    new evangelization and, 6, 7, 9,
        13, 39, 40, 47, 55–58, 61, 151,
        270, 288, 289, 295
    Novo Millennio Ineunte of, 57, 58
    Redemptoris Missio of, 5, 20, 32,
        55, 66, 76, 143
    Tertio Millennio Adveniente of,
        56–57
John XXIII (Pope), 65
Jubilee Year 2000, 56, 57

Kelley, Dean, 115
kerygma (gospel initial proclama-
    tion), 172, 266, 267, 269, 272, 278
    basic topics of, 225
    catechesis *vs.*, 223–225, 279, 280
    distinctiveness of, 279–280
    with faith, 280
    joint proclamation basis of,
        280–282
Kreeft, Dr. Peter, 18

laity, Christian
    evangelization and, 6, 7, 9,
        160–161, 222, 270
    responsibility of, 216, 270, 293
Langton, Stephen (Cardinal
    Archbishop), 166
Last Judgment, 178
Latin American evangelization, 5
law of God, 2, 3
Leo, XIII (Pope), 103
liturgy, Catholic, 2, 26, 269
love, Christian, 34
    evangelization and, 35, 37,
        252–253
Lumen Gentium, 23, 50, 65, 142
Luther, Martin, 3

mainline Christian denominations,
    276–277
marriage
    enrichment programs for, 241,
        245–246
    monastic life *vs.,* 89
married couples, evangelization of
    attraction, stage of, 189–192
    conversion, stage of, 192–194
    difficulty of, 188–189
    importance of, 196
    keeping/growing, stage of,
        194–196
Marshall, Sir William, 101–102,
    305n12
Mass, 239
    attendance at, 215
    different types of, 238
materialism, 205
McGavran, Donald, 113–114
ministry

dimensions of, 267, 269
of the word, 266
miracles
of disciples, 139–140, 141–142
of Jesus, 141, 142, 143
missiologists, 113
mission
of Catholics, 49–61, 64, 176, 265, 270–271
of church, 265, 267, 269–271
of Jesus, 265
in parish renewal, 235–237, 248, 249
The Mission, 30
"The Mission of the Redeemer: On the Permanent Validity of the Church's Missionary Mandate." *See Redemptoris Missio*
missionaries, 3, 30
early evangelization methods of, 98–99, 106
later evangelization methods of, 104–106, 306nn18–19
of Portuguese, 94–101, 303n3, 304n9, 304nn6–7
missionaries, African, 3
early, 95–100, 303n3, 304n9, 304nn6–7, 307n22
later period of, 100–106, 305n12, 306nn17–19, 307n22
monastic life, 89, 245
morality, 241
multicultural evangelization, 218, 219
Muslims, 31

National Pastoral Plan for Hispanic Ministry (U.S. Catholic

Bishops), 66, 218–219, 223, 226, 227, 228
Nazianzen, Gregory, 87–88
new evangelization. *See also* John Paul II; specific topics
characteristics of, 6–9, 39
early *vs.*, 6
evangelization and, 55
foreign missions *vs.*, 7
goals of, 160, 270
strategies of, 7–8
new millennium, 60
new life in, 56–57, 61
Newman, Cardinal John Henry, 14
nonsacramental Christian streams, 276–277
Novo Millennio Ineunte (John Paul II), 57, 58

oikos evangelization, 259–260
Origen, 85, 301n15
Orthodox Christianity, 117

paganism, 7–8, 98
parish
function of, 264
Hispanic integration into, 225–228
liturgical, 269
local church of, 250
mission of, 265, 267, 269–271
pastoral, 226
sacramental, 269
U.S. *vs.* Latin American, 226
parish, as evangelizing community
building, 269–270
duty of, 265–266
reason for, 264

transforming into, 271–273
vision of, 265
parish, evangelizing, 230, 250
    catalyst for, 255–256
    methods for, 254–256, 272
    outreach of, 253–255, 258, 261,
        267–268, 271–273
    planning for, 256–257, 261,
        271–273
    reasons for, 251–253
    strategies for, 258–263
    targets of, 267–268
parish renewal, 230–232, 249
    catechesis/evangelization in, 237,
        240–242
    Holy Spirit deeper release in,
        246–248
    mercy work/evangelization in,
        243
    prayer in, 233–235, 237, 247, 248
    servant leadership in, 243–245
    small faith communities in, 237,
        239–240
    social justice in, 237
    spirituality in, 245–246
    vision/mission in, 235–237, 248,
        249
    worship/community in, 238–239
parishioners, 272–273
pastoral leadership, 222, 270
Paul III (Pope), 97
Paul, Saint, 4, 5, 13, 32
    on Christ's love, 35
    on multicultural evangelization,
        219
Paul VI (Pope), 13, 264
    on charisms, 142

Evangelii Nuntiandi of, 5, 6, 8, 9,
        41, 50, 51, 52, 53, 54, 57, 65, 66,
        70, 219, 252, 279
    evangelization and, 4–5, 15, 49,
        289
    Synod of Bishops and, 51, 65
Pentecost, 44
    baptism and, 87, 90
Pentecostalism
    African attraction to, 120
    classical, 83, 91, 92
Pentecostals, 113, 117, 276, 281,
        284, 286
    church growth of, 113, 117, 118,
        119, 120, 121, 122
personal witnessing, 193
Peter, Saint, 15, 33
    Holy Spirit and, 43, 44–45
    miracles of, 139–140, 141
Philoxenus of Mabbug, 89–91
Poland, 212
poor
    evangelization of, 176–183, 185,
        186, 187
    helping the, 186, 243, 270
    Hispanic, 225
    identities of, 181, 185
    Jesus and, 176–177, 178, 183–185
pope. See selected popes
Portuguese
    early African missionaries of, 9
        4–100, 303n3, 304n9, 304nn6–7
    later African missionaries of, 101
    poverty, material vs. spiritual, 225
prayer
    evangelization and, 46, 215, 255
    Holy Spirit and, 46, 233, 248
    Jesus on, 233

in parish renewal, 233–235, 237, 247, 248
preachers, evangelistic, 165, 166
  Catholic, 167–168
preaching, evangelistic, 165
  Catholic techniques of, 168–172
  political/social change and, 166–167
  primary focus of, 172–173
pride, 19
priests
  evangelization and, 6
  servant leadership of, 244–245
  primary evangelization, 8
  prison evangelization, 212, 238
Prison Fellowship, 212
proclamation
  churches of, 2
  of gospel, 66, 218–219, 223, 226, 227, 228
  Protestant churches and, 2
Promise Keepers, 214, 217
proselytization, 9, 10
Protestant evangelization, 2, 4, 213
  in Africa, 100, 109, 306n17
  Catholic vs., 9, 10, 11, 49, 50, 109, 110, 125, 280, 306n17
Protestants, 2, 141, 281, 286
  church growth of, 117, 119, 121, 122

Ratzinger (Cardinal). See Benedict XVI (Pope)
Redemptoris Missio (John Paul II), 5, 20, 32, 55, 66, 76, 143
reevangelization, 8, 127, 223, 253
religious orders, 245
renewal, spiritual, 231, 232

retreats, Catholic, 231
Roman Empire, 14

sacraments, 241, 269
  Catholicism and, 2, 3
salvation
  for heaven, 24–25
  from hell, 23–24
  plan of, 19
  through faith, 17, 20–22
  through grace, 17, 18–19, 20
  through Jesus, 31
Satan, 161
Scripture reading, 215
Second Vatican Council. See Vatican Council II
secularization, 59, 60, 67, 68–69, 289–290
servant leadership, 243–245
Sheehan, Michael (Archbishop), 67
sign-gifts
  of disciples, 139–140
  and God's kingdom, 143
  meaning of, 139
  of Protestants, 141
sin, 19
Sixtus IV (Pope), 96
small faith communities, 237, 239–240
social justice, 237, 267, 270
Society of African Mission, 100–104, 305n11
Spirit. See Holy Spirit
spiritual gifts. See charisms
spiritual poverty, 225
spiritual renewal, 231, 232
Spiritual Renewal Services, 231
spirituality, Catholic, 245–246

"Spreading the Holy Fire" (Chicago archdiocese), 55
Ste. Marie parish, 230–249
street evangelization, Catholic, 150, 151–152
  considerations for, 158–159
  methods of, 155–158, 159
  targeting those for, 155
Synod, African, 107–109, 308nn26–27
Synod of Bishops, 50
  on evangelization, 51, 57
  Paul VI and, 51, 65–66
Syrians, 89–91

teenagers evangelizing
  challenges of, 197–198
  effective, 199–201
  large group, 201–203
  outreach, 203–204
  reasons for, 198–199
Tertio Millennio Adveniente (John Paul II), 56–57
Tertullian, 83–84
theological issues, 279–285
Thiandoum, Cardinal, 48
Third World, 120

unchurched adults, 69
unchurched Christians, 127, 128
United States
  Catholic population of, 222
  early immigrant Catholics in, 67–68
  Hispanic population of, 220, 221–222
United States Catholic Bishops
  Go and Make Disciples: A

National Plan and Strategy for Catholic Evangelization in the United States of, 54, 64–67, 69–78
  National Pastoral Plan for Hispanic Ministry of, 66, 218–219, 223, 226, 227, 228
Urban VII (Pope), 97

Vatican Council II, 50, 57
  John XXIII and, 65
Vatican I, 4
Vatican II, 11, 279, 286, 293
  evangelization and, 4, 9, 10, 65, 216, 277, 285, 295
  on salvation, 23
  on words/deeds, 142–143
Vaughn, John, 119
vision
  action and, 251
  in parish evangelizing, 255, 257
  in parish renewal, 235–237, 248, 249

Wagner, C. Peter, 114–115, 116, 122
Western culture, 290
word
  of God, 2, 15
  ministry of the, 266
World Christian Encyclopedia (Barrett), 117